The Complete Track and Field Coaches' Guide to Conditioning for the Throwing Events

Larry Judge, Ph.D., CSCS

ISBN: 978-1-60679-006-9
Library of Congress Control Number: 2008930710
Cover design: Studio J Art & Design
Book layout: Studio J Art & Design
Front cover photo: Victah Sailer@www.photorun.NET

Coaches Choice
P.O. Box 1828
Monterey, CA 93942
www.coacheschoice.com

I dedicate this book to my father, Dr. Ira Lee Judge. He was inspiring, encouraging, and motivating to all of the lives he touched. He showed many aspiring young athletes how to achieve their full potential through the feedback, insight, and guidance he gave. It was through his inspiration (with the help of his assistant coach, my mother, Joan) that I embarked on my journey into coaching.

Dedication

Acknowledgments

I have spent the best 21 years of my life coaching the throws events for track and field and training athletes in the weight room. From Indiana State to South Carolina to Wyoming to Florida and now Ball State, from walk-ons to Olympians, the struggles, laughter, triumphs, and tears, coaching has left me with the richest of memories. I have certainly enjoyed every place coaching has taken me. I think the championships, record-setting meets, and relationships are the experiences I will treasure most.

This work will follow my adventures of the past and hopefully aid the pursuit of future achievements and fond memories for others. This book is a labor of many years of hard work and learning from lots of mistakes, but nonetheless, a labor of love. I can remember my first workouts with my brother Mike at our house in Merrillville, training at just about every gym in Northwest Indiana, at Lew Wallace High School with my dad, and even in the driveway with my mom. For the blood and sweat of my former training partners, climbing the ladder in pursuit of the dream, I say thanks to my brother Mike Judge, Jeff Oresik, Dan Tolle, Bill Milner, Tom Smith, Pete Kutsakaris, Lenny Bernstein, Phil Santino, and Ken Bonner. I can honestly say that I learned the most about myself when the chalk was flying and the weights got heavy.

Along my journey, I have learned from so many individuals. I want to say thanks to each and every one of them, almost an impossible task due to the many people who have shared information and experience with me. Those from whom I have learned a great deal in person include (but are not limited to): my father Ira Judge, Rob Roeder, Jim Moody, Lafey Armontrout, Klaus Bartonietz, Rob Bell, Jean Burke, Bruce Craig, Bernie Dare, John McNichols, Curtis Frye, Bill Godina, Greg Kraft, Mike Stone, Meg Stone, Jeff Potteiger, Vern Gambetta, Jud Logan, Glenn McAtee, Kevin McGill, George Dunn, Dave Pearson, Dan Pfaff, Bud Rasmussen, Phil Santino, Steve Thomas, Mike Turk, Stuart Tougher, Yuri Sedych, Tom Smith, Mike Young, and Boris Zaitchuk. I have also learned much from the writings of A.P. Bondarchuck, Eberhard Gaede, Vern Gambetta, Oleg Kollodiy, Kevin McGill, Jimmy Pedemonte, Mel Siff, and V. Petrov. This book is a compilation of the ideas that I have drawn from my experiences, studies under these people or from studying their articles. I take credit only for the errors.

I also want to give a special thanks to Coach Tom Jones for being a great mentor, boss, colleague, and friend. We shared many great moments at the University of Florida.

Last but not least, I want to thank Jean Burke, Frank Caraway, Erin Gilreath, Jim Peterson, Rob Lasorsa, Glenn McAtee, Kevin McGill, and Liz Wanless for their help in putting this project together.

Larry Judge (far right) and his athlete Erin Gilreath (second from left) with Yuri Sedykh (far left), world record holder in the hammer throw, and Harold Connolly (second from right), 1956 Olympic gold medalist in the hammer throw

Larry Judge (left) with Tom Jones, former University of Florida head women's track and field coach

In 2003, at the indoor NCAA Division I Championships, something remarkable happened. In the women's weight, five athletes from Florida were in the top six in the results. A few days later, a teammate who did not throw in that event, broke the NCAA women's hammer record. You should know that the coach was the author of this book, Larry Judge.

I first met Larry in 1990 at the USATF Coaching Education Level II school out in Colorado Springs. At the end of the sessions, I turned to my co-teacher, George Dunn, and said, "We need to get Larry involved in Coaching Ed." In the prior nine years of teaching the coaching education programs, few students possessed the dedication to learning that Larry showed. He must have asked both of us over 50 questions, which required detailed answers. It was clear from the start that Larry was quite unusual in wanting to learn everything there was to know about coaching throwers.

So, from 1990 to 2005, it is fair to conclude that Larry succeeded in his task of becoming the best throws coach in the United States. It is impossible to achieve the results he has achieved without a consummate mastery of strength and conditioning.

This book joins his many publications, which have clearly made him the most prolific throws writer in the past 20 years. When I edited *Track Technique*, he sent in a super article on throwing the 35-lb weight. It is still an outstanding article, 13 years later. Around a year ago, I was reviewing old issues of *Modern Athlete and Coach*, an Australian track journal, and he had published an article in 1994 on how to use biomechanical analysis in the shot put. Like the article on the weight, it was very practical and useful for a coach—immediately.

You are holding a book that can help you create a training plan to improve performance in a month. Nothing is instant, but the ideas in the book will put you on the path to make steady improvement in throwing. Athletes and coaches need to understand how a plan can make a difference. It is also imperative for coaches, more than the athletes, to understand the science behind the plan. Larry has attempted to bring the science to the coaches, and in this book you will learn the terms and the basics of that science.

It was only a few years ago that the rubber medicine ball did not exist in the U.S. I had to ask a popular sports company to get me one from England. In no time, they sold over 10,000 of them. Larry will show you how to combine medicine-ball work with circuit training, lifting, jumping, and various other drills.

Coaches need to learn how to test athletes and diagnose problems. It is no longer enough to say, "Hit the weight room for 20 minutes," and then not give specific instruction. Larry's experience with elite throwers easily translates to the high school or college coach wondering how to put it all together.

The book will make you think, and you will not find a cookbook approach in these pages. It is impossible for anyone to just copy the workout of another athlete, and just think it will work. Books with sample workouts can be found, but that is simply not the correct approach.

An old high school friend contacted me recently and asked about his young son and a well-known drug, which is legal. Yikes, where did the young man come up with that? Well, he had attended a football camp at a college, and one of the "coaches" mentioned using this drug to gain weight. That situation is one of the problems with sports today, in that athletes are being told to seek quick gains. A book like this is the real alternative, an explanation of the complete conditioning program for a thrower.

As you read this book, think back to my experience in 1990 as I saw this young throws coach begin his incredible journey. You are about to start your own journey to achieving your goals and dreams as either a thrower or a throws coach.

Kevin McGill
August 2007
Coauthor of *The Throws Manual*

Contents

Before You Begin
Strength and Conditioning Coaches
Metabolic Classification of Track-and-Field Events
Neuromuscular Classification of Track-and-Field Events
Biomechanical Classification of Track-and-Field Events
Athlete Classification
The Biomotor Abilities

The Warm-Up
Flexibility
General Strength Development
Medicine Ball
Plyometrics

Technical Development
Technical Training in the General Preparation Phase
Technical Training in the Specific Preparation Phase
Technical Training in the Pre-Competitive Phase
Technical Training in the Peaking Competitive Phase
Implement Choice and Training Blueprint
The 10 Percent Rule
Light Implements
Heavy Implements
Using Heavy Implements in the Warm-Up
Balancing the Performance Model
Changing Implements
Throwing Intensity
Number of Throws Per Session
Maximum-Effort Throws
Designing the Training Blueprint: Choosing the Weight and
   Number of Throws
Program Design
Sample Training Program

Execution of the Power Clean
Common Technical Flaws in the Power Clean
Teaching Progression for the Power Clean
The Jerk
Technical Description of the Jerk

**Chapter 10: Psychological Preparation:
Getting Into the "Flow"**
    Flow Defined
    Role of the Flow State in Athletics
    Fundamentals of Flow
    Flow Skill Training Examples
    Application of Skill Training to Achieve Flow in the Throws Events
    Conclusion

Preface

The concept of an athlete's "talent" has been a theme woven throughout the history of sports. How much of an athlete's success depends on his genetic code? As time has passed, coaches and athletes have risen above their genetic destinies with sports expansion, as well as sophisticated training methods and technology. As a result, the past century and a quarter have seen frequent improvements in track and field records. Specifically, throwing-event records have progressed at a rapid rate due to three critical factors. The most important of these was a shift in emphasis on basic strength training. In the 1950s, throwers began using resistance-training methods to improve power and in turn improve throwing. Secondly, training time was extended in both time per week and weeks per year. This extension made for a more demanding training regime, but also for much more capable athletes. The third major change made in the 1950s was purely technical. Using new methods to throw had a huge impact on throwing velocities.

Strength training, one of the critical factors for superior throwing records, has come a long way from the time when coaches used a small group of standard exercises and lifts to help develop stronger athletes. In the past, the weight room was the domain of mostly football players, body-builders, and a few aspiring throwers. Early barbells had hollow globes that could be filled with sand or lead shot, but by the end of the century these were replaced by the plate-loading barbell we use today. The 1960s saw the gradual introduction of exercise machines into the still-rare strength-training gyms of the time. Weight lifting of yesteryear was a novelty and most athletes were advised that serious resistance training may hurt their flexibility and athleticism. Today, resistance training is accepted as a standard part of the preparation formula, so a trip to the weight room is a prerequisite for any dedicated athlete. Strength programs are specifically designed for each event group in track and field and often for different specialties within an event area. Contemporary training is not about just developing maximum strength. While specialized weight training provides great benefits to many athletes, any enhancement of strength and power can be severely restricted if general strength parameters, mobility, and posture are not also addressed. A multifaceted approach—combining medicine-ball work, body-weight circuits, controlled movements, abdominal exercises, dumbbell circuits, static lifts, Olympic lifts, body-building exercises, and throwing workouts with different weight implements—can provide physiological and biomechanical advantages that enhance performance for the present-day thrower.

Today, the competitive performance of a thrower in track and field is a very aggressive display of strength, power, and technique. The throws are complicated movements performed at high speed in a limited space. We classify the hammer, weight throw, shot put, discus, and javelin as the speed and power events. While each of these events is different, many of the qualities needed for success is the same. The backbone of any successful program is a well-organized regime of practice and training. Training goals in track and field can be accomplished through a variety of modes, but need to be specific to the demands of the event. In order to construct the optimal performance model for the thrower, a training program that systematically and progressively builds the proper physiological abilities necessary to achieve certain fundamental physical skills, eventually leading to the achievement of peak performance must be developed. Many coaches get impatient with athletes because they are not performing in competitive situations, and the coach fails to realize the true cause of an athlete's technical difficulties: the training plan.

Larry Judge with current and former athletes (from left to right) Candice Scott, Erin Gilreath, and Lisa Misipeka at the 2004 Olympic Games in Athens

An Introduction to Conditioning in the Throwing Events

Developing successful training plans is not quick, easy, or even a surefire link to achieving great results. The idea that successful coaches simply replicate past successful training programs is a myth. Great throws coaches instead rely on knowledge, scientific principles, experience, and intuition to develop a great strength and conditioning program. This view of strength training and conditioning for the throws athlete is not a cookbook; no magic recipe for developing these physiological abilities exists. Each athlete is unique, each coach-athlete relationship is different, and many strength training/conditioning paths may lead to the same goal. The coach who gains an edge over the training variables that plague other coaches commits to knowledge and never stops learning. The methods may be diverse, but each successful training program adheres to a number of concepts and themes. As a throws coach, once I had developed my own training plan, approximately 95 percent of my strength and conditioning program was set in stone. I kept that five to 10 percent open for variety, change, and new ideas/training techniques that I learned. I developed my own philosophy, adhered to it, and made incremental adjustments based on my experience, past results, and increased knowledge.

So instead of just listing numbers, percentages, and sample programs, we will take a comprehensive look at the strength-training principles that must be followed not only to make a successful throws program, but to keep one. Included are ways to address the biomotor elements for the thrower, including tips to supplement strength at the track, how to develop throwing workouts using different weight implements, guidelines for developing resistance-training programs, exercise prescription, exercise technique, detailed exercise-program guidelines, programming for injuries, and numerous tables to aid understanding.

Larry Judge and Candice Scott at the 2003 NCAA Outdoor Championships

Important Concepts in Exercise Science

© Victah Sailer@www.photorun.NET

Chapter 1

Before You Begin

It is reasonable to consider, briefly, important concepts in exercise science to help the throws coach in understanding how to construct basic training programs. An abundance of information is available on the Internet for designing resistance-training programs. The best place to start in the process of program design is with the scientific foundations behind the training blueprint. Competition in the throwing events has developed to such a degree that no athlete or coach can afford to neglect the application of scientific principles to the event.

The distance achieved in the throwing events is determined by the velocity of release, the angle of release, the height of release, and in some cases aerodynamic factors. To take advantage of these forces, the thrower must be properly conditioned and skilled to realize the static positions and the temporal patterns involved in the throw. Understanding the mechanics involved in generating the necessary power and momentum during the throw allows the throws coach to make adjustments when necessary and to devise procedures, which can measurably improve an athlete's performance. Velocity is often referred to as the critical factor in successful throwing. At first glance, it would be easy to say that velocity is not just the critical factor in throwing, but the main focus. This assessment, however, would be a mistake for two reasons: athletes always try to throw as hard as possible in competition, and having velocity as the critical factor would only tell the athlete "what to do" and not the "how to do it." The question is: how do we increase release velocity? The two primary ways to increase release velocity are: first, improve strength and power, and second, optimize technique to maximize the use of strength and power. Keep in mind that technique may be limited by strength and power capabilities.

The training plan of a thrower must address general fitness and strength, but must also provide a technical foundation and specific conditioning to ensure success for the throws-event athlete, depending on the event, in the indoor and outdoor seasons. Training methods within a session should be grouped correctly to enhance adaptation. Activities may be grouped by: speed and power-related activities, energy-system demand, and intensity of activity. Contrast between successive training sessions is important to enhance adaptation, avoid monotonous training, and prevent injury.

If a coach wants to draw a master training plan, the first concept to understand is that nothing ever goes as planned. Even modern technology will not be able to accurately predict how an athlete will react to each and every training module. A master training plan is properly designed, and must always be subject to adjustments and tweaks to suit the individual. Contingency planning is a very important and necessary part of the planning process. It is especially important to have contingency plans ready for individual training sessions. In such instances, having a solid foundation in the area of exercise science comes in handy. Those on-the-field decisions/adjustments require a combination of knowledge and experience. So how can a coach be effective at planning a program that fits the individual? The successful throws coach must be an active player in both the physical training and technical development. He should definitely be perceptive of the athlete's psychological disposition and state, anthropometric characteristics, and biomotor capabilities, and the physiological demands of the event.

Training a throws athlete correctly means being involved and understanding physiology, biomechanics, nutrition, sports psychology, and sports medicine. Ultimately, the goal is to provide information to the thrower on how he can improve his distance. As such, the coach has a need to establish associations with and verify previous research with the effects of release parameters, and to implement velocity and acceleration, temporal parameters, and athlete kinematics with elite-level throwing distances.

Strength and Conditioning Coaches

Many sports are borrowing training aspects from track and field. The "need for speed and power" is a phenomenon that is sweeping across the sports horizon. Strength and conditioning has become a discipline. High schools, colleges, and professional teams have hired strength and conditioning coaches and have spent millions of dollars on equipment and facilities. Organizations like the National Strength and Conditioning Association (NSCA) and the development of the Internet have helped make information on resistance training, conditioning, and other training modalities available to coaches in all sports. But, it should be kept in mind that strength and conditioning is still a profession

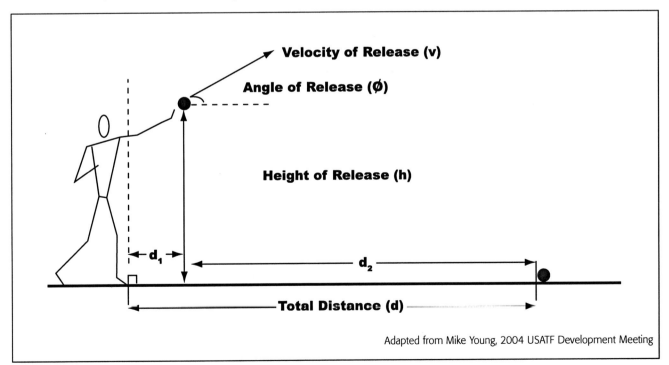

Adapted from Mike Young, 2004 USATF Development Meeting

Figure 1-1. Release parameters affecting the total measured distance of a throw

dominated by football and basketball (i.e., revenue sports) at the college level. Team sports are more concerned with a regular season and do not necessarily use a periodized approach to training. For this reason, it is important for the track and field throws coach to be knowledgeable in resistance training and other aspects of strength and conditioning. College strength coaches have taken over the strength and conditioning preparation of most sports, leaving the technical and tactical preparation to the specific sport coach. Should the throws coach hand over his strength and conditioning responsibilities to a professional outside the sport? The answer is simple. Technical competency and improvement in the throws is heavily influenced by an athlete's physical development. This gradual process includes an integrated training program on the track, in the throwing ring, and in the weight room. Without improvements in body composition and attention to improvement in the biomotor elements related to throwing, frustration will occur when trying to master the complex technical elements of the throws. All aspects of the training on and off the track and the competition calendar must be factored into the exercise prescription of the thrower. The throws coach must devise or be heavily involved in designing the strength and conditioning program. Ultimately, the throws coach must be the strength and conditioning coach.

Metabolic Classification of Track-and-Field Events

Not all head track-and-field coaches have a background in throwing events; most of these coaches have endurance running or sprinting backgrounds. Strength and conditioning coaches most often have a team-sport background. Since not all coaches have throwing expertise, knowledge of the energy systems is of utmost importance when choosing exercises, number of repetitions, number of sets, volume, intensity, rest between sets, and frequency and duration of weight-room and track training sessions for throwers (Table 1-1). Because the sport of track and field is a combination of many radically different events, the coach must understand how to manipulate these acute variables to match the energy requirements of a particular event. The key to designing a successful training program is having an understanding of how an athlete's body responds to and adapts to exercise and training. The three metabolic pathways available to replace ATP concentrations are: anaerobic phosphagen (ATP-CP) energy system, anaerobic lactate (glycolytic) energy system, and the aerobic energy system (Table 1-1). Adenosine triphosphate (ATP) is the immediate usable form of chemical energy for muscular activity and is depleted in 1 to 2 seconds. The anaerobic (ATP-CP) energy system (0 to 15 seconds) is depleted usually well under 20 seconds. An energy-rich compound called creatine phosphate (CP) is present in muscle. In the aerobic lactate (glycolytic) system (approximately 45 seconds to 2 minutes), as hydrogen ion concentrations increase, enzyme activity decreases, and glucose or glycogen is broken down to pyruvate to provide high-energy phosphates. The aerobic metabolism (at approximately 3 minutes and greater) is capable of utilizing proteins, fats, and carbohydrates for resynthesizing large quantities of ATP without creating fatigue. When designing an exercise program, a coach must consider the energy-system contribution to that athlete's given event. For example, when designing a program for a 5000-meter runner, much more emphasis would be put on rep/set/rest period combinations, stressing the lactic acid (glycolysis) energy system. On the other hand, for a 100-meter sprinter or shot-putter, a coach must train the ATP/PC energy system, the system used in short, powerful bursts. During the general preparation period, many coaches tend to overemphasize the development of endurance at the sacrifice of the crucial explosive qualities needed for the throws. Running one, two, or three miles as part of preparation-phase conditioning will develop the aerobic qualities within the cell. This approach is counterproductive. Don't mistake motion for achievement; mixed training brings mixed results. Specific preparation builds a specific base that brings specific results. Anaerobic fitness, the ability to produce ample energy using the body's anaerobic system, is more specific to throwing. Repeated bouts of high-intensity, short-duration activity helps develop the body's work capacity. Work capacity is the ability to withstand large training loads, and high training volumes increases work capacity.

Energy System Classification		
Energy System	*Duration*	*Events*
ATP-PC	Short (0 to 15 seconds)	Short dashes, jumps, throws
Glycolysis	Medium (15 seconds to 2 minutes)	400 m, 800 m, 1500 m
Aerobic	Long (2 minutes and up)	1500 m and up
Neuromuscular Classification		
Energy System	*Fiber Type*	*Events*
ATP-PC	Type IIb (fast twitch)	Short dashes, jumps, throws
Glycolysis	Type IIa (combination)	400 m, 800 m, 1500 m
Aerobic	Type I (slow twitch)	1500m and up
Biomechanical Classification		
Event Area	*Classification*	*Definition*
Running events	Cyclic	Repetitious act
Throwing events (SP, DT, HT, WT)	Acyclic	Motor skills
Jumping events, Javelin	Acyclic combined	Repetitious act, followed by motor skill
Hurdle events	Acyclic combined	Repetitious act, followed by motor skill

Table 1-1. Classification of events in track and field

Neuromuscular Classification of Track-and-Field Events

Knowledge of the neuromuscular classification is another significant variable when designing a resistance-training program (Table 1-1). A coach should understand the three different types of muscle fiber: type IIb (fast twitch), type I (slow twitch), and type IIa (combination). Each athlete has a different fiber make-up and will react a little differently to the chronic variables of the periodized resistance-training program. Because throwing is such a short duration event, coaches hope all throwers have mostly fast-twitch fibers. Most do, but all throwers are not created equal; some throwers have more fast-twitch fibers than others. A coach can identify an athlete's dominant fiber type initially by performing non-invasive field tests. As the athlete performs the tasks of different mesocycles throughout the training program, the coach can make further determinations of the athlete's dominant fiber type. The coach can then tailor the sets and repetitions to fit the athlete. Does the athlete make the most strength gains on sets of eight or sets of three? Those athletes responding well to higher-rep sets will have more slow-twitch or combination fibers. A coach can then tailor a strength program to the muscle-fiber make-up to help an athlete optimize strength gains. Also, exercise selection and rest periods between sets are an important consideration for muscle-fiber types and will be discussed later in the chapter. The series of neuromuscular factors involved in strength production must be considered when programming. Throughout all the training, coaches must always pay special attention to the development of the basic neuromuscular and biomechanical qualities required in throwing.

Neuromuscular Factors Involved in Strength Production

- Biomechanical/anthropometric factors

- Motor-unit activation pattern (intramuscular activation)

- Motor-unit recruitment

- Muscle action pattern (intramuscular activation)

- Muscle cross-sectional area

- Motor-unit activation frequency (rate coding)

- Motor-unit type (muscle-fiber type)

- Neural inhibition

- Synchronization (ballistic movements)

- Use of elastic energy and reflexes

Adapted from Stone (2004)

Biomechanical Classification of Track-and-Field Events

The coach must identify the dominnt mechanical components of a given event. Specific event training must correlate to areas of the body that are involved in the event. Even within the throwing discipline, athletes use different muscles for each specific throwing event. The percentage must be broken down into the contribution of the legs, trunk, and arms. (Table 1-1) Because of time and energy constraints, specificity is very important when constructing the resistance-training program. Examine event strength demands, and ask the following questions when formulating a program.

- What muscle groups are used in your event?
- What are the movement requirements?
- What is the direction of the application of force?
- What is the range of movement?

All of the throwing events require a good deal of lower body and core development, but each event has other areas of the body that require additional emphasis in the training program. A hammer thrower, for example, would spend more time developing the musculature of the legs and back, while a shot-putter would be concerned with strengthening the chest, shoulders, and triceps. In the javelin, the pull-over may be classified as a primary exercise and should be emphasized in the training plan. In the javelin and hammer, the development of upper-body mass in the chest and shoulders in many cases is counterproductive because of losses in mobility.

It is important to be aware of the basic biomechanical principles of throwing when making decisions for the training plan repertoire. Try to relate activities in the training program to these basic principles of throwing. It will help tie the weight room and throwing together more effectively and will give the coach a cue system that the athlete can internalize and understand. Following are the basic biomechanical principles of throwing:

- Involve the whole body.
- Achieve a summation of forces.
- Apply force in the direction of the throw.
- Achieve a long range of motion.
- Transfer body weight.
- Keep the center of gravity over the base.

The best place to begin is by performing a need analysis. For example, if an athlete has problems getting into and holding key positions in the throw, then this athlete may be limited by his physical capacity. Capacity can only be improved through *targeted* training.

Athlete Classification

The training program for the youth athlete must be designed to work in concert with the natural maturation process. Age may be the most important variable to consider when determining appropriate training activities. Table 1-2 illustrates a progression for training a young thrower.

Athletes age 6 to 11 are taught only very basic skills. Interest-awakening activities should be emphasized; the young athletes should be allowed to play and have fun. Energy-system fitness should not be stressed, as the body does not respond to such training at these ages. Prior to puberty, children have a less-developed ability to support anaerobic metabolism. Training can include very basic body weight calisthenics. Athletes age 11 to 13 can be subject to a variety of training activities. Important skills include basic Olympic-lifting techniques and throwing drills and techniques. The theme at this age should be learning the concept of training. Athletes in late adolescence (ages 15 to 18) are ready for more specific and demanding training, as well as higher training volumes. Energy-system fitness training can be introduced at this time. Boys and girls are both developing quickly at these ages, and they are capable of performing more complex activities. Consideration now needs to be given to the training structure in relation to event specific requirements. Coaches need to consider the athlete's muscle-fiber profile. Higher intensity weight training is appropriate because more advanced anaerobic training can be done at these ages. The training load for adolescents should be gradually increased in the following order: training frequency, training volume, training density of the stimuli, and training intensity of the stimuli. The relationship between the volume of general training and the volume of specialty training of young throwers should follow the basic percentage guideline outlined in Table 1-3.

When examining the level of intensity for strength exercises for young throwers, it is important to use light weights and emphasize proper technique. Table 1-4 offers a general percentage guideline for choosing intensity for resistance training.

Stage	Emphasis	Age	Periodization	Training Content
1	Play games	6 to 11	No periodization	Basic biomotor
2	Multi-event development	11 to 13	Single	Motor learning
3	Event group development	13 to 15	Single	Physical skills
4	Specialization	15 to 18	Double	Individual programs
5	Performance	19 to 25	Double	High intensity
6	Continued performance	26+	Double	Adaptive strategies

Table 1-2. Progression for training a thrower

Age	15 yr	16 yr	17 yr	18 yr	19 yr	Top Athlete
General Training Percentage	55	50	40	35	30	25
Specialty Training Percentage	45	50	60	65	70	75

Adapted from Bartonietz (2004)

Table 1-3. Percentage guidelines for general and specialty training volumes

Age					
Level of Intensity	15 yr	16 yr	17 yr	18 yr	19 yr
90-100%	—	05	10	15	20
75-89%	20	30	40	50	55
60-74%	80	65	50	35	25

Adapted from Bartonietz (2004)

Table 1-4. Percentage guidelines for intensity for resistance training

Training age, different from an athlete's chronological age, is a concept used to calculate the specific training background of a particular athlete. Understanding the concept of training age is especially important in a specialized discipline like throwing. The training age of an athlete is determined by the number of years he has consistently performed sport-specific training with progressively increasing loads. In the case of a high school athlete, the training age may only be a certain number of months. In other words, an 18-year-old athlete who has been training seriously for two years, but who has only been participating in track and field four months out of the year, has a training age of eight months, rather than two years. In the case of a multisport athlete, only a fraction of the year is spent on throwing. If a multisport athlete decides to specialize, his training age can often double in one year of dedicated sport-specific training. This approach often causes a large enhancement in performance because of additional time spent on sport-specific preparation. College freshmen in the United States often see a noticeable increase in performance during their first year because of the additional training time.

Athletes are classified as follows: The beginner has less than one year of consistent throwing/strength-training experience, the intermediate athlete has one to two years of consistent throwing/strength-training experience, and the advanced athlete has more than two years of consistent throwing/strength-training experience.

Chronological age and training age affect what type of resistance training is prescribed for the athlete. Someone with a training age of two years or less would concentrate on technique and perform strength-building lifts in a slow and controlled manner. The emphasis in the power exercises would be on proper technique with light weight. Once an athlete has three to five years of resistance training under his belt, repetitions in the 1 to 5 RM range (85 to 100 percent of the 1 repetition maximum) are used to develop maximal strength by training the nervous system. According to Stone (1997), some of the changes in the nervous system associated with resistance training include: increased neural drive to the muscle, increased synchronization of motor units, increased activation of contractile apparatus, and decreased inhibition by the protective mechanisms of the muscle. However, these great performance changes only occur when an athlete has the proper technical pattern pre-established.

Figure 1-2. Great performance changes only occur when an athlete has the proper technical pattern pre-established.

Athlete Age Classifications

Chronological age: The number of days, months, and years that have elapsed since birth.

Biological age: The individual's stage of development in relation to physical maturity. Children within the same chronological age banding can differ by several years in their level of biological maturation.

Developmental age: The complex interaction between physical, emotional, psychological, and social development.

Training age: The number of years that an individual has been in specific training for any related sport.

Activity	Grades 7-8	Grade 9	Grade 10	Grade 11	Grade 12
Resistance training		X	X	X	X
Olympic lifts	X (Technique)	X	X	X	X
General strength work	X	X	X	X	X
Plyometrics		Ground level	X	X	X
Sprints	X	X	X	X	X
Heavy implements			X	X	X
Specific endurance		X	X	X	X
20 throws	X	X			
30 throws			X		
40+ throws				X	X
Technique drills	X	X	X	X	X

Adapted from Godina (2006), USATF Level II Curriculum

Table 1-5. Training for the throws: age-appropriate workout guidelines

The Biomotor Abilities

Periodization will not be effective without addressing the five biomotor elements in the training program. The biomotor elements are: strength, speed, coordination, endurance, and flexibility. All of these elements can be addressed in a conditioning/resistance training program. The goal is to develop all biomotor qualities in a systematic, sequential and progressive manner for optimum development of the individual's performance capabilities. Keep in mind with beginners and intermediate level athletes the training program may stress all five of the biomotor elements equally because of the emphasis on general strength and conditioning. While specialization is necessary and appropriate at times, balanced development will lead to better long-term progress.

When considering intermediate- to advanced-level athletes, the five biomotor elements are stressed fairly equally in the preparation phase only. Closer to the competitive season, the training program should highlight the demands of the specific event and the individual; therefore, only two or three of the biomotor elements may be emphasized and the others simply addressed (Tables 1-6 through 1-8). Remember, mixed training brings mixed results. When constructing the training plan, you have to make choices during each mesocycle, and you cannot train everything equally. Specialization in certain areas of training must be accompanied by a decrease in other areas to maintain a constant training load.

On the other hand, too much specialization can be harmful. Be careful to develop your athletes in a specific but balanced manner. The overdevelopment of a given quality at the expense of other important qualities will have a detrimental effect on performance. Make sure you build a solid foundation, but

Training Unit	Dosage
Strength/power training	High-volume/low-intensity
Specific endurance	800-meter run, general strength circuits
Speed	Bounding/sprints/60- to 80-meter sprints
Plyometrics	Ground-level jumps, 3x5 vertical jumps, 2x1 standing long jump
Drills	Event-specific, three sets, 10 reps, all movements with standard implement
Throws	Overweight implements for standing throws only (without reverse) Full-technique throwing with standard shots for technical development

Table 1-6. Biomotor emphasis: general preparation phase

Training Unit	Dosage
Strength/power training	Medium volume/medium intensity
Specific endurance	400-meter run, active warm-up
Speed	40- to 60-meter sprints Agility drills for foot speed Plyometrics Drills using 12- to 18-inch boxes
Drills	Hip pops with and without, glides with crossbar, glide and stops, throws with weight vest
Throws	3x5 full at 80-percent intensity, 1x5 full at 95 percent. The majority of the throws (70 percent) should be performed between 10 and 20 percent heavier than the standard implement; 30 percent of the throws with the standard implement to keep in touch with the competition rhythm.

Table 1-7. Biomotor emphasis: pre-competitive phase

be very energy-system and event-specific conscious when constructing workouts. Overemphasizing the endurance portion of the program is a common error when training for the speed and power events. Overemphasis of endurance can hinder strength, speed, and coordination development.

The five primary biomotor abilities can each be expanded into a more detailed list of specialized qualities. No biomotor quality has been explored in scientific research studies more so than strength. Entire industries have evolved around this concept through the endless search for a faster way to athletic excellence. The rest of this chapter will examine the specialized qualities of strength that must be developed for success particularly in the throwing events.

Training Unit	Dosage
Strength/power training	Medium to low volume Medium to high intensity
Specific endurance	Not an emphasis here; recovery is the emphasis.
Speed	20- to 40-meter sprints, block starts Agility drills (all timed) Underweight implements
Drills	Emphasis on dynamic movements and rhythm. Improve block and release mechanics.
Throws	Reduce volume, use the standard and light implement 5x5 full at 85 percent intensity, 1x5 full at 95 to 100 percent (stay in on every attempt). Use 15 percent heavy, 60 percent standard, and 25 percent light implements.
Meet preparation	Simulate meet conditions prior to each competition. High intensity throws (3 to 6), staying in the ring.

Table 1-8. Biomotor emphasis: competitive phase

The development of strength presents a unique puzzle: so many other biomotor and biomechanical factors have to be accounted for while addressing this particular quality. In the throwing events, strength is often the main difference between beginners and advanced level throwers. Many approaches can be taken toward developing this very fundamental quality. A detailed description of the strength-related biomotor abilities is as follows:

- *Absolute strength* is the ability to produce great force, regardless of speed of movement. Absolute strength qualities determine greatly an athlete's ability to withstand stress and impact, and are an inherent and contributing part of all other types of strength. High resistances normally characterize absolute strength-developing activities.
- *General strength* is the ability to overcome the resistance of an athlete's own body. Body control is an important part of general strength. General strength-training activities involve no external loading, using bodyweight as the sole load.
- *Power* is the ability to produce force quickly. In power situations, resistance is present, and speed of movement is needed. Power-training activities combine resistance and speed of movement.
- *Elastic or reactive strength* is the ability to produce force using the stretch reflex. Training elastic strength normally involves plyometric and/or jumping activities. All muscle possesses the potential for elastic strength development.
- *Strength endurance* is the ability to sustain force production. Strength endurance is a concern in stabilizing postural muscle groups, which must

be able to remain effective throughout the course of an event. Strength-endurance activities require either high repetitions of movement or extended stabilization.

All training, regardless of the time of year or event, must address the five biomotor elements: strength, skill, speed, flexibility, and endurance. Keep in mind the synergistic relationship between all biomotor qualities; therefore, all components must be trained during all phases of the year, but the proportion will change significantly with training age, event specialization, and priorities of the particular training period. Specialized training increases in the latter stages of the training year, and is more appropriate in the latter part of an athlete's career. The extent to which each biomotor ability is trained should depend on the particular demands of the event. The biomotor elements are presented in the order of descending importance for the beginning- to intermediate-level thrower. Adjustments can be made on an individual basis.

Strength is defined as the ability to overcome outside resistance. Stronger athletes are able to hold the positions necessary, as technique can only be mastered if muscle contractions and relaxations can be coordinated and synchronized to produce maximum acceleration of the implement. Lifting exercises are a good expression of strength, and they are easily testable. For a thrower, the ability to squat, bench press, snatch, and clean large weights is important. Heavy implements reveal weaknesses in the thrower's technique and specific strength. However, also being able to move and execute technique with the implements is extremely important.

Skill represents proficiency in accurately performing the skill of throwing the shot put, discus, javelin, hammer, and weight under competition conditions. The coach assesses the skill level as he compares the thrower's skills against technical norms. Also, comparing performance at practice against performance in the meets will reveal if the skill is stable under competition conditions.

Speed is the rate at which general and specific skills can be performed. For example, a hammer thrower must be able to turn rapidly (specific skill), or a javelin thrower must be able to run fast with the implement keeping the javelin in position, and execute the withdrawal, cross steps, plant, delivery, and follow-through. This factor can be measured by throwing of light implements. Also, being able to perform general skills (sprinting, agility drills) rapidly is a plus.

Flexibility. Suppleness or range of movement in joints or combinations of joints is important for all sports skills, including the throws. A hammer thrower must have good range of motion in the shoulder girdle to obtain maximum radius and a good range of motion in the ankles to allow for proper turning. Additionally, the thrower must have good flexibility in all the muscles that connect to the hips and vertebral column in order to prevent injury to the spine. An athletic trainer can perform range of motion tests, and problems can be identified and corrective exercises can be prescribed for the thrower.

Figure 1-3. A thrower must have a combination of coordination, balance, and strength, plus a good range of motion and good flexibility.

Endurance is defined as specific work capacity. Not many throwers have a lot of general endurance; send them on a three- to five-mile run, and most would not come back—ever. However, an athlete who throws 30 to 50 times in a session must have a high level of specific endurance to complete all those throws with good technique. Add in some weight lifting and other conditioning, and you are really tapping into the thrower's stamina. Distance running is not the way to address this biomotor element.

© Victah Sailer@www.photorun.NET

Figure 1-4. To be successful in the glide shot put for men, the thrower must possess incredible physical tools.

Strength
Development
at the Track

© Victah Sailer@www.photorun.NET

Chapter 2

After reviewing basic physiological foundations of designing a training program, a coach needs to perform a need analysis for his athletes. A good place to start is with examining general strength and overall throwing fitness. The enhancement of strength and power can be severely restricted if general strength parameters, mobility, and posture are not addressed. It's not just about the weight room anymore; properly preparing a thrower encompasses a lot more than just how much an athlete can bench press, squat, or power clean. In the throwing events in track and field, when speaking of body mechanics to describe sport posture and technique, this term refers to both the static and functional relationships between body parts and the body as a whole. The concept includes over 200 bones and some 600 muscles not to mention the endless chains of fascia and various connective-tissue systems. Efficient body mechanics is a function of balance and poise of the body in all positions possible—including standing, lying, and sitting, during movements and in a variety of mediums. As a general statement, aside from the obvious rotary motions of the shot, disc, and hammer, all the events in track and field have a heavy linear emphasis in their execution. Joint or body torques are certainly involved in any movement, but the average coach ignores the training for dynamic stability in the medial to lateral plane (coronal plane). When coaches translate weight-room work to the field, several variables can interrupt the transition, and weight training may not be as effective as it could be to improve throwing. An athlete's throwing ability is enhanced when these variables are utilized instead for a smooth transition. Throwers need general athleticism. To bridge the gap between the weight room and the throwing circle, throwers' strength can be developed and supplemented out at the track. As the athlete acquires more efficient postures during very simple motor tasks, more advanced skills tend to evolve at a quicker rate, and long-term repetitive injury

Figure 2-1. Throwers must be strong throughout all three planes of movement. The waving is an excellent exercise for working the frontal plane.

patterns lessen or are eliminated. From knowing how to warm up, to establishing general strength, to developing flexibility, and even throwing to get strong, a coach can produce superior results and better prepare an athlete. The coach should use a multifaceted approach to conditioning throwers at the track that includes the following: flexibility, medicine-ball work, body weight circuits, plyometrics, sprint work, release efforts, and multithrow exercises.

The Warm-Up

Various forms of warm-up exist for practice, training, and competition activities of athletes. A well-designed warm-up will bring about various physiological changes that will enhance the training activity or competition. Although the need of a warm-up might be clear, the specific elements that should be included in the warm-up may be less obvious. Whether or not some sort of warm-up should be performed prior to activity is certainly not a new idea. Research as far back as the 1950s and 1960s showed that a pre-activity warm-up could be beneficial to vertical jump performance. Anderson (1980) built on this idea by stating that some sort of general warm-up should be conducted before any other type of activity. Specifically, he suggested that a light jog of 200 to 400 yards be performed, followed by static stretching. Researchers began to explore the physiological bases behind warming up. These findings gave more support to the belief that a general warm-up may decrease the chance of injury during the following activity. Hedrick (1992) pointed out several physiological responses to a warm-up activity that have a direct relation to improved performance. The first response was the friction between the contractile filaments during the contraction of muscles . This friction resulted in an increase of tissue temperature within the body, aiding the body's need to increase circulation for the raised oxygen requirements. Yet another physiological benefit of a pre-activity warm-up is that it can decrease the occurrence of abnormal electrocardiogram responses at the onset of activity. Ninos (1995) suggested that 5 to 10 minutes of easy, low-level aerobic activity, such as cycling or jogging, should be performed before stretching. He claimed that the best way to know the body's internal temperature has been raised is the onset of perspiration. Low-level jogging or cycling can also allow the muscle to reach a greater length. Ninos (1995) also drew this conclusion: if the muscle can reach a greater length, one may assume that the risk of "pulled" muscles would be decreased. Research involved with pre-activity warm-up began another thread: what happens when athletes neglect a warm-up? Mann and Jones (1999) pointed out that many athletes who begin activities without some sort of warm-up will have muscles that are at a minimal core temperature, and therefore, are not properly prepared for activity. If the body is not prepared for the activity, the threat of injury may in fact be at a higher level. The three findings from Hedrick (1992), Ninos (1995), and Mann and Jones (1999) all add validation to the premise that pre-activity exercises should actually "warm" the muscles up. The type of warm-up utilized should be specific to the task demands. An effective throwing warm-up also progresses from general to specific. Once the warm-up gets under way, the thrower is constantly moving. The warm-up is very active with various total body movement exercises followed by short rest periods. The point of the warm-up is to raise the core temperature of the muscles. For each degree that the athlete raises the core temperature of the muscle, about 13 percent efficiency is gained. The general strength parameters, mobility, and posture must be addressed in the warm-up, or throwing power can be severely restricted. The throwing warm-up includes a great deal of remedial and ancillary work in the training schedules because the warm-up is a big part of developing specific endurance, flexibility, and core stability for the thrower. Each workout should always have a remedial injury prevention component, which is often most easily addressed in the warm-up.

Special consideration for other "at risk" joint complexes must be programmed into the warm-up. The ankles and feet are often a weak link in technical execution. You cannot run fast, jump, or throw far unless you have a strong foot and ankle. The development of better training shoes and reliance on the improved footwear has made the feet an area prone to weakness. You must prepare the foot for the stresses of plyometrics and other high-impact activities and the high velocities involved in throwing by performing foot-strengthening conditioning exercises. You can have your athletes warm up and do sprint drills, general strength circuits, and jump circuits in bare feet on the grass. Warming up with no shoes on is a great way to build strength in the feet and ankles. You can also have them perform low-level, single-leg hops and other special exercises to build up the feet and ankles. Prescribe exercises for these and other at-risk areas as a part of the thrower's warm-up.

Each session begins with some easy walking in bare feet on the grass. An assortment of walking exercises can warm up the legs, back, shoulders, and arms. Backwards walking, walking carioca, side shuffle, and rotational walking exercises that include twisting and chopping movements are a great starting point. The warm-up intensity is then increased by performing some light jogging. The jogging can range from 200 to 800 meters, and it is a slow jog that may last three to eight minutes, depending on the fitness level of the athlete and the throwing event. Athletes often wear headphones during this part of the session to visualize the day's activity and increase excitability. Active flexibility must be incorporated into the warm-up training as part of the warm-up, and it should follow light activity. A thrower should roll his hips, neck, shoulders, ankles, and back. Joint-flexibility exercises are followed by some sprint drills (Table 2-1). Combining the sprint drills into warm-up routines of varying intensity helps the coach choose the warm-up that fits the day's activities and conditions. A lower intensity warm-up would be used for a morning workout or an afternoon recovery session. Low-intensity skips, squats, lunges, and rotational walks are suitable. A warm-up that stimulates the nervous system would precede a high-intensity throwing day. This high-intensity warm-up could include squat jumps, lunge jumps, bounding, and high-intensity skips for height and distance. Sprint exercises involve various movements horizontally through space, whereby limbs are placed through unique ranges of movement under varying thresholds of velocities and force considerations. An example of

Sprint Drills (Three Different Warm-Up Combinations)		
Warm-Up A	*Warm-Up B*	*Warm-Up C*
Skip with crossarm F and B Windmill skip F and B Crossover skip Alternate side shuffle Carioca Strides	B-skip Fast-leg butt kick Fast-leg cycle Fast-leg knee lift Straight leg bound Carioca (high knee) Strides	A-skip B-skip Straight leg bound Flex leg bound Butt kick Carioca (high knee)
Mobility Exercises		
Dynamic Flexibility (Five of Each)	*Dynamic Flexibility Hip Series*	*Hip Mobility (Hurdle Drills)*
Head rotations Arm circles 　(front/back and in/out) Hip rotations Side bends Knee rotations Eagles Scissors 　(frontal and sagittal) Hip circles Leg swings 　(frontal and sagittal) Scorpions Ankle circles	Leg swings 　(frontal and sagittal) Trail leg windmill Lunge exchange Side bends Donkey kick and leg whip	Hurdle walkover with 　alternate lead leg; spacing 　ranges from rail to rail to 　one-foot gaps. Hurdle walkover with 　constant lead leg Multidirectional walkovers 　(i.e., two hurdles forward, 　then one backward)
Upper-Body Flexibility With the Javelin		
Side bends	Place the javelin on the traps, curl the hands over the top, and bend the torso toward the ground. Bend toward the left and then to the right.	
Twists	Place the javelin on the traps, curl the hands over the top, and twist the torso 180 degrees to the left and to the right.	
Rotator-cuff stretch	This exercise loosens up the front deltoid, and it is very specific to javelin throwing.	
Dislocates	The athlete grips the javelin with the hands close to the ends. The athlete takes the javelin over the head and behind the body while still holding on to the javelin. The object is to be able to move the hands in closer and closer and still take the javelin overhead.	
Hip pops	Place the javelin on the traps, and curl the hands over the top. The athlete then assumes the power position and turns the drive leg in the direction of the throw.	

Table 2-1. Warm-up activities for throwers

sprint drills that are performed as part of the warm-up include: high knee, heel-to-glute, A skips, B skips, and carioca. General strength exercises can be performed following each sprint drill. Three to five sets of various abdominal movements can be included daily as part of the warm-up to ensure the core as well as the upper and lower body is warm. The last part of the warm-up includes some easy strides. An athlete should never overexert the warm-up in a meet situation and should establish a pre-meet routine based on the warm-up the protocol used in training. Make sure the total warm-up lasts between 30 minutes to one hour, as it takes about 45 minutes to warm-up the soft tissue in the body.

General Guidelines for a Thrower's Warm-Up

- Mark a distance of 30 meters with cones for the athletes to move between.
- At the end of each shuttle, the athletes complete a set of exercises/drills (e.g., half squats, side lunges, split jumps, etc.).
- Athletes move the length of the shuttle, using a variety of running drills (e.g., skips forwards and backwards, high knees, walking lunges, crossovers, etc.).
- Shuttles can start with low intensity and slowly increase intensity.
- This work is continuous for 10 to 15 minutes.
- Ensure a permanent heart rate of 150 bpm (approximately).

Using High Intensity Activities in the Warm-Up

In an activity like throwing, which requires explosive strength, performance factors that should be addressed during the warm-up include optimal stiffness of the series elastic component and rapid activation of the contractile apparatus (Chiu, 2003). Another form of warm-up, known as potentiation or postactivation potentiation, is receiving an increased amount of attention from the sports-science community. The contractile history of a muscle influences the mechanical performance of subsequent muscle contractions. Fatiguing muscle contractions impair muscle performance; whereas, non-fatiguing muscle contractions, typically at high loads of brief duration, may enhance muscle performance. Postactivation potentiation (PAP) is the increase in muscle force and rate of force development as a result of previous activation of the muscle. The implementation of high-intensity contractions as a component of the warm-up prior to a training session or a competition has been suggested to improve performance. Olympic weightlifting exercises, squats, jump squats, heavy medicine-ball throws, and throws with heavy implements are activities that could be used as part of the warm-up of a thrower. The exact protocol of exercise for inducing potentiation is currently unknown.

Flexibility

Research pertaining to pre-activity warm-up and stretching and post-activity stretching has evolved over the past few decades. The second pre-activity debate involves what type of stretching is performed (if performed at all) prior to activity. Current research shows that some of the activities suggested a few decades ago are no longer suggested practice. Two topics that have been at the center of these debates involve two common practices: pre-activity warm-up and pre-activity stretching. Flexibility protocols have been an area of focus for researchers in the past few decades. Researchers have been trying to assess the athletic benefits of performing a general warm-up prior to activity and attempting to pinpoint what (if any) type of stretching should be performed before activity to then maximize practice and performance.

The ballistic-style of stretching popular in the 1960s was slowly replaced in the early 1980s with a focus on static and/or PNF stretching. Cornelius (1984) favored PNF stretching over ballistic stretching, stating that the explosive nature of ballistic stretching created a higher risk for injury and can cause soreness. PNF stretching, he concluded, will result in greater flexibility.

The pre-activity stretching routine suggested by Anderson (1980) contained a variety of static stretching for the groin, hips, ankles, and lower back. These types of stretches before activity would allow the muscles the opportunity to move freely and easily. Wallace (1984) also preferred this static type of stretching due to its ability to produce plastic changes in the muscle-tendon unit. Beaulieu (1984) also favored static stretching, but also points out that no one stretching technique, at that time, had been shown to be more effective than the others.

As suggested by Prentice (1984), the current trend has found that these static and/or PNF stretching tactics are better suited following activity, not before it. Several other studies have shown that using static stretching as a pre-activity warm-up has no effect on performance. Nelson, Kokkonen, and Arnall (2005) found that static stretching actually lowered the muscular strength endurance in 22 college students by 28 percent. Another study on adults aged 18 to 34 years found vertical jump performance to be 5.6 percent lower following static stretching as compared to no stretching at all (Wallman, Mercer, McWhorter, 2005). A similar study (Unick, Kieffer, Cheesman, and Feeney, 2005) found no difference in vertical-jump performance from either static or ballistic stretching as compared with no stretching. One final study by Cramer (2006) found no effect on peak torque of leg extensors from static stretching. This research all suggests that static stretching should be avoided prior to activity, a stark comparison to research from a few decades ago.

A currently well-accepted theory for pre-activity was not widely mentioned in research until the 1990s. Flexibility research strayed from concepts of static stretching and involved the notion that a pre-activity warm-up should contain some sort of "dynamic flexibility" or "activity-specific warm-up." Dynamic flexibility is defined as "the act of quickly moving a joint through its range of motion with little resistance" (Fredrick and Szymanski, 2001, 22). Zentz et al. (1998) described what they called a "specific" warm-up as involving "skill applications actually used in the sport" (51). Some of the examples of these specific warm-up exercises include throwing a ball, shooting a basketball, swinging a bat, and throwing with a heavy implement.

Mann and Jones (1999) state that types of dynamic warm-up routines are designed "from analyzing the movements associated with a particular sports activity and developing stretches to enhance flexibility and balance for that activity" (53). They explained that most static stretches can be easily transformed into dynamic stretching. For example, instead of having an athlete push against a wall with his leg stretched behind him in order to stretch the calf, have him walk on the balls of his feet for 10 yards, both forward and backward. Static stretching does very little to raise the internal temperature of the muscle, but having the athlete perform a dynamic movement can help to raise the core temperature. Other lower-body dynamic stretches involve a series of front, side, and rear lunges that actively warm-up the hips, knees, ankles, and all of the surrounding muscle groups. Mann and Jones (1999) also suggest a series of upper-body dynamic activities such as arm circles and arm swings as well as the act of throwing, as previously mentioned by Zentz et al. (1998).

Research supports dynamic stretching over other types of pre-activity. The research has attempted to prove its superiority by showing that it can better prepare athletes for certain athletic activities. Yamaguchi and Ishii (2005) found dynamic stretching to be better than static stretching or no stretching at all for leg extension power in male students. In another study, athletes were tested on a t-test, underhand medicine-ball toss, and a five-step jump test. Their results were significantly greater when dynamic stretching was performed prior to the tests than when static stretching was performed. Little and Williams (2006) also found agility performance to be greater following dynamic stretching as opposed to static. This research suggests that dynamic stretching should be included as part of a thrower's warm-up.

Flexibility, an essential ingredient of a successful thrower, is often a challenge—especially in males. One of the by-products of functional hypertrophy is the maintenance of flexibility. Flexibility is primarily important to increasing the efficiency of muscle contraction and preventing injury. Long-term repetitive-injury patterns lessen or are eliminated with proper flexibility training. Flexibility in the shoulders, arms, and torso is necessary to get into the proper positions when throwing. However, athletes can sometimes lose range of motion in these crucial areas with years of targeted resistance training. In the past, it was generally assumed that lifting weights can decrease flexibility and make a person muscle bound. It is now generally believed that lifting weights will increase flexibility if three basic rules are followed: the exercises are performed through the full range of motion of the joint, the muscles responsible for flexing as well as extending the joint are exercised, and flexibility exercises are included as part of the lifting program.

Subsequent to a proper warm-up, flexibility-exercise sessions should start easy and should always include dynamic exercises (Table 2-1). Static and dynamic flexibility are two different things. Dynamic flexibility, the most common type of flexibility, is the range of movement around a joint, and it raises the core temperature of the muscle. This type of flexibility is performed at the beginning of the training session.

General flexibility exercises must be followed by more specific exercises related to throwing or weight lifting, depending on the activity. These exercises are referred to position drills and are generally related to the technique of the specific throwing discipline. Walking South African drill is a great example of a specific warm-up drill for a discus thrower. Hip pops (Figure 2-2) warm up the hips, knees, and ankles in the power position for the discus and the shot put. Breaking down the turn in the hammer into position drills at each of the key degree points is a great way to prepare for further hammer activity. An excellent way to warm-up the upper body for a javelin thrower is to perform event-specific dynamic flexibility exercises. For the javelin thrower, you can use internal and external rotation exercises in which the javelin is gripped near the point and the tail is placed under the arm. A dynamic flexibility exercise performed as part of the warm-up is called the dislocate drill. The athlete grips the javelin with the hands close to the ends. The athlete takes the javelin over the head and behind the body while still holding on to the javelin. The objective is to be able to move the hands in closer and closer and still take the javelin overhead. Light medicine-ball work is an excellent way to increase dynamic flexibility and warm up the athlete for a training session, and it can be combined with sprint drills as well. In the weight room, doing warm-up sets with a broomstick or bar or performing a light complex workout is a great way to prepare for activity. An active flexibility routine, such as performing Olympic lifting derivatives with an Olympic bar, works well prior to throwing and lifting workouts.

Figure 2-2. Hip pop drill (starting position)

Post-Activity Flexibility

Some static stretching must be incorporated into the training as part of the cool-down and should follow activity. This aspect of training is essential for all athletes, because it allows freedom of movement of all joints and enhances muscle elasticity. Following the resistance-training program, gradual stretch-and-hold methods should be used to elongate elastic elements. Stretching should be done after each training session to take advantage of muscle spindle fatigue, prevent soreness, and enhance muscle tendon elasticity.

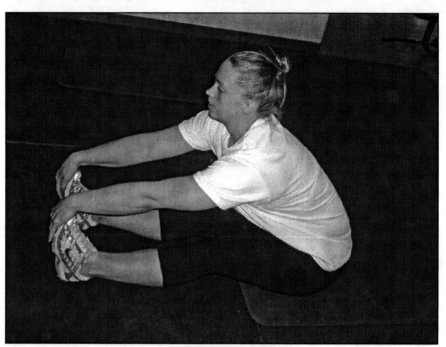

Figure 2-3. Static stretching should consist of gradual stretch and hold methods.

Figure 2-4. Static stretching should always be performed post-exercise.

The preparation phase is the most prudent time to work on improving a thrower's flexibility. The sit and reach test (Figure 2-5) is an excellent way to test hamstring flexibility. To test other areas of the body, a good place to start is by conducting tests like the functional movement screen or the comparative-range-of-motion assessment. These tests can be performed by someone such as an athletic trainer or a physical therapist, but the coach should always be involved. In this type of assessment, the ranges of motion of all major joints are compared to norms and also between the two sides of the thrower's body. The information gained from this type of measurement will allow for the rational planning of a flexibility/conditioning routine. All too often, throwers work flexibility patterns that are already acceptable and ignore patterns that are substandard. It could be argued that it is better to have poor flexibility in all your joints rather than having good elasticity in some joints and poor movement in others. If the thrower's symmetry is compromised with muscle and strength imbalances and tightness in only certain areas of the body, the athlete is at risk. When all the joints are tight, they share stress equally, but when only a few joints don't move as they should, the stress is placed squarely upon them, and they become overstressed. A well-planned flexibility routine, along with soft-tissue work from a physiotherapist and chiropractic care, can help correct this predicament.

General Strength Development

General strength exercises are strength movements that involve no external loading. Body weight serves as the only loading agent. In throwing, the athlete must be able to manipulate his body weight in free space with an implement. Therefore, the first step in the conditioning process is to effectively manipulate his own body weight by performing basic calisthenic exercises. A highly sedentary lifestyle exhibited by today's society has precluded the acquisition of these general qualities that were found in abundance several generations ago.

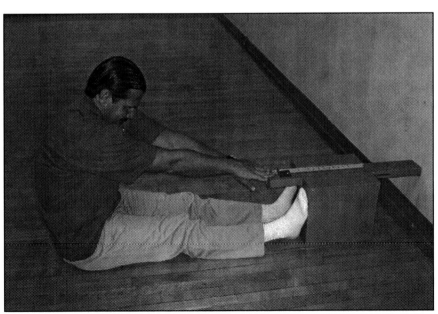

Figure 2-5. The sit and reach test is an excellent way to test hamstring flexibility.

Calisthenics were once part of the basic physical education curriculum that has vanished from the education system. General strength exercises can be used to help the athleticism of the new sedentary generation, and can also improve coordination, strength endurance, energy-system fitness, and even flexibility. General strength maneuvers can take the form of general calisthenics (such as push-ups, sit-ups, squats without weight, etc.), abdominal or spinal work, or special stabilization exercises (such as physioball work or Pilates). These exercises can be grouped together in a circuit (Table 2-2) and can be performed as part of the warm-up or done as a conditioning circuit on the track or in the weight room.

Pedestal
The athlete starts with 10 seconds of holding each position with the body in perfect alignment. After the athlete can hold the positions, he starts performing 10 repetitions on each leg, maintaining alignment.

- Prone, elbow stand, single leg raise
- Supine, elbow stand, single leg raise
- Prone, hand stand, single leg raise
- Supine, hand stand, single leg raise
- Lateral, elbow stand, single leg raise
- Lateral, hand stand, single leg raise
- Prone, flexed knee, elbow stand, hip lift
- Supine, flexed knee, hip lift
- Crunch, low reach
- Crunch, low reach with twist

General Strength Circuit #1 (Outside)		General Strength Circuit #2 (Weight Room)	
Crunches	X30	Hanging leg raise	X30
Clap push-ups	X10	Chin-ups	X10
Leg toss	X20	Roman chair sit-up	X20
Push-ups	X15	Dips	X15
V-ups	X20	Russian twists	X20
Leg scissors	X20 in-and-out	Lunge walk	X10 steps
Push-up toe walk	X10 steps		
Side crunch	X10 each side		
Decline push-ups	X10		
Wrestler's bridge	X5		
Single-leg squats	X10 each leg		

Remedial Shoulder Strength Circuit (Javelin)	
Crawling forward and back	X10
Crossover crawl	X10 each way
Arm step-up forward and back	X10
Reverse arch-up	X5

Table 2-2. General strength activities

General conditioning and general body strengthening are basic requirements for all athletes. Circuit training is a good way to control athletes' conditioning and add variety to programs. Circuit training, either with or without weights, not only can improve general strength, but with different exercises can boost specific strength and specific endurance as well. The effect on the cardiovascular system is strong if the circuit is done with short rest periods, and as a result circuit training has a good effect on improving body composition. Circuits can be controlled by:

- Type of circuit: timed or repetition based
- Number of exercises (usually 6 to 8)
- Types of exercises
- Sequence of exercises
- Number of repetitions of each exercise
- Number of repetitions of each circuit
- Amount of rest between exercises and/or circuits
- Circuits are designed to meet the aims of particular training phases.

Example Circuit

Station 1: Leg exercise (e.g., body weight squats)
Station 2: Abdominal exercise (e.g., crunches)
Station 3: Step-ups, holding light dumbbells to a small box
Station 4: Back-muscle exercise (prone position; paddle with arms and legs)
Station 5: Straddle side hops over a towel
Station 6: Chest shoulder and triceps exercise (e.g., push-ups)

Work: 20 seconds   Rest: 20 seconds   Sets: 2 to 3

General strength exercises can be performed anywhere and are an excellent exercise prescription for holiday periods when facility issues arise and can interrupt training.

Medicine Ball

Because of the nature of throwing, medicine-ball training often comprises a large percentage of the auxiliary training. Discus great Al Oerter attributed much of his throwing success to medicine-ball training. Dribbling a heavy medicine ball against a concrete wall, Oerter conditioned his upper body with "talking arms." The result: four gold medals! Medicine-ball throws can be categorized as supplemental or specific training for the throws because medicine balls can not only be used for extraneous preparation exercise but also in the specific throwing pattern. Medicine-ball preparation exercises are used to strengthen the abdominals and the torso. These exercises will help improve the biomotor qualities of flexibility and strength. The use of medicine-ball drills can be valuable in adding an increased load to full-body muscle groups as well. These drills are particularly useful for developing ballistic strength in the trunk, back, and shoulder girdle.

Figure 2-6. The medicine-ball sit-up with a twist is a multi-planer exercise that works the trunk in the sagittal and transverse planes.

Medicine balls come in a variety of sizes and weights. In most cases, athletes should start out with lighter balls, and as higher physical conditioning levels are obtained, increase the load of the balls. The standard rule-of-thumb emphasizes technique over ball weight. Using a ball that is too heavy will cause breakdown in skills. Sets, reps, and recovery time are also important and are specific to the athlete's individual needs. Too many sets or reps, or not enough recovery time could cause fatigue and unacceptable skill performance. It is also important to perform each drill with both sides of the body. Medicine-ball preparation often consists of a combination of supplemental exercises with a 1 to 5 kg (2 to 11 lb) ball (Table 2-3). Athletes should pair up and follow the exercises listed in Table 2-3. Ten repetitions should be performed in each exercise. As the athletes progress, the number of repetitions should be increased, and a second set can be added or a heavier ball should be used.

During the peaking phase, medicine-ball exercises are great for developing speed strength. Unlike free-weight exercises such as the bench press, medicine-ball throwing involves no deceleration phase. Release work using a medicine ball can be performed for all of the throwing events that emphasize the velocity of release. Specific medicine-ball exercises for each throwing event are performed in the same manner as the particular throwing event. For the shot-putter, another means of increasing upper-body strength popular with throwers is to lie on the ground face up. A partner then drops a medicine ball down toward the chest of the athlete, who catches the ball (pre-stretch) and immediately throws it back. This exercise is high-intensity and should only be used after some basic conditioning has been completed. Medicine-ball work is the foundation of a javelin thrower's training. A progression for a javelin thrower would include: standing throws, three-step throw, five-step throws, two-step

Medicine-Ball Exercises (10 repetitions each)		
Have the athlete start with a 3k ball and increase when he can do each exercise under control.		
#1 Competition Phase	*#2 Preparation Phase/ Pre-Competitive Phase*	*#3 Preparation Phase/Pre-Competitive Phase*
Catch and throw Back-to-back partner pass Over-and-under pass Sit-ups Seated side throw	Standing overhead forward Hip catch and throw Good morning V-sit Catch and throw Hurdle reach Partner exchange hip Prone catch and toss Knee toss Seated roll Arm-add-abs	Standing shoulder catch and throw Reach and hike Back toss Seated oblique twist catch and throw Leg toss Torso circle Kneeling overhead forward Leg-adductors-abdominals Prone overhead back Partner exchange, kneeling overhead back Arm-adductors-abdominals

Event-Specific Medicine-Ball Drills

Hammer

Modified Hammer Throw: Start with ball on hip opposite the throw/delivery side. Start transferring weight from backside to delivery side by turning the back foot, while twisting the body's core. Finish by throwing/delivering the ball at shoulder height with the body weight balanced over the delivery side. This throw can also begin at shoulder height instead of by the hip.

Shot Put

Puts: Start with ball behind one hip with more weight on that leg. Throw ("put") the ball while turning and reaching toward the direction of the throw. Finish the drill in a balanced position.

Putting exercises can also be performed in the weight room on an incline bench. Another great putting exercise is to perform a three-step javelin approach and finish with a putting motion. The athlete will face a wall and hold the medicine ball with the throwing hand behind the ball and the free hand on the side for support. Starting with the left foot, the step pattern would be left, right, left/plant. The athlete would plant and put the medicine ball against the wall. The emphasis is on rhythm, a strong block, and keeping the hand over the deltoid for a clean arm strike. This drill has great crossover for those multievent throwers who may participate in the javelin and shot put.

Javelin

Wall Throws: Stand six to eight feet from the wall. Swing the ball to an overhead position, stretching the upper extremities. Throw the ball, aiming one to two feet above the bottom of the wall, using the core.

One-Step Wall Throws: Start with the ball at the belly button. Swing the ball to an overhead position, and step forward with one foot toward the wall. Shift weight completely over the front throwing leg, using the core to throw. Aim one to two feet above the bottom of the wall.

Discus

Side Throws: Begin at 90 degrees to the wall, with ball held away from the body behind the hip, and more weight on that leg. Deliver the ball at hip height, with weight transferred to the front leg. Catch the ball, and repeat. Use a light (1 to 3k) ball to work on arm whip.

Table 2-3. Medicine-ball circuits

walk-in full throws, and full throws. For the discus thrower, the athlete can perform high-velocity discus releases against the wall with a 1 or 2 kg (2 to 4 lb) medicine ball, emphasizing an explosive release. These slinging throws can be performed on the knees and standing. The hammer thrower can also perform multiple releases against a wall, working both the left and right sides.

Advantages of Medicine-Ball Training

- A large number of exercises can be performed in a relatively short period of time.
- All muscle groups are worked through a full range of movement that is required for the throwing events.
- Training loads (weight of ball, number of sets and repetitions) are individualized to the age and stage of the athlete and training period.
- Dynamic and plyometric work with selected exercises can be event-specific, ending with maximal speed of release through a full range of movement.
- Weight of balls can be varied with lighter balls used to increase the speed of execution.
- Sessions are fun, especially for groups of athletes.

Figure 2-7. Medicine-ball drop

Plyometrics

Plyometrics are a training method thought to be developed in Eastern Europe for emerging elite athletes. Together, the Latin root words *plio* ("more") and *metric* mean measurable increases. These "jumping" exercises have actually been around for decades and involve an eccentric contraction followed immediately by a concentric contraction. The term "plyometrics" was first coined not in Europe but instead in the United States by track coach, Fred Wilt.

Plyometrics involve simultaneous voluntary and involuntary muscle contractions. Therefore, more motor units are called upon during a single contraction of this type than would be used in either the voluntary or involuntary contraction alone (Table 2-4). One of the limiting factors in improved performance is eccentric strength, and one of the benefits of plyometrics is the development of eccentric strength.

The athlete should perform each exercise for a prescribed number of repetitions or time period, and then rest. The athlete should start with a 3:1 work:rest ratio.	
Jump Circuit #1	**Jump Circuit #2**
Star jumps 180-degree jumps 360-degree jumps Speed skater Line hops Dynamic step-ups Single-leg butt kick	Lunge jumps Tuck jumps Butt kick Lateral squat jumps Downhill jumps Straddle jumps
Jump-Rope Circuit	

30-second warm-up
15 seconds each:
  • Regular jump
  • Side-to-side
  • Front-to-back
  • Double jump
  • Skipping
30-second cool-down	

Competitive-Phase Plyometrics	
5x5 Boxes (double-leg hop) 3x5 Rotational boxes (sides, 180 degree, 360 degree) 5x Depth jumps 5x Hurdle hops (use the baby hurdles) 5x Standing broad jumps (jump into the sand) 5x Tuck jumps	
Combinations	
Quarter squat and overhead back throw with medicine ball Parallel squat with concentric jumps Bench press with medicine ball drop Mid-thigh high pull with a medicine ball throw for height Seated dumbbell twist with seated side med ball throw	

Table 2-4. Multijump exercises

Plyometrics play a vital role in strength/power sports like the throwing events in track and field. Plyometrics have long been considered to provide event-specific training in the mechanics of performance, including the need to improve RFD. Plyometrics have been shown to improve force production at high velocities and to increase the maximum rate of force development. It is a well-known fact that muscle contractions are more powerful when preceded by the muscle pre-stretch plyometric exercises create. Verkhoshansky (1986) suggests that traditional weight programs that incorporate plyometrics are superior to those that do not. Combining weight training and plyometrics develops speed-strength, the "amount of internal strength which the neuromuscular (the body's electrical system) is able to mobilize per unit of time."

Some prerequisites must be developed in order to make this mix of plyometrics and weight training work at maximum efficiency. If force = mass x acceleration, then particular care should be taken with heavy athletes. It is up to the discretion of the coach to assess strength in relation to bodyweight and use safe methods with all athletes. A simple rule of thumb to determine if an athlete is ready for plyometrics: the athlete must be able to squat approximately one-and-a-half times his body weight (Chu, 1983). It has been suggested that athletes who weigh over 220 lbs (100 kg) should not perform depth jumps higher than 18 inches (45 cm). In addition, plyometrics should not be used by athletes with orthopedic injuries. In the author's opinion, throwers should not do very much single-leg jumping, excepting javelinists. Although authorities have placed many qualifications upon the use of plyometric training ultimately, the wisdom of the coach and close training state observation are prerequisites to the use of this type of training. Written guidelines can never replace visual control by the coach.

The basic jumping skills employed when performing plyometric exercises can be classified as follows:
- Hop: one foot to the same foot
- Step: one foot to the other foot with ground contact
- Bound: one foot to the other foot with flight phase
- Jump: one foot to both feet, or both feet to both feet

Plyometric exercises can be grouped according to the strength qualities developed: exercises that are designed for developing elastic strength (low-hurdle jumps, low-drop jumps), exercises that develop concentric strength (standing long jump, high-hurdle jumps), and exercises that develop eccentric strength (higher drop jumps, depth jumps). Plyometric exercises should be sequenced to reflect the period in the annual plan.

Progression of activities should take place from soft surfaces to hard surfaces. Harder surfaces encourage high rates of energy return. The exercise progression is as follows: double-leg to single-leg jumps, in-place to moving jumps, unweighted to weighted jumps, jumps with a pause to jumps to continuous jumps, and low-amplitude to high-amplitude jumps. Ground-level

Figure 2-8. Plyometric exercises help develop concentric strength, which is needed for the standing long jump.

plyometrics should be introduced initially and used in the high-volume preparation phase to build the foundation for more intense plyometrics. When in doubt about volume, intensity, or frequency, it is best to be conservative in program design.

For most throwers, the beginning box or hurdle height should be relatively low and increased gradually. Proper form and body mechanics should be should taught and be constantly monitored. When performing a box jump, the athlete should step off the box in a relaxed state, not jump. The optimal height of the box should not result in a landing where the heel is forced to the ground by momentum. Biomechanical data supports the idea that high-force production corresponds to a "bridging" action of the foot on ballistic action (Chu, 1983). Contact is made on the outside edge of the mid-foot, then the athlete rolls onto the inside edge of the forefoot (fifth metatarsal to the big toe). Toe-first contact results in a lack of force produced. Coupling times refer to the transitional time between eccentric and concentric action (Chu, 1983). The research is contradictory in this area, but generally, the time it takes to reverse action must be very short in order to take advantage of the increased force production. Two very effective cues for coaching plyometric exercises are: "quick off the ground" or "jump off the frying pan." Shoes should be suited to the foot and provide good support for beginners and good energy return for advanced athletes.

Plyometric training is very individual and must be tailored to the specific athlete for whom it is intended. Every athlete has different concerns and needs. Because of individual variations, cookie-cutter plyometric programs are a sure way to hurt athletes. Medical histories, training age, strength, muscle imbalances, and the individual athlete's throwing events are some of the variables that will dictate the specific design of the program. In general, females need more biomotor training in the area of strength development. Work more low-intensity plyometrics with female athletes, and hold off on high-intensity work until a large training base is established. Keep in mind, most females have a larger quadriceps angle (Q angle) than men that posturally presents with an increased valgus (shin out) stress at the knee.

Many experts in the field suggest that moderate jumps can be included in the athletic training of very young children. However, great care needs to be exerted when prescribing any training procedures for preadolescents. Because of the relatively immature bone structure in preadolescent and adolescent children, the very great forces exerted during intensive depth jumps should be avoided.

It is important to keep track of plyometric volume and intensity. Count the number of foot contacts in a workout to track the volume. Quantify the intensity for plyometrics: heavy (depth jumps), medium (concentric jumps), light (sprint drills, easy strides). It is wise not to perform too many repetitions in any one session since a plyo session is a quality session, with the emphasis on speed and power rather than endurance. Coaches should split the work into sets with ample recovery in between. As a general rule, athletes should perform two sessions a week with 48 hours recovery between sessions. Jump circuits, and low-intensity plyometrics can be included as part of the warm-up progression during the preparation phase. Each exercise must be performed with an elevated level of effort. High intensity must dominate the plyometric training session because exercises are to be performed at 95 to 100 percent effort. However, athletes must keep a balanced relationship between stress and recovery. Insufficient recovery is the most common cause of injury in plyometrics. Generally one to three minutes between sets and three to five minutes between exercises is sufficient recovery within a single training session. Always watch the execution of technique, and always discontinue an exercise or end the workout if technique breaks down. The "more is better" mantra when applied to plyometric work will rapidly negate any training effect only to produce acute bone, joint, or soft-tissue injuries. The one common major error in the use of jumping exercises is that it is often assumed "the higher/further, the better." When athletes are advised to bound or jump, often the focus is on the distance or the height. Worldwide, you will find boxes in gyms well beyond reasonable heights, but will rarely find low (20- to 30-cm, or 8- to 12-inch) boxes. Going for distance or height is only one objective in reactive strength training, while the other and more important objective must be minimizing ground contact times.

Preparation-phase plyometric exercises include various ground-level plyometrics like jump circuits, many types of bounding drills and bleacher/stairs work. Many of these exercises are used throughout the training program to build a base for later high-intensity work that includes hurdle hops, benches, and boxes of various heights.

Figure 2-9. Concentric jump

A specific plyometric exercise, a series of depth jumps, is very helpful, but also very demanding on an athlete's body. Depth jumps should only be performed after a good strength and conditioning period and lower intensity ground-level plyometrics such as skipping and bounding. The beginning height should then be relatively low and increased gradually. The optimal height of the box should not result in a landing where the heel is forced to the ground by momentum. The athlete should fall off the box in a relaxed state, not jump. The dosage of depth jumps should not exceed two to three sets of four to eight repetitions for the lesser conditioned athlete and four sets of five to 10 repetitions for the well-conditioned athlete. The rest intervals between sets of maximal plyometric exercises should be about three to five minutes for speed strength development. During this rest interval, the athlete can do some easy running and relaxation exercises. Depth jumps are used late in the preparation period of a yearly cycle, but can also be used during the competition period about once every 10 to 14 days, and not later than 10 days before a competition.

General Guidelines for Plyometric Training

- Go for short ground contact times. The consequence: small obstacles, short distances.
- Always remember: it is quality that counts.
- Stop it the moment quality gets worse.
- Don't overestimate the relevance of the number of jumps.
- Make sure that exercises are age-related.

Developing Special Strength and Speed in the Ring

© Victah Sailer@www.photorun.NET

Chapter 3

A critical part of the preparation program for the thrower is technical training. Technical development is an integral part of the daily training routine of a thrower and must be periodized like all the other aspects of training. The first three stages of technical development are acquisition, modification, and stabilization. Athletes must acquire new skills, and they may need to modify their existing technique and stabilize these patterns for execution under competitive stress. Once the technique is stabilized and before the peak of competitive technical training, coaches should take advantage of building special strength and speed by using overweight and underweight implements. Special exercises for throwing are exercises using a substantial overload (greater than the standard implement) with a movement that is identical to, or very similar to, parts of the complete competition throwing movement. Training to improve throwing strength that is specific to the positions in the throw can only be accomplished by incorporating special strength work into the strength and conditioning program of the thrower. When the technique is stabilized and the athlete is rested, speed can be developed by using light implements in training. The fourth and final stage of technical development is the peaking competitive technical phase. Peaking competitive technical training can best be described by "less is more." Throwers have a variety of options in training to improve performance; it is the coach's responsibility to harmoniously periodize technical training with the other training units to train athletes most effectively. Following a periodized plan for technical training is another way to edge closer to success. This chapter will address technical preparation for the thrower.

Technical Development

Technical training takes place throughout the whole training year, and as the year and training phases progress, the objectives of technical training will change. No matter the event, some basic rules for technical training must be followed. First of all, athletes must be relatively well recovered (also have in mind yesterday's training). It makes no sense to schedule technical training if the athlete had a tough weight-lifting squat session the day before. Each technical training session must have a clearly defined objective for both coach and athlete. Once the objective has been established, it is important to tailor feedback to that objective. It's a very bad habit to name an additional fault on every throw. Limit the number of feedback cues. No athlete is able to perceive and realize several comments at a time. A coach can measure the athlete's competence by the ability to sort throwing errors, and the sense to start with the basic fault and correct causes accordingly. When making corrections, it is always good to use the "positive sandwich" with beginners. Start the conversation with something positive, make the correction, and then end the dialogue with something positive. This approach will help the athlete stay energized and confident. The number of sessions, the number and kind of exercises, and the volume and intensity will vary according to the training period. Technical training is divided into four stages:

- Acquisition
- Modification
- Stabilization
- Peaking competitive

Acquisition Phase

The acquisition of new skills or technical elements starts in the general preparation phase. This phase is particularly important for beginners or youth athletes. Youth athletes are consistently learning new skills and new techniques. New elements must blend with the athletes' physical qualities. Practices should emphasize a large number of repetitions of the correct movements. Teaching progressions are used with facilitated conditions. Athletes will be receiving a lot of feedback during this phase (Figure 3-1). Youth athletes or beginners are not the only athletes utilizing new skills. During this phase, advanced athletes will learn new techniques or at least elements (for example, a glide shot-putter beginning to learn the rotary shot or a hammer thrower adding a fourth turn).

Figure 3-1. Mastering the power position through constant repetition of various power position drills with and without the shot put is a way to teach proper mechanics in the acquisition phase.

Modification Phase

Modification of an existing technique is a very difficult and often long-lasting process. This conversion may be even more difficult than new skill acquisition; existing movement patterns and neuromuscular patterns interfere with new desired pathways, and the athlete will unfortunately execute old and bad habits. Coaches must commit to destroying old patterns before creating new ones. One method to do so is overcorrection. Overcorrection means teaching something that exceeds the desired pattern outcome. As an example: the "wrap" of a javelin in the set position gives the thrower more time to apply force during the delivery action and thus increase speed of release. At first teach, employ an "exaggerated" wrap, and then give the thrower time to find the best amount of wrap they feel is the most effective to apply their power and at the same time throw through the javelin line. The old and the new model will mix to produce the best the desired outcome for the individual thrower. Effective modification should begin with an early start in the general preparation period. The left arm drill (Figure 3-2) in the hammer is a drill that is used to help the athlete fix the bad habit of dragging the ball. A lot of repetitions are required during this phase. One of the advantages of teaching an event from scratch is a coach does not have to "unteach" bad habits. In the U.S. collegiate system, coaches often teach the hammer and javelin events to athletes who have never thrown. This method allows coaches to teach the proper technical model from the beginning.

Figure 3-2. Left arm drill

Stabilization

Once acquired, new skills must be stabilized. Stabilization is accomplished with a high volume of throws with varied weights. Most of these throws (60 to 70 percent) are executed at a medium throwing intensity of 88 to 92 percent of training max. This intensity is optimal to stabilize the technical pattern. A few easy repetitions are used to warm-up, and approximately four to six maximum effort throws are completed as part of the workout. With many repetitions, athletes will perform very well in training, executing a superb technical pattern. Consistent training results usually mean the athlete is ready to put their training to the test of a competitive situation. Some athletes respond differently to the stress of competition. For many athletes, as soon as it comes to competition, the old bad habits are back. This result is an indication that new skills are not yet stabilized against disturbances. Competitive conditions may be complicated by:

- Unusual times
- Unusual weather
- Unusual surfaces (fast, slow, uphill, downhill)
- Fatigue
- Stress

Introducing these disturbances into the practice may help the athlete overcome these obstacles. This type of training should be conducted after the modification phase. It is a great way to add a little variety and change to a workout.

Unusual Times

Athletes may be required to compete internationally with little time to adjust to a time change as severe as 7 to 12 hours difference. Training at international competition times may help an athlete adjust. Often times, the throws may have qualifying rounds at 8 in the morning, or may compete in a final that begins at 8 at night. Again, practicing at these times in training will help ready an athlete for the time difference. Having morning practices, or working at later hours under the lights, is a great strategy to start the adjustment process.

Unusual Weather

It is important to maintain training in bad weather. You have no guarantee that no rain or heavy wind will be present during competition. This possibility must be rehearsed by training in all weather conditions. Have an occasional cold-weather session to help prepare the athletes for all conditions. Don't be afraid the throw a bucket of water on the ring in training to help prepare your athletes.

Unusual Surfaces

The surface of a ring or runway can vary from facility to facility. At a newly constructed championship venue, the throwing rings are often the last thing completed. This situation can make the surface unpredictable. The green concrete on a newly poured circle can be very slippery. Runways in the javelin are not 100 percent even (Figure 3-3). Sometimes, they are slightly uphill or downhill. Some are in better condition than others, which makes a big difference for run-up and plant. Coaches can prepare for these factors by arriving at competition sites early to allow athletes to practice on the different surfaces. If arriving early cannot happen, finding a surface that mimics this new surface may be a possible solution. Make sure your athletes bring more than one pair of shoes. They should have a pair that works best on a slow surface and one that works best on a fast surface.

Fatigue

Throwers experience fatigue in competition. Travel to competitions usually accounts for the majority of fatigue in athletes. Sometimes, the fatigue

Figure 3-3. The condition of the runway in the javelin can have an impact on the distance of a thrower's approach run.

originates from the preparation for the trip prior to departure. Nevertheless, athletes must have experience throwing max competitive efforts in a fatigued state. Competitions do not always run on time, and an athlete's rhythm may be disrupted by long periods of time in between throws. Training an athlete in these conditions will help an athlete prepare for these types of situations.

Stress

Competition is considerably different from practice. Athletes may be feeling all types of pressures unique to competition. Holding competitive situations frequently between team-mates will mimic the pressure. Schedule developmental competitions, and have the athletes follow the expected protocol of a major competition. Modify the warm-up, and challenge the athletes to hit a certain distance on their first three attempts. Doing so will give more meaning to a competition that may not have an otherwise formidable opponent.

Peaking Competitive Technical Training

In the throwing events in track and field, unlike other sports such as gymnastics, it is an error to overemphasize technical details during the last weeks before a major competition. Coaches pressing certain technical cues in the last remaining weeks are making a mistake: what is the hope that those things which did not work for months will work at the very last minute? Instead, emphasize work on rhythm and speed rather than technical details. Working with the current technical pattern, go for speed and distance in short practices. The throwing intensity remains high, but the volume should be cut in half two weeks before the target competition. It is the quality of each throw that counts. An athlete should leave practice feeling good with some "gas in the tank." Make sure you stop the practice well before the technique breaks down. Remember that all the work is already done, and "the hay is in the barn." The following tables provide guidelines for technical development during the different phases of training.

Technical Training in the General Preparation Phase

The general preparation phase (GPP) is the period of the year for acquisition and/or modification of new skills or technical elements:

- Number of repetitions should be quite high.
- Use light and regulation weight implements to teach technique.
- Try to find adequate drills to work on details apart from the circle or runway.
- When using standing or throws off a short approach, never forget the speed aspect.
- Use overcorrection.
- Advanced athletes would begin working with heavy implements.

Technical Training in the Specific Preparation Phase

The specific preparation phase (SPP) is the period of the year to finalize acquisition and/or modification of new skills or technical elements:

- Throwing volume and intensity should increase.
- Gradually, have the athlete reduce the number of partial technique throws toward the end of SPP phase,
- By the middle of the SPP, greater emphasis should be placed on heavy implements
- Make sure that the technical elements blend with the athletes' physical qualities.

Technical Training in the Pre-Competitive Phase

The pre-competitive phase (PCP) is the period of the year when stabilization of technique should be emphasized:

- This period is of a high throwing volume.
- Intensity (i.e., run-up speed) should increase.
- At the end of the PCP, only a very few standing throws, one or two turn throws, or throws off a short approach are used.
- Continue to emphasize heavy implements, and gradually introduce regulation and light implements by the end of the PCP.
- Make sure that the technical elements blend with the athletes' physical qualities.

Technical Training in the Peaking Competitive Phase

The peaking competitive phase (CP) is the period of the year when speed and rhythm should be the emphasis:

- Stop working on technical details at the latest two weeks before the major competition.
- Think globally, and work on rhythm instead of specific parts of the throw.
- Emphasize speed by using light and regulation implements at high intensities.
- Use minor competitions to rehearse special aspects (e.g., pre-competitive routine, number of warm-up throws).
- Introduce certain stress factors to stabilize the technique.

Implement Choice and Training Blueprint

Various implement weights can be used for the improvement of core control as well as strength, power, speed, and technical development. Implements are specified as light, normal (competition-weight), and heavy. Each of these implement types has a place in your training program. An implement that is different from the competition weight can help work on a specific part of the technical pattern. For example, a heavy implement teaches patience and a long range of motion. A lighter implement works on a quick reaction in the circle and increased speed of the overall rhythm of the throw. Overweight implement training at the beginning and middle portions of the season builds strength, and underweight implement training at the final quarter builds speed. The use of variously weighted shots, hammers, weights, discuses, and javelins should be structured like a lifting workout with designated sets, repetitions, and a percentage of maximal effort.

Figure 3-4. Discus throwers can benefit by using overweight and underweight implements to build power and speed.

The 10 Percent Rule

Varied weight implements should be introduced after the athlete grasps the basic technical model. The question that is often asked when training with various weight implements is: "How heavy or light should I go?" Beginning- to intermediate-level throwers should conform to the "10 percent rule" (Table 3-1) when using varied weight implements. The 10 percent rule means the weight should be plus or minus 10 percent of the standard implement. Keeping the weights within 10 percent of the competition implement will allow the beginner to adapt to this type of training system and will not disrupt the competition rhythm. As a thrower becomes more advanced, he will use much heavier implements. Ultimately, implements that do not exceed the standard weight by 20 percent can be used in the full glide. The use of a heavy implement increases intensity and may have a positive effect on transformation, as long as ideal posture/technique is not altered. Light and heavy implements greater and less than 10 percent of the competition weight are thrown in training with the notion that the improvements in specific speed and specific strength will transfer to the competitive implement, allowing for a better rhythm and a more forceful acceleration during each movement.

The 10 Percent Rule			
Weight	Men	Women/Girls	Boys
Standard	16 lb (7.26 kg)	4 kg (8.89 lb)	12 lb (5.4 kg)
Overweight	18 lb (8 kg)	10 lb (4.5 kg)	14 lb (6.4kg)
Underweight	14 lb (6.4 kg)	8 lb (3.6 kg)	10 lb (4.5 kg)
Adapted from Dunn and McGill (1991)			

Table 3-1. 10 percent rule

Most throwers will throw implements of two to three different weights during each six- to eight-week training period. Too many different weights in a training phase may overwhelm an athlete's nervous system instead of developing the proper pattern for each throwing implement. Varying weights aid the development of the "right reflexes." Technique can only be mastered if muscle contractions and relaxations can be coordinated and synchronized to produce maximum total effort relative to throwing.

Light Implements

Implements that are lighter than the competition weight offer less resistance, allowing the athlete to throw at a higher rate of speed than can be achieved with a heavier implement. Light implements can be used to condition the body's nervous system to learn how to handle the higher rates of speed required for long throws. This technique is known as specific speed. The reaction in the middle of the circle is often an area of the throw that always can be improved. In the glide shot put, a slight pause will be made in the middle of the circle as the athlete prepares to rotate lift and drift. The key is to make sure the pause is as slight as possible, and lighter implements drill a faster reaction time into an athlete's body. Throwing light implements far means throwing with the same rhythm as the competitive weight, just a little faster. Some athletes have a tendency to try to overpower or muscle light implements and fail to work on technique. For intermediate or advanced throwers working on specific speed, the light implement should be used in training only after the following conditions have been met:

- Technique is stabilized (efficient pattern is established).
- The athlete is highly motivated.
- The athlete is fit and or in top physical condition.
- The athlete is fresh (absence of a high workload).

The use of light implements requires a high degree of coaching scrutiny and input, due to the various ways in which their use interacts with and affects the competitive movement. With such an implement, the degree of difficulty of the movement is not heightened, but the coordinative demands are greater; likewise, although throws with light implements are "easy" to execute, they are necessary in developing a heightened level of acceleration throughout the various phases of the throw.

How many throwers "can't" throw light implements well? Such throwers will never reach their true potential with the competitive-weight implement until they are able to develop the speed and rhythm required to throw the light implements far. Simple logic suggests that if the athlete wishes to throw 21 meters (68'10") with the 7.26 kg (16 lb) or 20 meters (65'7") with the 4 kg (8 lb, 13 oz) shot put, he must first be able to throw something of less weight that distance.

Lightweight implements are great for teaching young children/beginners the throwing pattern. When the improvement of throwing technique is the objective, lightweight implements create at least two teaching advantages: the movement is generally easier to perform, and greater mastery of the implement is possible. The competition weight may be too heavy for young athletes to handle to establish a technical pattern. Moving to a lighter weight will not sacrifice a young thrower's ability to perform with heavier shots later in their career; it will only set up an appropriate technical pattern instead of bad habits. For example, 8 or 10 lbs (3 to 5 kg) for boys, and 6 or 8 pounds (2.5 to 3.5 kg) for girls, in the shot put usually works best. Insist that younger athletes using lightweight implements also use correct form.

Heavy Implements

Achieving success in the throws is similar to the pursuit of success in the weight room: a consistent training regime that incorporates a system of overload, progressive resistance, and recovery. Implements that are heavier than the competition weight offer more resistance and therefore require the athlete to generate more force against the ground. Heavy implements teach the athlete to be patient during each phase of the throw and to use long applications of force against the ground to accelerate the implement. The heavy implements help the athletes improve their technical pattern in addition to specific strength. Often times, the athletes can muscle the lighter implements, but when using the heavy shots in the full throw, for example, athletes must concentrate on proper technique because they won't be able to muscle the overweight implement. Throwing heavy implements makes the thrower strong in a way that is very specific to the technical pattern of the event. It helps develop special strength in the core that gives the thrower the ability to stabilize the midsection during high-velocity throws. Control and kinesthetic awareness of the legs and the right side of the body in the power position is critical. The larger implement weight induces increased electrical activity in the involved muscles, consequently working the muscles in a fashion that improves the coordinative potential of the movement: in short, facilitating better recruitment of functional motor units.

Figure 3-5. Throwing the 35-pound weight

Using heavy implements causes the athlete to recruit fast-twitch fibers. Strength and power gains are not only related to cross-sectional muscle size, but to the ability of the central nervous system to properly activate those muscles. The concept of post-activation potentiation (PAP) will be discussed later in this chapter. Just keep in mind rate coding and synchronization are important aspects of intramuscular coordination. Recruitment gradation of total muscle force based on need will be met by the addition or subtraction of active motor units. Small neurons (lowest firing threshold) are recruited first. Demand for larger forces are met with the largest motor units. Developing the fast-twitch fibers is the best way to develop speed. Developing specific strength through the use of heavy implements will cause the recruitment of the largest motor units and the most fast-twitch fiber. This type of training will bring the quickest improvements. The athletes feel very confident with the competition implement after using the heavy implements for their full technique. The heavier implement must be used at a time of year when the athlete's conditioning level is elevated. When the performance level with one implement becomes stabilized, the other weight is then used in training (variability of stimulus).

However, when throwing heavy implements, the athlete is throwing at a slower rate of speed than he would with the competitive implement. A word of caution: if too high a percentage of heavy shots/hammers/discuses/javelins are thrown, the athlete learns to move slowly, and in extreme cases, the nervous system becomes "set" at that one speed. Cases can occur where an athlete can throw a whole range of different weighted implements close to the same distance. Such athletes have developed a "speed barrier" and must take special action in training to restore the ability to react quickly. Heavier shots are also tougher on the wrist and hand, and they can break down a young, weak, inexperienced thrower and hurt their confidence at first. Let the young thrower work up to the heavy implements.

Using a training regime that incorporates a system of overload, progressive resistance, and recovery will allow the thrower to make steady progress and build a base for future success. As the season progresses, the ladder (weight of implements) can be adjusted downward for more speed work. About three weeks out from a major competition, start to use light implements in training. This approach will help the athlete develop a faster temporal pattern. Using a system of overload training helps create magic in the throw. The object is to make the competitive implement feel light on the day of the competition. When the competitive implement feels light, the athlete will have the confidence to throw far.

Using Heavy Implements in the Warm-Up

Some debate exists within the field concerning the validity of the use of heavy implements in training and during the throwing warm-up prior to competition. The biggest criticism is the effect on the rhythm and timing of the movement. Critics believe heavy implements will disrupt the timing of the movement and set the nervous system to a slower speed. I have witnessed the opposite. Using heavy implements to warm up is a concept that I have used very successfully throughout my coaching career. Although I have never tested this concept scientifically, I have witnessed some incredible results using this technique. First, we would order heavy implements that were in line with competition specifications. In the shot put and hammer throw, we would warm up with an implement that was 2 kg heavier than the competition implement for one or two trials. I then would have the athlete drop to an implement 1 kg below for the competition weight for one or two trials. The athlete would not touch the regulation implement until the competition started. I was trying to take advantage of a concept called post-activation potentiation (PAP). The jump from the heavier to a lighter competition implement often produced some very good results on the opening throw.

Several researchers have addressed this topic in the literature, but further study is needed in this area. Following is a basic explanation of the scientific rationale behind using this technique with your athletes. In essence, throwing heavier implements in the pre-meet warm-up works because the contractile history of a muscle influences the mechanical performance of subsequent muscle contractions. Fatiguing muscle contractions impair muscle performance; whereas, non-fatiguing muscle contractions, typically at high loads of brief duration, may enhance muscle performance. Post-activation potentiation (PAP) is the increase in muscle force and rate of force development as a result of previous activation of the muscle. The proposed mechanism for PAP is phosphorylation of myosin regulatory light chains, which renders actin-myosin more sensitive to Ca^{2+} released from the sarcoplasmic reticulum during subsequent muscle contractions.

Although PAP is a well-known property of muscle, the impact of PAP on human performance is less understood. The research is equivocal to date as to whether PAP enhances human performance. According to Sale (2002), PAP by increasing the rate of force development may increase the acceleration and hence velocity achieved with loads. This effect of PAP would be to shift the force-velocity curve upward and to the right, which may potentially enhance strength and speed performance. In theory, a brief, high-intensity contraction preceding a brief maximal effort during an athletic event that involves throwing may increase the rate of force development. Increasing the rate of force development would in turn increase the strength and speed attained during the performance of an athletic event that involves a brief maximal effort (e.g., throwing an implement), which would manifest as improved athletic performance.

Balancing the Performance Model

As mentioned previously, many coaches get impatient with athletes because they cannot perform the ideal technique, and the coach fails to realize the training plan is at fault. One of the most helpful tools for the coach and athlete is comparing the distances achieved under training conditions with implements of various weights. The relationship of distance thrown when comparing the light, normal, and heavy implements can reveal what the priority should be for the specific training. The expected relationship is approximately 10 percent per kilogram of weight change. If you know what to expect, you know what to change about the training based on deviations from the expected pattern. Suppose in the following example, instead of throwing 15.84 meters (52 feet) with a 5 kg (11 lb) shot put, 18 meters (59 feet) with a 4 kg (9 lb) shot put, and 20.16 meters (66 feet) with a 3 kg (6.6 lb) shot put, the athlete is throwing 16 meters (52 feet), 18 meters (59 feet), and 19 meters (62 feet), respectively. This significant deviation from the normal suggests that whatever this athlete has been doing in training has produced a performance model that is not balanced. This athlete is very good with the heavy shot put and very poor with the light shot put. If this athlete can bring performance back into balance by improving the best training result with the light shot put, the athlete may throw much farther. It is also a good idea to periodically execute standing throws with the light implements to work speed (Table 3-2). By changing the percentage of the various implements thrown during the course of training, the athlete can correct the specific speed problem.

Changing Implements

At any time during the session, the coach can easily adjust the plan to address the needs of the athlete. It is recommended that the thrower "master" each task in the progression before proceeding to the next. In the end, the athlete will develop a consistent technical pattern that will allow him to remain calm and focused during competition. You can work a ladder system of throwing, starting with a heavy implement and moving to a lighter implement as the athlete tires and technique deteriorates. The number of throws is usually predetermined, but the coach should make adjustments on the field when necessary. Specific training for the shot put works the same way or very similar to the weight room. When an athlete begins throwing an implement, he initially gets good stimulation of the nervous system. However, after a number of sessions with the same shot put, the body adapts, the brain becomes "bored," and he fails to make improvements in his performances. Continuing to throw this same implement is unwise and leads to stalled development. Once the results plateau, it is time to change the implement weight to get new stimulation.

The time it takes for this plateau to be reached varies. If your athletes are throwing 30 to 35 throws a day, four-five days a week, you would need to make a change every six to eight weeks. Some throwers take less time to adapt, and others take more time. This time is often based on the athlete's training age. Advanced throwers tend to adapt quicker than beginners. The only way to tell is to have your throwers keep careful track of their progress with a training journal.

Throwing Intensity

Throwers engage in serious and methodical resistance training as part of their workout, using percentages of a maximum to control the intensity of weight-lifting sessions. Surprisingly, many throwers do not know how to use different intensities (distances) in training for the throws. Training throws should be divided into three categories: weak/light intensities, medium intensities, and maximal intensities. Each intensity should be allotted time during the training session, and the proper throws of the right intensity used at the right time can

Heavy Implements	
Intent	For greater hypertrophy of the muscular regions (specific strength) For improvement of the elastic reactions when reaching the power position When technique is stable and the focus on technical training is less

Points of Emphasis	*Power position*: To build functional strength
	• Throws from simplified positions
	  ✓ Frontal (power position) throws or releases
	  ✓ Feet parallel frontal throws to build core strength and torso torque
	  ✓ Frontal throws (power position) with two hands with weights, puds (kettlebells), plates, or medicine balls
	
	Full throw: For athletes with a solid technical pattern
	• Magnification of and attention to the execution timing
	• Greater elastic reaction

Standard Implements	
Intent	*Power position*: Set up the positions for the full technique *Full throw*: Verification of the technical pattern • Addressing competition rhythm • Increasing consciousness of the full movement • Confirmation of the training results
Points of Emphasis	Simulation of the competition environment Staying in the circle on every attempt Throwing with intensity and maintaining proper technique
Light Implements	
Intent	Technical coaching and focus (function of the movement) Improvement of sport-specific speed • Throwing-arm velocity • Velocity of the hip To be performed during the period of the attainment and apprehending of technique
Points of Emphasis	*Power position*: Have the athlete focus on these points mainly when using the standing throw in the shot put and discus: • Work on reaction of the lower limbs. • Work on speed of rotation of the hip. *Full throw*: The same issues are addressed in the full throw. Because of the reduced execution times, the coordinative aspect assumes particular importance.

Adapted from Piga (1981)

Table 3-2. Implement selection and training design: a guideline for using different weight implements

very positively influence training productivity. If the thrower does not understand, compare this system to the weight room.

Weak/light intensity is 50 to 80 percent of the maximal distance with the implement being thrown. Medium intensity is 80 to 95 percent of the maximal distance, and maximal intensity are throws averaging 95 to 100 percent or more of the previous training best. It is important to note that these percentages are based on the results from practice. It is not uncommon for throwers to improve the training result by as much as 5 to 7 percent in a competition. For example, a high school thrower with a competition best of 19.65 meters (64.5 feet) with the 5.45 kg (12 lb) shot put may never have thrown farther than 19 meters (62 feet) with that same weight shot put in training. Base your training intensities on training results.

Research shows that the optimal order of throwing intensities is: light or weak followed by maximal and then medium. The weak throws are used to warm up the body and the nervous system to prepare for the maximal effort(s) to follow. Medium is the best intensity for learning and correcting errors. It also has a high level of transfer to the maximal attempts without the same fatiguing effect that the maximal attempts have on the thrower's mind and spirit.

It is important for athletes to learn to control the intensity of throws in the low-stress training environment if they are to control the intensity of throws in the high-stress competitive environment. Mastery of the event of shot put is indicated in part by the ability to dial up certain throws: ask an experienced thrower who is a good competitor and has a practice best of 19 meters (62 feet) to throw 18 meters (59 feet) and that athlete will be able to oblige you with fairly good accuracy (16.50 to 17.50 meters, or 54 to 57 feet). It is a good idea to have some reference arcs or markers on the field and to place cones out at the distances that need to be achieved. The thrower can be challenged to come as close to the cone as possible without going over, even trying to land throws right on top of the cones. Setting up a throwing range with cones or reference arcs is a great way to control practice intensity. When calculating ranges, keep in mind that percentages should be based on practice personal bests, not competition personal records. Using cups at various distances for target throwing in the javelin is a way to work on control and technical development.

Having your athletes take some maximal attempts each time they throw is a great idea. First, the structure of weak/maximum parallels the warm-up and competition process they will follow on the meet day. How many times have you seen someone throw farther in the warm-up than in the meet? This issue is one of control, and it is easily solved by having your throwers practice controlling intensities in training. Second, if your throwers know the maximum they are capable of each day, it is a great way to prevent overtraining. If you are seeing a pattern of steadily decreasing throws over time, you are witnessing overtraining at work. This tells the coach it is time to decrease the loads and intensities or to add a recovery module to the training plan. The coach should also make sure the athlete is doing his part off the field.

Number of Throws Per Session

Throwing volume should be tracked just like weight-room volume. The number of throws per session (as well as week/month/year) should be carefully planned. How many throws an athlete takes in a session will depend on:

- The age of the athlete (how old)
- Fitness state (less fit athletes cannot take as many quality throws)
- Training age (the longer your athletes throw the shot put, the longer their sessions can last while still being productive)
- The time of year (you would not want the athlete to tire himself out with a lot of throws the day before the championships).

As a general guideline, follow the recommendations laid out in Table 3-3.

Experience	Age/Level	Number of Full Throws
One year or less	14 to 15 years old	10 to 15
Two years or less	16 to 17 years old	15 to 20
Three years or less	18 to 19 years old	20 to 25
Four years or less	Intermediate to advanced	25 to 30
Five years or more	Elite	35 to 40
Eight years or more	International elite	45 to 50

Table 3-3.

Some elite athletes may take up to 50 throws per session, sometimes doing two sessions a day. Remember, these throwers are special people, who are very fit, who have been throwing a very long time. These throwers also know that they cannot continue these sessions when technique begins to break down and the throws become sloppy. An athlete should never do more throws than he can do well: 20 throws done with proper technique is more productive than 20 throws done with good technique followed up with five poorly done throws.

Maximum-Effort Throws

It is pretty much common knowledge that maximum lifts are not attempted on a daily basis in the weight room. The argument is that performing one-repetition maximums is too dangerous. A plan has to be employed to determine when near-maximum or maximum throwing efforts should be performed in training. Most of the throwing volume in a training session is performed at a percentage of the training maximum. These sub-maximum efforts are focused on improving technique and throwing fitness. However, in selected workouts, it is important to perform several efforts at near-maximum intensity. Alternating sessions by performing high-intensity throws with each shot put is one approach. However, if the performance model is unbalanced, you may want to consider near-maximum throwing, alternating days with the light and normal (specific speed problems) or alternating days with normal and heavy (specific strength problems). If the imbalance is extreme, perhaps near-maximum throws with just the light or just the heavy may be the right protocol. When the athlete is fatigued or not motivated to throw at near-maximum intensity, it is better to not max than to do a maximum throw that will erode confidence. If the result from a max is going to be very poor and the coach knows that in advance, maxing serves no point and should be avoided. Make the practice a technical one, with technical goals. Two to three throws per practice at near-maximum is the optimum if the athlete has the proper fitness level and mindset.

Designing the Training Blueprint: Choosing the Weight and Number of Throws

In traditional training plans based on the notion of periodization, one trend is to plan the training from general to specific over the course of the year. In throwing training, a more appropriate way to approach this issue is to plan a training progression from specific to more specific. For example, very heavy implements can have a positive effect of specific strength and power if they can be thrown with good technique and rhythm. However, the direct transfer to the competitive movement is not perfect. In fact, throwing heavy implements can sometimes disrupt the athlete's competitive rhythm. Therefore, it is advisable that as the most important competitions approach, the shot puts thrown in training be more like the competitive implement. Table 3-4 offers a specific example for a 20-meter adult male shot-putter:

September to December		January to March	
Light	6 kg (13.25 lb)	Light	6.5 kg (14.3 lb)
Normal	7.26 kg (16 lb)	Normal	7.26 kg (16 lb)
Heavy	10 kg (22 lb)	Heavy	9 kg (20 lb)
April to June		**July to August**	
Light	6.75 kg (14.8)	Light	7.0 kg (15.4 lb)
Normal	7.26 kg (16 lb)	Normal	7.26 kg (16 lb)
Heavy	8 kg (17.6 lb)	Heavy	7.5 kg (16.5 lb)

Table 3-4. Sample progression for a male shot-putter

The shot-put weight should be changed when the thrower has adapted to that particular weight. When your brain is presented with a new stimulation, it reacts with heightened responsiveness at first, and gradually becomes less and less responsive over time. All the elements of a training plan are stimulation for the brain.

Figure 3-6. Training with heavy implements for specific strength and power can be very beneficial for the glide and rotational shot putter.

Program Design

You can structure throwing workouts in many ways to achieve the desired training effect. The easiest example to illustrate this approach is with the shot put. This concept can be used in setting up training for all of the throwing events.

Playing the Percentages (Based on Training Results)		
Light intensity	50 to 80%	At the start of each workout
Maximum intensity	95 to 100%	After the technical pattern is set
Medium intensity	80 to 95%	At the finish of each workout

Table 3-5. Training intensity for throwing workouts

Only throwing a light implement during a session will improve specific speed. Throwing the light shot put immediately followed by the normal shot put will not only improve specific speed, but will also lead to a better transfer of that specific speed to the normal-weight shot put. Compare two possible training sessions:

Session A
10 throws with light shot put
10 throws with normal shot put
10 throws with heavy shot put
(33 percent light, 33 percent normal, 33 percent heavy)

Session B
15 throws, alternating light and normal
15 throws, alternating normal and heavy
(25 percent light, 50 percent normal, 25 percent heavy)

Session B is more effective for two reasons. First, a greater possibility for the transfer to the competition-weight shot put exists since the light shot and competition shot are alternated. Second, half of the workout is done with the normal shot put, making the workout specific to that implement. The structure of this typical session provides a baseline for any changes that might be needed. If the expected differences show that the athlete is very deficient in specific speed, two sessions that can correct this problem:

Session C
15 throws, alternating two light shot puts and one normal shot put
15 throws, alternating two normal shot puts and one heavy shot put
(33 percent light, 50 percent normal, 16 percent heavy)

Session D
21 throws, alternating two light shot puts and one normal shot put
10 throws, alternating one normal shot put and one heavy shot put
(45 percent light, 39 percent normal, 16 percent heavy)

Even in extreme cases where specific strength is very well developed, it is not advisable to drop the heavy shot put completely from the thrower's sessions. Heavy shot puts should be included to assure the maintenance of the specific strength. In the most extreme cases where specific strength is the overriding quality, you could have the thrower alternate these two sessions:

Session E
15 throws alternating two light shot puts and one normal shot put
15 throws alternating two normal shot puts and one heavy shot put
(33 percent light, 50 percent normal, 16 percent heavy)

Session F .
30 throws alternating two light shot puts and one normal shot put
(66 percent light, 33 percent normal)

The closer the training shot put is in weight to the competition shot put, the greater the transfer from training to the competitive action.

Sample Training Program

The following is a sample workout session for a 18+ meter female shot putter. She is throwing 15.84 meters (52 feet) with the 5 kg (11 lb), 18 meters (59 feet) with the 4 kg (9 lb), and 20.16 meters (66 feet) with the 3 kg (6.6 lb)—all achieved in training. She is a good competitor and has thrown the 4 kg (9 lb) shot put 18.58 meters (61 feet) in competition. She has a balanced performance model: the light and heavy shot puts go the distances that you would expect. She is having some small problems with patience in her power position and transition using the hips. What would a throwing session look like for her?

General Warm-Up
Jogging and active flexibility x 15 minutes

Specific Warm-Up
Position drill (hip pops) 3 x 3
Glide and position drill 3 x 3

Throwing Session
5 sets, alternating 4 kg x 17 m +/- and 5 kg x 14 m +/-
4 throws with 4 kg for max (17.81 m, 18.02 m, foul, and 17.63 m)
5 sets, alternating 3 kg x 19.50 m +/- and 4 kg x 17.50 m +/-

Keep in mind that this workout is for one athlete for a given day. Think of it as an example of how a throwing workout can be structured. A throwing workout at a different time of the year would vary in the number of throws and the weight of the implement.

Figure 3-7. Advanced female shot putters can benefit from training with implements as heavy as 16 lbs. (7.26 kg).

Developing a Resistance-Training Program

© Tony Duffy/Getty Images

Chapter 4

Important Concepts

In throwing, the purpose of strength training is not to produce weightlifters; however, it is reasonable to briefly consider important components of their basic training programs. By understanding the basic physiology of training throwers and knowing how to bridge the gap between weight room and field, a coach has an edge on achieving the desired results. However, the proper resistance-training program can make or break throwing improvement. A successful training program is a combination of many different strength-training concepts interlocking to form one regime. Each concept is dependent upon the next: intensity and volume cannot be maximized without the proper recovery, recovery is not effective without a periodized training approach, and a periodized training approach is nothing without the right load percentage. The list continues. Ultimately, periodization is an erudite attempt at prediction of future performance based on evaluation of previous competition and training results. A coach must have a thorough understanding of all training concepts to form a successful training and throwing program.

Common Questions When Developing a Resistance-Training Routine

The coach must ask himself some specific questions before constructing a resistance-training regimen. One of main questions you must ask before getting started is why do your athletes train? The simple answer is: to throw far. Sometimes, you need to remind your athletes of this goal, as some throwers get a bit carried away and overdo it in the weight room. However, from a physiological standpoint, athletes train to get a response and, ultimately, an adaptation. Is there a difference, and if so, what is it, and why is understanding the difference important? A response can be defined as a reaction or the sum total of reactions to a stimulus or treatment. According to Lamb, it is defined as a "temporary adjustment in physiological function brought on by a single exposure to exercise." An adaptation is an adjustment of an organism to a change in the environment. Further, says Lamb (1984), it is "more or less a persistent change in structure or function, caused by repeated bouts of exercise." These and other questions should deal with some of the basic physiological principles of resistance training, and each one of these questions will be covered in detail in this book. A number of questions are common sense, while most require some planning and organization by the coach. The following section includes some examples of questions that are part of the planning process.

The first question is what helps you make your exercise choices? The best answer would be with factors such as the following: structure, function, training age, diagnosis, attitude, protocol, and available equipment. Do you use "normative" data as a basis for your decision? If so, what data do you have? Who produced the data? If you base your prescription on data, do you also base your outcome on data? Where do you get your indications and contraindications of exercise: medical diagnosis, functional diagnosis, athlete's attitude, athlete's appearance, protocols, normative data, and personal opinion? These questions should be part of the process of planning your training regime.

A series of important questions dealing with exercise selection and exercise technique are also part of the planning process. When observing exercise technique, what is the difference in movement quality and quantity? What is the ratio of qualitative tests to quantitative tests you normally employ prior to exercise prescription? How do you measure quantity? How do you measure quality? What insight does the ability to observe, analyze, and describe movement quality and quantity provide. This skill can be useful in determining function, training activities, and technique? Attention to movement kinematics is imperative in the ring and the weight room.

The final series of questions you must ask when designing a resistance-training program deal with the particular demands of the event. What are the demands of the event in terms of energy system and technique? What type of equipment and facilities are needed? What is the status of the athlete in relation to the objective of the workout (i.e., overuse, injuries, etc.)? How does this unit of training fit with the other units in the session and the microcycle? What type(s) of exercise(s) is required to meet the objective? How much time is available for the resistance-training session? What is the required volume, intensity, and load? What is the speed of movement, and how long should the rest period between sets be?

It is always good to perform a self-analysis. Identify your strengths and weaknesses with regard to exercise prescription and progression. Is it education, equipment, time limitations, or something else? What is needed to make improvements? Try using the following four categories to rank and describe your program:
- The ability to observe, analyze, and describe movement quality and quantity
- Knowledge of neurodevelopmental sequences and motor-control issues
- Orthopedic evaluation and manual or soft-tissue skills
- PNF-type approaches using movement and positioning for input and facilitation

Types of Exercises

It can be argued that to most effectively enhance strength or power attributes for a specific sports activity (such as throwing in track and field), the training program should contain exercises that address the concept of mechanical specificity (Stone, 2007). The benefit of exercises with mechanical specificity is not limited to movement pattern or velocity considerations, but also includes peak rate of force, peak force, and positional characteristic development (Stone, 2007). Also, a training exercise similar to the actual physical performance increases the probability of transfer from the weight room to the field. Mechanical specificity emphasis should be the foundation of the exercise choices during your in-season competition/peaking phase program in the throws.

The application of free weights as a means of developing physical capabilities for the throws has long been a common practice. The use of other forms of resistance equipment and machines has become popular in recent years. While any variety of resistance applied against working muscles can enhance the strength of that muscle group, when training throwers, the use of free weights is superior to fixed-position machines.

Olympic lifts are the core of a thrower's resistance-training program. Numerous studies and review articles have reported evidence and logical arguments for the use of explosive exercises for throwers. Schmidtbleicher has characterized explosive exercise as having maximum or near-maximum rates of force development. These types of exercises (such as throwing) are not only marked by high force development, but are high-velocity movements. The specific explosive exercises chosen should include global exercises that work explosiveness in more than one muscle group all at once, like the movement in each one of the throwing events. The snatch and clean and their derivatives have potential for power outputs higher than the so-called "power-lifting exercises" (squat, bench press, and dead lift) or more appropriately termed "strength" lifts. The clean and snatch are two of the exercises that will change between blocks of training. The many derivatives of these exercises can be changed to reflect the goal of the training cycle. For example, you can choose between doing a snatch from the floor, from the knee, with a close grip, with a wide grip, or with dumbbells.

For all of the throwing events such as shot put and discus, strength lifts for lower-body and upper-body strength development areas also necessary. Within each muscle group exists many available exercises from which to choose a set of exercises. Back squats, front squats, quarter squats, step-ups, lunges, one-legged squats, and many other exercises are very effective in building leg strength. The upper body can be trained using the many derivatives of the bench press, such as wide- or narrow-grip bench press, incline bench press, and pressing exercises with dumbbells.

Another great sport-specific exercise for throwers that meets the criteria of mechanical specificity is the mid-thigh high pull. It is a derivative of the power clean, where the athlete performs an explosive shrug (second pull) from the mid-thigh position in the power rack, allowing for maximum power development. During the second pull, peak force, rate of force development, power, and bar velocity are at their highest values. Heavy weights can be handled in training without the wear and tear of the full movement. In terms of force and rate of force development, the shot put and pulling movements can be used as an example of integrating movement patterns and overload. These two movements share common time frames and similar ground reaction forces, and largely use the same muscles (Stone, 2007). Using an explosive

Figure 4-1. The upper body can be trained using the many derivatives of the bench press.

performance such as the shot put as an example, comparisons indicate that pulling movements can provide a power overload. Elite throwers can generate approximately 54 W/kg during execution of the shot put (Bartonietz, 1996). Using the optimum percentage of 1 RM for the pulling movements can produce power outputs up to 20 percent greater than the power generated in the shot put, thus providing an overload. Bartonietz (1996) suggests that power summation is a primary factor separating elite throwers from inferior throwers.

Other exercises employed during the in-season competitive training period, such as bench press throws (using a smith machine) and multiple repetition jump squats, may provide an excellent alternative or supplement to the traditional Olympic weightlifting-style movements for the development of speed strength. Athletes with mobility or orthopedic issues who are unable to perform Olympic lifts can use these exercises to build speed strength. The power produced during jump squats or bench press throws will not exceed that of the Olympic lifts, but these "derivative exercises" can serve as supplemental alternative in the peaking phase. Jump squats are an excellent way to build explosive power. Other specific training methods to increase force at high rates of muscular contraction include medicine-ball and power-ball drills and other high-speed, low-intensity resistance-training exercises such as snatch-and-release and press-and-release lifts in a sand pit with light resistance at high speed.

Thematic Approach to Resistance Training

The organization of training is really nothing more than an application of the classical management process of planning, implementation, and evaluation. Failing to plan is planning to fail—especially in a sport like track and field.

Primary Lifts	Secondary Lifts	Auxiliary Lifts
Bench press Squat Power clean Jerk	Snatch Mid-thigh pull Incline bench Behind neck press Leg press	Flies Lunges High pulls Shrugs Close grip bench Triceps extension Chins Curls Crunches

Muscle Groups

Body Part	Possible Exercise
Total body	Power cleans, snatches, mid-thigh pulls, jerks
Chest	Bench press, incline press, dumbbell flies
Legs	Squat, lunge, leg press, leg extension/leg curls
Back	T-bar rows, bent-over rows, behind-the-head pull-downs
Shoulders	Behind-the-neck press, front-shoulder press, shrugs
Biceps	Two-arm curls, one-arm curls
Triceps	Triceps push-down, close-grip bench press, dips
Calves	Toe raises, reverse toe raises, straight or bent leg
Abdominal/lower back	Crunches, sit-ups, back extensions

Resistance-Training Exercises for the Development of Speed Strength

Behind-the-neck jerk
Mid-thigh clean pull
Jump squats
Smith machine bench-press throws
Snatch and release (in a sand pit)
Push-press throws (in a sand pit)
Narrow-grip hang snatch
Hang snatch
Hang clean

Table 4-1. Exercises in a weight-training program for the thrower

Throwing in particular uses a periodized approach to training. This approach requires the coach to plan training by working back from the most important competitions to the pre-season. When setting up an annual plan, the coach should have a theme for each year of the plan. Each training cycle affects the next; all aspects of training must be laid out in advance. A specific theme for each mesocycle should be implemented to properly utilize the thematic approach, and the resistance training must match the other aspects of training. The key to successful periodization is the timing, sequence, and interaction of thematic training stimuli to allow optimum adaptive physical response. These periodic changes and interaction of the training scheme are accomplished by manipulating chronic and acute variables (Table 4-2). For example, a successful coach would not plan sets of 10 for the final preparation for a championship. Of course, an athlete performing high-repetition sets would experience more fatigue as he developed muscular endurance. The goal of final preparation in the competition phase is to maximize fitness and skills and minimize fatigue on the day of that crucial competition. These objectives are met through systematic planning of all segments of the training year before the year begins.

As the year ends and the coach has implemented his training plan, he must then evaluate. A well-organized coach keeps accurate records of both training

Phase Potentiation Sequencing: *Strength/Endurance > Strength > Strength/Power > Speed/Strength*			
Meso/Block 1: Emphasis on strength and endurance/basic conditioning			
Meso/Block 2: Emphasis on squat and bench-press strength			
Meso/Block 3: Emphasis on pulling strength			
Meso/Block 4: Emphasis on power/speed development			Adapted from Stone (1997)
Sequencing: Emphasis on Power and Speed Development In-Season *Mesocycle and Macrocyle Progression*			
High volume to low volume Less specific to more specific			
Chronic Variables			
Phase	*Time*	*Number of Reps*	*Length*
		Strength Lifts / Olympic Lifts	
General preparation	Pre-season	10 6	4 weeks
Special preparation	Pre-season	5 3	4 weeks
Specific preparation	Pre-season	8 5	4 weeks
Pre-competitive	Pre-season	6 4	4 weeks
Competitive	In-season	5 3	4 weeks
Peaking	Peak	3-2 2	3 weeks
Transition	Between seasons	10 6	1 week
Pre-competitive	In-season	6 4	4 weeks
Competitive	In-season	5 3	4 weeks
Peaking	Peak	3-2 2	3 weeks
Transition	Active rest		2 weeks

Table 4-2. Mesocycle sequencing

goals and what actually occurs during each training phase. Goals should be set based on the previous year as well as the results of the pre-season testing. Athletes must try to improve their functional biomotor abilities (Table 4-3), including weaknesses as well as their strengths. The goals that are set should be demanding yet realistic. Quantification and accurate record keeping are essential to training plan improvement. Whether an athlete has or has not met these training and competition goals at the end of the year may be the window into what training methods should be changed for the upcoming season.

Strength:	Defined as the ability to overcome outside resistance.
Skill:	Proficiency in accurately performing the skill.
Speed:	Rate at which general and specific skills can be performed.
Flexibility:	Suppleness or range of movement in joints or combinations of joints.
Endurance:	Defined as specific work capacity.

Table 4-3. Biomotor abilities

Proper use of the periodized program can take the guesswork out of constructing a training program by isolating the factors that influence athletic performance. Keep in mind that periodization is not an exact science and must be individualized to each person's competitive and training environment, training age, and ability level. The track and field coach who understands the concepts of resistance training will experience better results with the periodization plan.

Testing

A number of non-invasive field and laboratory tests can be used to evaluate the training state of track and field athletes. These tests measure biomotor qualities, analyze the pre-training state of an athlete, and analyze training effects while a program is in progress. The variables that can be easily measured include the following: anthropometric measurements, body composition, lower body anaerobic power and capacity, upper-body neuromuscular performance, leg extension and flexion strength, and upper- and lower-body repetition maximums. Before initiating a resistance-training program, the coach must select a battery of tests to determine the training state of the athletes. Physical testing and performance trials every 4 to 8 weeks will evaluate the effectiveness of the training cycle. Tests include the standing long jump, overhead back shot throw, between-the-legs forward shot put throw, flying 30 m (100'), vertical jump, standing triple jump, sit-and-reach test, and the seated medicine-ball throw. Lifting tests on the Olympic and strength lifts are also used to assess training performance. A possible combination of tests could include body composition, weight, vertical jump, one-leg vertical jump, overhead back shot put throw, standing triple jump, standing broad jump, 30-meter (100') sprint, and the selected repetition maximum in the bench press, squat, and power clean. It is often advisable to start with a test like the functional movement screen to detect any imbalances or abnormalities before any performance measures are taken.

Figure 4-2. The overhead back shot-put throw can be a foundational exercise for a testing regimen for the thrower.

During the preparation phase, throwing-performance tests keep athletes motivated and inspire competition between teammates. Instead of contesting full competition implement throws, a variation such as the standing throw or partial movement challenges the athletes, but also keeps the competitive tests fresh. The mental aspect of competing is often ignored in training programs. Competing within the team at these specific tests will not only expose physical preparation, but mental preparation as well. Using scoring tables for the tests will make it even more competitive.

Test what is trained. Perform full technique tests with overweight implements in the fall. For example, a female thrower would be tested in the 5 kg (11 lb) shot put and hammer throw, 1.4 kg (3 lb) discus test, and 25 lb (11 kg) weight throw test. The theme of that particular training block determines what tests should be used.

The Importance of Strength in the Throws

Strength has been described by Stone et al. (1997) as the basis of high-level performance in track and field. But, why is strength so important in the throws? Stronger athletes are able to hold the positions necessary to master technique. Optimal technique is a set of muscle contractions and relaxations coordinated and synchronized to produce maximum acceleration of the implement. A stronger thrower will be able to advance to a higher level technically and will achieve superior levels of performance. Several factors contribute to strength (many of them genetic) including: muscle-fiber arrangement, muscle cell activation, enzyme concentrations in the cell, sensitivity of the golgi tendon organ, the ratio of fast-twitch to slow-twitch fibers, musculoskeletal leverage, coordination of movement, and the number of myofibrillar elements in activated cells.

The majority of strength, conditioning, and technique work for the thrower are geared toward increasing force to achieve this objective. Schmidtbleicher indicates that maximum strength is the basic quality affecting power output. It is also important to understand the relationship between maximum strength, rate of force development, and power in throwing performance. The main objective in throwing is to create the highest release velocity possible. Keep in mind the cause-and-effect relationship between force and velocity. In the arena of track and field throwing, the term "power" seems to be the current buzzword. Speed strength is the ability of the neuromuscular system to produce the greatest possible force in the shortest possible time and is usually defined as exercises producing high-power outputs. Power is the ability to apply a specific force at a target velocity, or vice versa.

Figure 4-3. The back squat is a foundational lift in developing lower body strength for the thrower.

Strength is exhibited when muscles act to produce force. Muscle action can take four different forms:

- Isometric: the muscle gains tension, but does not appreciably change its length.
- Concentric: the muscle gains tension and shortens.
- Eccentric: the muscle gains tension and lengthens.
- Plyometric: a concentric action is immediately preceded by an eccentric action, thus taking advantage of a stretch-shortening cycle.

Muscle actions are supported by a number of different physiological and biomechanical mechanisms. Various mechanisms are involved in muscular strength. Two primary factors which govern muscle activation and the gradation of strength are the number of motor-units recruited and the frequency of motor-unit activation which can be termed "rate coding." These two factors normally work together in increasing force production. The exact degree to which one mechanism is emphasized over the other during muscle activation depends upon the amount of force required and the size and type of muscle being activated.

The percentage of strength and power movements in the resistance-training program will vary based on the stage of training, but strength training will always remain a major element of the training program. The main objective in throwing is to create the highest release velocity possible. The majority of strength, conditioning, and technique work for the thrower is geared toward increasing the force necessary to achieve this objective. Many experts in the field agree that maximum strength is the basic quality affecting power output. Choosing exercises and training volumes that positively affect these components is of utmost importance. The search for these elusive athletic ingredients has led to one of the most heavily debated subjects in the field of strength and fitness. At times, these augmented physical demands exceed physiological norms, and the athlete's functional state and ability to work are diminished. The tremendous number of variables involved in maximizing performance and the training effect makes the training procedure a very complex puzzle. It is a very fine line between adaptive stress and destructive stress. The track and field coach must understand the principles and concepts of resistance training to be able to design a comprehensive training program for the thrower.

The value of good strength training for the thrower can never be underestimated, but it is also possible to overemphasize this biomotor element. Throwing any implement that is heavier than normal, or doing any technical drill with added resistance is going to improve specific strength—as long as the movement pattern is correct. While it is possible to begin pre-season training with heavy implements, it is often better to save the heavy throwing until some adaptation to training has occurred. Additional drill work with heavy implements and less throwing is preferable during this early period of training. Throwing kettlebells (also known as puds) during this time is recommended. Not only will this activity improve specific strength, but it will also help to condition the body for the demands of the in-season training. The pre-season is also an excellent time to work on the lifting technique of the thrower. It is necessary to perform all lifts correctly, not only for safety reasons, but also to improve effectiveness. Do not turn your throwers into Olympic lifters or power-lifters, but instead assure that they have good basic technique in all the lifts that you will use during the upcoming year.

The Load

The stress placed upon the body in training is called the load or stimulus. Experimental research and empirical evidence have shown consistently that the amount of resistance used for a specific exercise is probably the most important variable in resistance training. The level of tension imposed upon the muscle is critical for obtaining a strength-training response, for an athlete to physically get stronger.

The load of each strength-training workout is based on a percentage of a repetition maximum, and it is the most important factor in determining the volume and intensity of a particular training session. For example, the maximal weight that can be lifted correctly five consecutive times without significant rest would be known as the 5 rep max (5 RM). An intensity zone of 85 to 100 percent for 1 to 5 RM produces minimal muscle-mass increases, but is particularly effective to train the synchronization of the motor units that make up an athlete's nervous system. For effective speed strength development, loading 80 to 90 percent of RM (2 to 5 reps) is recommended for Olympic lifts, whereas for bench press, 50 to 60 percent of RM is desirable. It is important to maintain appropriate technique regardless of training load, for both safety and performance purposes. Winchester et al. (2005) was able to demonstrate that at the same training load, power output can be significantly improved through improved technique in the power clean exercise. For an exercise like the jump squat, 30 to 40 percent of maximum may be more appropriate. The percentage for jump squats must also take into consideration the athlete's body weight. For example, a 100 kg (220 lb) athlete with a 1 RM squat of 180 kg (400 lb) should perform jump squats with only 12 kg (26 lb) loading [total system weight = 280 kg (100 + 180); 280 kg x 40% = 112 kg (247 lb), only 12 kg above body weight]. Keep in mind that all percentages are only guiding values and may be influenced by training status, sex, muscle group, and exercise.

The SAID principle (specific adaptation to induced demands) simply states that the body will adapt to the demands placed upon it. It means that the nature of loading must challenge the athlete's present training status in order to force the body to overcompensate for the new training load. The load is directly related to the amount of tension placed on the working muscle. This planned tension in the muscle is an essential component in both hypertrophy and strength development; the degree to which the body will adapt depends on the stress placed upon it.

However, for the body to overcompensate with even more gains, some type of recovery must be built into the program. The time in which this process occurs can encompass weeks or months. It takes about two weeks for any training stimulus to take effect. It is also important to consider how the stresses that occur outside training can effect recovery and subvert the best designed training program. Elite athletes are always training on the edge, but overdoing it can lead to a condition referred to as overtraining. To avoid overtraining, you must include variety and change in your athletes' regimens. Specifically, the program must change every 3 to 4 weeks. Keep in mind the highly trained athlete will adapt quicker. Monthly testing can help monitor the training state of the athlete. The effects of overtraining are reversible, but the process takes time.

One must never disobey the "law of reversibility," especially when training females. This law states, "If you don't use it, you lose it." The body will return to an untrained state of homeostasis when the training stimulus is removed. Loss in strength can happen within just a few days of too much rest, but a coach may not actually see the decrease for about two weeks.

Types of Loading

A variety of methods can be used to periodize the load of the resistance-training program (Table 4-4). The type of exercise and the time of year help determine the load. For example, the mid-thigh pull exercise is performed at 85 to 95 percent of maximum in a ladder progression. In the final mesocycle, after performing a top set, three sets of five speed repetitions are performed at 50 percent. According to Stone et al. (1997), among good-strength power athletes, peak power is at maximum values somewhere between 0 and 40 percent of 1 RM in the squat. In an exercise like the jump squat the athlete performs as many repetitions as possible in 10 seconds with 30 percent intensity. Listed in this section are different loading methods. No matter what type of systematic loading is used, overload must be followed by recovery for supercompensation to occur.

Linear Progression

Linear progression is the application of progressively increasing intensity: the weight percentage goes up. As intensity increases, volume or the number of sets decreases. Load intensity starts out low and is increased progressively with each workout. This progression is accomplished by increasing repetitions within each set or increasing the amount of resistance used instead of increasing the number of sets. This type of loading system is excellent for a short duration of training like a high school season. The positive changes in the nervous system in the first six weeks of resistance training make this method of load work well in the short term. If this type of system is used over an extended period of time, an elevated chance of overtraining can occur.

Light-Heavy System

The resistance training workouts in this system of loading will alternate light and heavy days in a microcycle, and each body part will be worked biweekly. Each

	LINEAR PROGRESSION				
	Percentage System				
	(Estimate One Rep Max)				

Week	Workout 1		Workout 2	
1	70%	4x5	75%	5x5
2	80%	4x5	85%	5x5
3	85%	3x5	85%	4x5
4	90%	1x5	90%	2x5
5 Start sets of 8				

LIGHT-HEAVY SYSTEM
(Using sets of 10 on strength lifts and sets of 5 on power lifts)

Percentage for Bench and Squat
(Estimate 10 Reps Max)

Week	Workout 1		Workout 2	
1	75%	4x10	85%	4x10
2	80%	4x10	90%	3x10
3	85%	4x10	95%	2x10
4	80%	4x10	100%	1x10
5 Start sets of 5				

Percentage for Cleans
(Estimate Five Reps Max)

Week	Workout 1		Workout 2	
1	75%	4x5	85%	4x5
2	80%	4x5	90%	3x5
3	85%	4x5	95%	2x5
4	80%	4x5	100%	1x5

LIGHT-HEAVY SYSTEM (WEEKLY)
(Estimate one rep max for power clean, jerk, snatch, squat, and bench press)

Week 1	Week 2	Week 3	Week 4
Set 1 60%	Set 1 60%	Set 1 60%	Set 1 60%
Set 2 65%	Set 2 65%	Set 2 65%	Set 2 70%
Set 3 70%	Set 3 70%	Set 3 70%	Set 3 75%
Set 4 75%		Set 4 80%	
Set 5 75%			

WAVE-LIKE LOADING

Example 1: (90%, 95%, 100%) 2-3 sets of 3-2-1 reps
Example 2: (85-88%) (90-92%) (94-97%) 2-3 sets of 5-3-2 reps
Example 3: (Bulgarian System)
- 3 sets of (5x85%, 3x90%, 2x95%, 1x90%, 3x90-92%)
- 1 set of (1x102-105%)
- 3 sets of (5x85-88%)

Table 4-4. Loading methods

workout will be based on a percentage of a repetition maximum for the particular mesocycle. The system will include one workout of medium intensity at 70 to 75 percent and one workout of heavy intensity at 90 to 100 percent per week. An example of this system is listed in Table 4-4.

Wave Loading

Wave loading is a system of alternating sets of greater loads with sets of lesser loads to stimulate the nervous system. This type of system is used by competitive Olympic weightlifters and is widely used in Bulgaria. The neural drive is increased to drive the larger (high-threshold) fibers necessary to move the maximal loads, and a carryover effect occurs on the next wave in which the lighter load is used. Athletes experience faster, more crisp reps when moving from the heavier load to the lighter load. By the time the athlete reaches the heaviest set, the rep feels lighter and faster because the wave loading stimulated the nervous system. Wave loading is very effective in the peaking phase, because it is a neural workout. The wave-loading system is less effective with higher rep workouts that require a musculature stimulation over a neural stimulation. The Bulgarian method begins with high-intensity exercise, working down to resistance against body weight. Following is an example of wave loading: 90 percent (4 reps), 95 percent (3 reps), 97.5 percent (2 reps), 95 percent (4 reps), 90 percent (4 reps) (for maximal strength).

Time-Controlled Speed-Strength Methods (TCSSM)

Time-controlled speed-strength methods (TCSSM) control the duration of the rest intervals between the sets and between the repetitions. The duration of rest between sets should be 5 minutes. It is desirable to work in an intensity zone between 50 and 60 percent. Using TCSSM, the number of repetitions are established by feedback of the time per rep and the recovery time between reps. After the first repetition, it is important that the second, third, and subsequent reps are executed with a speed reduction of below 10 percent of the first rep in the preparation period and below 5 percent of the first rep in the competition period. To do this reduction, the lift must be done with speed. These reps are sometimes referred to cluster sets.

Other Important Strength Training Methods

Contrasting load method: The use of heavy and light loads in the same training session is referred to as the contrasting load method.

Russian complex: The Russian method involves a continual alternating between heavy and light loads in the same training session (quarter squats and overhead back with a medicine ball).

Absolute strength: Two sets of two to three repetitions at 90 percent of 1 RM. The eccentric and concentric movements are executed slowly. Have the athlete rest 3 to 4 minutes between sets and 4 to 6 minutes after the second set.

Drop jumps: Two sets of 10 repetitions (height needs to be established to suit the individual). The athlete should rest 3 to 4 minutes between sets. The complex is repeated two to three times per training session with 8 to 10 minutes rest between complexes. Rest 3 to 4 minutes between sets and 5 to 6 minutes after all sets.

Timed squats: The athlete should perform as many repetition squats as possible in 10 seconds at 60 percent intensity (for explosive strength).

Jump squats: The athlete should perform as many repetition squats as possible in 10 seconds at 30 percent intensity (for explosive power).

Jump-ups: The athlete should perform as many repetition jumps as possible in 10 seconds without any load (for speed strength).

Intensity and Volume

The load of resistance training is quantified as the volume and intensity of training. Proper manipulation of the volume and intensity along with planned periods of recovery are the essence of periodization. Volume and intensity are integrally related and cannot be separated. One factor is dependent on the other at all times.

Intensity is the strength of the stimulus or the average or absolute amount of weight lifted per repetition. Intensity is quantified, displayed in numbers of kilograms or pounds, in terms of a percentage of a one repetition maximum. Strength coaches recently have been using the repetition maximum (3 rep maximum or 10 rep maximum) as the basis for the percentage system. Examples of intensity quantification are listed in Table 4-5.

Volume is the amount or quantity of training performed. In resistance training, it can be expressed in the sum of repetitions. This quantification can be broken down further by classifying the repetitions as being specifically for strength or power. Another way to calculate volume is by figuring the amount

Intensity = Percentage of Maximal Effort				
Quantification of Intensity for Training				
Intensity	*Weights*	*Running*	*Throwing*	*Plyometrics*
Heavy	90-100%	Sprint	Max effort	Depth jumps, etc.
Medium	80-85%	Sprint	90% of best	Concentric jumps
Light	70-79%	Stride	85% of best	Sprint drills
Easy	<70%	Jog	>80% of best	Strides

Table 4-5. Intensity quantification examples

of work completed or tonnage: number of sets multiplied by number of reps multiplied by amount of weight. Volume is a major factor when balancing a program to prevent injury, and it has a direct effect on both hypertrophy and strength development. When two athletes of comparable strength are on the same basic program, the athlete who performs at a greater volume will always be stronger. When coaches want to plan a low- or medium-intensity workout for recovery, it is important to understand the concept of volume. If the number of sets is too great on the low- to medium-intensity session, the volume will be too high. This approach makes a planned recovery workout into a high-stress session. Be careful not make light days into heavy days by increasing volume. Be mindful of all the important resistance-training terminology when constructing a program (Table 4-6).

Intensity: The average or absolute amount weight lifted per repetition. (It could be one rep max (RM) or 5 RM or 10 RM, etc.)

Volume: The amount of work performed during the lifting exercise. The athlete loads X number of reps or X number of sets or number of repetitions.

Number of sets: Normally, three or six sets per body part are performed. Warm-up sets should not be counted. Multiple sets are better for gains than single sets.

Repetition continuum: The load used is probably the most important. Reps of six or less are used for strength/power training, and 12 to 15 repetitions are used for endurance and less strength. However, doing two reps or one rep maxes are not as good as four to five reps for strength/power gains.

Rest periods: When training for strength/power, rest periods are generally 3 to 5 minutes between sets. When training for endurance, rest periods are generally less than 1 minute.

Maximum voluntary contraction: A maximum voluntary contraction is a repetition to near failure. It is an important characteristic of all weight-training programs. Have the athlete try to recruit the max number of fibers by going to fatigue.

Frequency: Number of training sessions per week. Recommend three times per week for beginners, and as the athlete gets more training under his belt, he can train up to six times per week (split program). Advise the athlete to train each body part at least two times per week and to have two days between body parts.

Table 4-6. Resistance-training terminology

Figure 4-4. It is important to have a reliable training partner to help with spotting and motivation during resistance-training sessions.

Figure 4-5. Having your throwers train as a group can really help build team chemistry and increase intensity.

Chronic and Acute Variables

Chapter 5

The Repetition Continuum

Certain numbers of repetitions develop certain physical qualities. The load based on a percentage of a repetition maximum is the most important factor in this repetition continuum. The number of repetitions completed is the single most important acute-exercise variable. If you seek muscle-mass increases for your athletes, repetitions from the hypertrophy method (8 to 12 RM range) seem to produce the best results. The ideal number of repetitions for the development of strength and power is six. For endurance, a range of 10 to 15 repetitions is ideal. If maximal strength is also a concern, you should restrict your athletes to the three- to five-rep range. Repetitions should always remain below six on Olympic lifting movements, unless performing a derivative like rack clean pulls from the mid-thigh. Repetitions of three or less are ideal for the Olympic movements. For peaking, one to three repetitions are ideal. Because sets of one to three reps put great stress on the neuromuscular and endocrine systems, they are best used for short periods (one to three weeks)—and only by highly qualified athletes. Bones, joints, and other connective tissues are also heavily stressed with "high-intensity training" and may be injured with overexposure to intense loads. After about three weeks on one to three reps, most athletes will not be able to maintain their peak and begin to lose strength.

When designing an annual plan, it is best to change the number of repetitions performed every three to four weeks. This approach will keep the body from adapting and eventually hitting a plateau. Each number of repetitions will hit the muscle fiber a little differently; therefore, changing the number of repetitions will promote increases in strength and size. Anecdotal evidence of muscle soreness in fit elite throwers, when the number of repetitions is changed, helps confirm the positive effects of periodizing the stimulus. Changing the number or reps hits the muscular and nervous system a little differently, causing micro tears and soreness. But after a week or two, the body adapts, and the same or an even more intense workout of the same number of repetitions causes much less muscle damage, fatigue, and soreness. After another week, it is time to change the number of repetitions again because the body has become accustomed to the workload. Every athlete has a different fiber make-up and may react more favorably to a particular number of repetitions. Controlling the number of repetitions in each set is definitely a way to control when an athlete peaks. However, you must also think about the number of repetitions in each session on each exercise.

A good rule of thumb to use is to make sure that you are doing at least 20 to 30 repetitions per session when performing a primary exercise. This number is only a general guideline, as the number of repetitions during a session may go up slightly during the preparation phase and go down slightly during the peaking phase. Warm-up sets below 60 percent do not count in this number. Most of the strength-building work will be performed between 80 and 90 percent of the one repetition maximum. The total number of reps can be broken down into four sets of five, eight sets of three, or four sets of six. The number of repetitions is, of course, dependent on the time of year. Performing a sufficient number of quality repetitions is usually not a problem until the peaking phase, when the number of repetitions in each set is dramatically decreased. Make sure extra sets are programmed for adequate volume during the peaking competitive phase. Always keep in mind that the higher the intensity of the session (95 percent and higher), the lower the total number of repetitions will be for that workout (Table 5-1). Another common question for coaches is the relationship between the number of repetitions and the percentage of one repetition maximum. The strength-training zone requires you to use loads in the range of 60 to 100 percent of 1 RM. The relationship of percentage loads to number of repetitions (rounded up) is presented in Table 5-1.

Number of Repetitions	Percentage of 1 RM
12 reps	60-70%
10 reps	65-75%
8 reps	70-80%
5-6 reps	75-85%
4- 5 reps	80-90%
2-3 reps	85-90%
1-2 reps	95-100%

Table 5-1. Percentage loads and repetitions

Training beginners has a theme: focus on technique. Beginners should start their resistance training program performing 8 to 10 or more repetitions using light weight on the static movements and four to six repetitions on the Olympic lifts. The focus is on concentrating and performing the exercise correctly.

Figure 5-1. When teaching the power clean, always start with light weight and work on proper technique. Make sure the athlete catches each rep with the elbows up. Training beginners has a theme: focus on technique

Prediction of the One Repetition Maximum

It is sometimes difficult to determine the one repetition maximum without actually testing. Table 5-2 is a helpful tool to determine the one repetition maximum for your athletes. Take the number of repetitions completed, and use the rep factor multiplier x the resistance used, and you will get an estimated one repetition maximum. For example, the estimated 1 RM for seven reps at 90 lbs resistance is 110 lbs (1.23 x 90). This formula will help you with a number to base your workout percentages from.

Reps Completed	Rep Factor
1	1.00
2	1.07
3	1.10
4	1.13
5	1.16
6	1.20
7	1.23
8	1.27
9	1.32
10	1.36

Table 5-2. Calculating the one repetition maximum

Maximum Voluntary Contractions

Maximum voluntary contractions are an important characteristic of all weight-training programs. A maximum voluntary contraction is a repetition to or near failure. Maximal voluntary contractions can be defined as the individual's attempt to recruit as many motor units as possible for the purpose of developing force. A maximum voluntary contraction does not necessarily equate with a 1 RM load; it could mean the completion of the last repetition of a 5 RM load, where six repetitions are impossible to perform. In that case, the last repetition of the set is done by a muscle reaching a fatigued state, at which point maximal force is being developed by the muscle. It is recommended that at least one session per week include a maximum voluntary contraction.

Number of Sets

For weight training to be effective and to control intensity volume, the number of repetitions and the number of sets share an inverse relationship. As the number of reps increases, the number of sets decreases and vice versa. In choosing the number of sets, keep in mind that in the first few weeks of training very little training volume (one to two sets) will bring about ample amounts of performance because adaptations are mostly neural. The neural adaptations are the improvement in muscle recruitment and an increase in the firing rate of the muscles. These neural adaptations will normally take place for about the first six weeks of training.

After about the first six weeks, a multi-set system (three to six sets) with specific rest periods between sets should be employed. This increase should be progressive. The primary exercises that target the larger muscle groups should be worked more extensively to achieve optimal results. Because of the larger load used in primary exercises, multiple warm-up sets may be employed. These sets do not count as part of the total volume.

As an athlete improves his skill level and matures in training age, more sets will be needed to bring about super-compensation and performance improvement. To maintain the quality of training stimulus, no more than 30 to 36 sets per workout should be performed. Better results are achieved if the total amount of sets is kept at about 20 to 25. A common guideline is to perform no more than eight sets per body part or 20 to 30 repetitions on each primary exercise. For optimal results, workouts should be kept between 45 minutes and 1 hour and 15 minutes. According to Stone (1987), the testosterone level begins to drop if the workout extends too long. The number of sets is the key loading norm in controlling overtraining.

Rest Periods

Rest and recovery between sets and between workouts must be as carefully planned as the weight-training workouts themselves. Frequency is the term designated to describe the amount of workouts per week, also determining the amount of rest between sessions. This topic will be discussed in a later section. Rest periods between the sets of a weight workout are often too long when athletes are casually working out or too short when an athlete rushes through his workout. An athlete who understands the benefit from set recovery will get the most out of his training workout. In general, rest periods should last between two to six minutes, with the average being three to five minutes. It takes the body about three minutes to replace 97 percent of the ATP used in a set of resistance-training exercise. For the strength/power athlete, three to five minutes should be taken between sets on strength and power exercises. On body-building exercises, where the goal is the improvement of body composition, 90 seconds to two minutes is sufficient. For endurance, 30 seconds to one minute between sets is optimal.

Each type of exercise has optimal rest periods. Rest period length can make or break explosive training. If rest periods are inadequate, fatigue hampers motor learning. Because explosive training has a strong motor-learning component and high levels of type II fiber recruitment, inadequate rest retards performance. On the other hand, too much rest between sets may result in loss of body temperature, loss of nervous system facilitation/stimulation, which can decrease the performance of the next set, and an increased likelihood of injury. Neural fatigue, associated regression of motor skills, and accumulation of metabolic waste are other side effects of rest periods that are too short in duration.

Strict management and recording of rest periods on major exercises like the squat, bench press, power clean, and snatch is essential for consistency of record keeping and for determination of program outcomes. If the rest period changes, the program has changed. Rest-period manipulation may serve as an effective stimulus for program variation (e.g., cluster sets on power cleans). Unplanned, inadequate rest periods can result in the progressive activation of alternative energy systems (i.e., fast glycolytic/lactic acid system), followed by the aerobic energy system. Activation of the aerobic energy system encourages glucocorticoid release (cortisol, cortisone, etc.).

These hormones are antagonistic to strength, power, and hypertrophy development. Aerobic training can be counterproductive for throwers trying to make improvements in the weight room. Without proper rest, an athlete also experiences an inability to maintain optimal levels of muscle tension. When targeting type IIb fibers, inadequate rest will result in forced recruitment of type IIa, and, eventually, type I fibers. Essentially, a coach may design a program to train a certain muscle fiber, and inadequate rest periods may instead train different muscle fibers, which will significantly affect speed of movement, strength, and muscle tension. Keep in mind that mixed training brings mixed results.

Speed of Movement

Strength is increased more rapidly in intermediate to advanced athletes if training includes various tempos of execution than if exercises are performed at one speed. Lifting with tempo should be understood and coached. Athletes grasp the meaning of tempo faster if the coach or an experienced athlete lifts with those trying to learn as a visual demonstration.

Strength-building exercises are designed to build maximum strength. Simply, this process involves executing a lift with heavy load in a slow, controlled manner. The tempo is slow and controlled. If the number of repetitions is too great, it increases the duration of the slow, controlled lift, which can cause a problem. If a set lasts more than 60 seconds, the stress on the energy system becomes progressively more aerobic and the capacity to maintain muscle tension is lost.

Whether your athletes are using machines or barbells for bodybuilding, utilizing small muscle groups, or performing any strength exercises, the weight should be raised without any jerking or explosive movements and then lowered under control. A reasonable training pace is one to two seconds for the lifting (concentric) portion of the exercise and three to four seconds for the lowering (eccentric) portion of the movement will ensure that speed of movement is not ballistic in nature and that momentum does not play a significant role in the efficiency of the exercise. (This technique is sometimes referred to as simply "up two, down four.") Fast, jerky movements should be avoided as they place undue stress on the muscle and connective tissue at the beginning of the movement, substantially increasing the likelihood of an injury. Fast lifting on static or strength lifts, also cheats you out of some of the strength benefits. When lifting at a fast pace, momentum (not the muscle) is doing a good deal of the work.

When someone is described as being "explosive" on an athletic field, the athlete performs, moves, or reacts quickly or forcefully. Development of muscular power depends on the improvement of maximum strength as well as the contraction speed, according to the particular needs of the performance structure under competitive stress. While the contraction speed of an exercise used for developing strength is performed in a slow and controlled manner, power exercises are performed in a rapid, explosive fashion. As an athlete becomes more advanced, the contraction speed on the strength lifts can be increased. A positive correlation can be found between strength and speed of movement at all loads. The closer a given load is moved to maximum velocity, the greater the intensity and the greater the training effect on a neuromuscular basis. Training at 30 to 60 percent of 1 RM may provide greater improvements in force production at higher velocities. When using high-intensity training, an effort should be made to accelerate the load as fast as possible, even if the weight moves slowly. This acceleration is done during the concentric or shortening phase. This technique is beneficial for developing the various manifestations of power. This type of training will aid in reducing the amount of time needed for maximal motor-unit recruitment, will help improve synchronization of motor units, and will facilitate movement qualities similar to those required in most events in track and field.

Although explosive training is very helpful for throwing athletes, some say it does have its drawbacks. Opponents of explosive training sometimes counter that explosive training poses inherent risks to its participants. Because of the highly technical and athletic nature of exercises designed to build power, coaches are concerned about the possibility of injuries and may avoid teaching these power lifts.

Also, most power or speed lifts incorporate momentum. Using momentum to lift a weight increases the internal forces encountered by a given joint; the faster a weight is lifted, the greater these forces are amplified. An injury occurs when the forces exceed the structural limits of a muscle, bone, or connective tissue. No one knows the exact tensile strength of muscles, bones, and connective tissue at any given moment, and unfortunately, the point of discovery is often too late. Performing explosive training on strength lifts should only be done in one or two mesocycles per annual plan. Speed sets of five repetitions at 50 percent of 1 RM can performed at the end of each exercise to build speed strength. To be effective, these sets must be performed with maximum intensity. This type of training should not be introduced to beginners.

Aside from all the scientific facets concerning muscle physiology and specificity, lifting weights in a rapid, explosive fashion is not recommended for bench and squat beginners. First of all, explosive lifting introduces momentum into the movement, which makes the exercise less productive and less efficient for the beginner who does not have a sound technical base. After the initial explosive movement, little or no resistance is encountered by the muscles throughout the remaining range of motion. In simple terms, the weight is practically moving under its own power. The muscles had resistance for the first part of the exercise, but not for the final part of the exercise. When weights are lifted explosively, tension is on the muscles for the initial part of the movement, but not for the last. In effect, a reduction in recruited muscular force occurs, and the potential strength gains are reduced accordingly.

Beginners should be taught a slow, controlled tempo on strength building lifts. The tempo of strength-building lifts should remain slow until an adequate technical and strength base has been built. The former Eastern Bloc coaches who have had enormous success coaching the throws recommend training at a moderate to slow tempo for the first year.

Frequency

Determining optimal recovery time between training sessions is an important variable in maximizing the adaptive process. Frequency of training, defined as the number of training sessions per week, will play a role in recovery time. Resistance-training principles suggest that the frequency of training should be as high as possible without causing adverse effects. It is important for the coach to understand individual differences among athletes who are involved in a resistance-training program. In some cases, female athletes can actually be worked as hard as, or even harder than, their male counterparts.

A variety of protocols are available for program design. You can find many ways to break up the routine. Be cautioned: a lot of the resistance-training protocols still being used in the United States today have their origins in bodybuilding. Many of these classic protocols can be effective in the transition and preparation phases when the athletes are building a necessary strength base. The classic approach to resistance training has been three resistance-training sessions per week on alternate days for each muscle group. This type of system has the athlete work the total body on a Monday, Wednesday, and Friday. For more advanced athletes, it is common practice to have multiple training sessions per week. This approach is referred to as a split routine in which an athlete trains multiple days and trains different exercises/muscle groups each day. In the split routine, each muscle group is usually trained twice per week. Another way to structure the resistance-training routine is called the push-pull routine. One the first day, the athlete performs all of the pressing movements (squat and bench press), and on the second day he performs all of the pulling exercises (clean, snatch, high pulls). The nervous-system routine is yet another strategy. On day one, all high-intensity multi-joint exercises are performed (clean, squat, pulls, bench press). On day two, all auxiliary or body-building lifts are performed. Day one is a high-intensity day that puts a lot of stress on the nervous system. Day 2 is a recovery day for day one and is a lower-intensity day, stressing the metabolic system. Neural days include all exercises that demand the nervous system. Metabolic days include all exercises that do not stress the nervous system. Perhaps defining this type of training into a neural day and metabolic day is overly simplistic, but this system of training is very easy to manage and easily understood by the athletes. Table 5-3 provides fundamental guidelines for this type of system that includes all training activities.

Neural Day	Metabolic Day	Recovery Day
Technique	Hurdle mobility	Balance
Multiple throw	Technique	Stability
Multiple jumps	Work capacity	Easy strides
Speed development	General strength	Technique
Olympic lifts	Medicine balls	Ice tank
Primary lifts	Auxiliary lifts	Massage
Secondary lifts	Bodybuilding	

Table 5-3. Training guidelines for a nervous-system workout routine

The athletes can easily understand that neural days involve sprinting, jumping, multiple throws, and explosive lifts, while metabolic days involve upper-body work, core strengthening, mobility, and agility. Table 5-4 presents a basic guideline of exercises that can and cannot be used together.

Compatible	Not Compatible
Speed and Olympic lifts, core, secondary lifts	Neural work within 48 hours
Speed and multiple jumps	Multiple jumps back-to-back days
Multiple jumps and multiple throws	Sprints on back to back days
Balance any day	Coordination with general strength
Core work any day	

Table 5-4. Exercise compatibility guidelines

A common way to break up the body parts in the resistance-training program is to work the upper body on Monday and Thursday and the lower body on Tuesday and Friday. Another combination in pre-season fall training designates Monday and Thursday as chest, shoulder, and triceps days, Tuesday and Friday as lower-body days, and Wednesday and Saturday as back and biceps days. Many of these particular resistance-training routines are often based on the training program of a body builder. These types of protocols are probably more effective for the off-season and preparation phase when building the base.

Figure 5-2. Bodybuilding exercises like bicep curls should be performed in the preparation phase to help balance all of the emphasis on developing the triceps muscle for the shot putter throughout the season. This type of base building work helps prevent overuse injuries.

Coaches also must be cautioned to be aware of the law of reversibility when training—and especially when peaking—female athletes. The law of reversibility simply states, "If you don't use it, you lose it." Because of differences in the amount of muscle mass, distribution of muscle, and hormonal levels, females may be subject to reversibility at a faster pace than males.

Recovery

Recovery is almost as important as the load itself. A tired athlete is not a successful athlete. Factors like resistance-training experience and the ratio of body weight to weight lifted are factors that can have an effect on recovery time. You can examine the intensity of the weight lifted compared to the athlete's body mass and lean body mass when constructing your annual plan. At first, many females will likely have a low intensity relative to body mass and lean body mass and consequently can increase the frequency and intensity of workouts. It is important for coaches to understand this concept in order to get the full strength potential out of their athletes.

Multiple daily sessions are a prerequisite for the elite athlete. It is not a choice as the athlete increases in training age; it is a requirement. Every training program must include built-in intra-workout recovery. Self-massage, shaking, and stretching as well as intra-workout nutrition in the form of hydration is the most basic and practical form of intra-workout recovery. This regimen helps keep the quality of training as high as possible. Carefully consider the ratio of the number of workouts to the hours trained. Recovery drinks and bars should be consumed within 30 minutes post workout.

Recovery sessions and microcycles of active rest must be built into the training program. Rest days are usually scheduled midweek and on the weekend. Every three to four weeks, you should include some built-in restoration time. This period would consist of two to three consecutive days off. A common practice when constructing resistance-training programs is to use three- to four-week mesocycles followed by a one-week unload microcycle. During the unload week, the volume and intensity is decreased and alternative activities are performed. It is an excellent time to test your athletes at the end of a training cycle and at a week of low volume.

Many factors besides the training regimen can affect recovery. Often times, the coach is unaware of these outside factors; but a coach that establishes a trusting, open, and honest relationship with his athletes about their outside influences not only can accurately train an athlete according to his recovery, but can also have a better chance at convincing an athlete to make the weekend-rest commitment to track and field instead of a taxing social life.

Core Training

Many functional activities in throwing and training for the throws require the trunk stabilizers in the core to transfer force from the lower extremities to the upper extremities and vice versa. One of the most neglected areas of the body in training also happens to be one of the most important. Control of the core will allow you to move faster, change directions quicker, be more explosive and become a better athlete in general. Trunk movements are the vital link in the body's kinetic chain, especially for throwers. The energy transferred from the core to the upper body results in a great amount of torque, which in turn exerts great demands on the musculature of the core—especially in the throwing events in which movements are performed with high accelerations.

Defining the Core Region

It is important to first identify the anatomy involved in the region commonly referred to as the core. The "core musculature" can be defined generally as the 29 pairs of muscles that support the lumbo-pelvic hip complex in order to stabilize the spine, pelvis, and kinetic chain during functional movements (Fredericson, 2005). The primary muscles responsible for the quick, ballistic, and rotational movements are the external and internal obliques, rectus abdominis, transversus abdominis, and the erector spinae. Utilization of these muscles allows the trunk to flex, extend, and rotate (Marieb, 1992). Over the last decade, strength training has evolved to emphasize the strengthening of core muscles as a means of improving performance (Brown, 2006). However, most of the claims are anecdotal as limited research is available to support these claims (Faries, 2007). Coaches have, through convention, included some level of torso preparation in their athletes' conditioning programs because empirical data seems to have shown that training the trunk and pelvic musculature is advantageous (Hedrick, 2000). Popular training programs for the abdominal muscles often emphasize global strength gains by using the rectus abdominis muscles as prime movers. Sit-ups, crunches (and their derivatives, with or without rotation), and leg-raise exercises often form the bases of many core-training programs (Norris, 1999). Exercise protocols sometimes neglect proper conditioning of the local or stabilizing system though low intensity slow movements and progress too quickly into more explosive global exercises (Faries, 2007). Hagins and associates (1999) showed that a four- to six-week lumbar stabilization program improved the ability to perform progressively difficult lumbar stabilization exercises (Hagins et al. 1999).

While specialized training provides great benefits to many athletes, any enhancement of power can be severely restricted if general strength parameters, mobility, stability, and posture are not also addressed (Chard, 1987; Chiu, 2003; Fry, 1992; Hides, 2001). Cholewicki and associates recognized that "active control of spine stability is achieved through the regulation of force in the surrounding muscles, consequently, co-activation of agonistic and antagonistic trunk muscles stiffen the lumbar spine and increase its stability" (2000, p. 1380). Stabilization training is often neglected in specialized sports preparation (Norris, 1999). If the extremity muscles are strong and the core is weak, an adequate summation of forces cannot be created to perform efficient movements (Tse, 2005). It has been proposed by Souza and associates that the spine can become unstable because of feeble trunk-stabilizer muscles (Souza, 2001).

To avoid this potential problem, the development of core stability, endurance, and strength should be a primary training goal for all sports (Faries, 2007). Poor mobility, strength imbalances, overuse injuries, and a lack of general coordination can often be traced back to deficits in the mid-torso (Tse, 2005). Sports movements occur in multiple directions, and as a result, athletes must possess lumbopelvic stability in all three planes of motion (Leetun et al., 2004). Lumbopelvic instability can be both the source and the product of an injury (McGill, 2004). The core is used in sports as a rigid and stable segment to dissipate force or transfer energy (McCarrol, 1982); however, it must sustain a balance of mobility to adapt to situations and circumvent injury (Voight and Cook, 1996; Oliveto, 2004). A majority of studies support the efficacy of training the various areas contributing to lumbopelvic stability in reducing the incidence of injury (Barr, 2005; Cusi, 2001; Hides, 2001; Tse, 2005).

Substantial core stability and endurance research has been carried out in the physiotherapy/rehabilitation discipline (Tse, 2005). The studies have centered on spine pathology and the reduction of lower-back pain (LBP). The incidence of LBP in athletes is not unusual, and its occurrence has been well documented in a variety of sports that consist of multiplanar movement—including football, golf, gymnastics, running, soccer, tennis, and volleyball (Brody, 1987; Chard, 1987; Hutchinson, 1995; Johnson, 1999; McCarrol, 1982; Nadler, 1998; NCAA, 1999; Saal, 1988; Wadley, 1993). A good number of sports engage in rotational movement; however, training programs sometimes undertrain this rotational component (Hedrick, 2000). Although core-strength exercises are often introduced into an athlete's exercise sequence to avert LBP, converse to what is commonly thought, data suggests that trunk-muscle endurance (not strength) is related to LBP symptom reduction (Biering-Sorensen, 1984). In theory, core stability training will lead to better maximal power and thus more proficient use of the muscles of the shoulders, arms, and legs, better body balance, and a lesser risk of injury. Although many queries still need to be answered regarding the effects of augmented core endurance/stability on serving to avert LBP, the evidence points in the direction of core endurance and stability having positive benefits for reducing LBP (Biering-Sorensen, 1984; Luuto, 1995).

Enhancing the function of the critical torso muscles in a way that spares the spine from damage serves as the training program objective. Choosing the proper exercises is critical to training program success. The next section will introduce a multifaceted approach to core training for the throwing events in track and field, which includes medicine-ball work, body-weight circuits, slow controlled movements, weighted abdominal exercises, dumbbell complexes, Olympic lifts, and ballistic release work.

The Exercises

Saal and Hodges describe the enormous loads on the spine during daily activities, and the role the abdominal muscles play in stabilizing the spine during these activities (Hodges, 1996; Saal, 1990). The loads on the spine increase as athletes engage in sports and the ensuing preparatory training. Abdominal training of the local system (the group of muscles in the core that stabilizes the spine against these loads) should be the cornerstone of any core-stabilization program. Isometric, dynamic, and unstable training to develop the deep muscles of the abdominals involved in core stability can help protect the athlete from LBP (Hodges, 1996; Saal, 1990). Research consensus does not claim one ideal set of core-training exercises, but does suggest general guidelines for exercises that emphasize trunk stabilization in a neutral spine, while also emphasizing mobility at the hips and knees (Axler, 1997; Barr, 2005; McGill, 1998). More specifically, McGill suggests that the ideal core exercise would challenge the muscle while imposing minimum spine loads with a neutral posture while challenging elements of whole-body stabilization (McGill, 1998, 2002). This ideal exercise may not exist, but a multifaceted approach may be among the best ways to benefit from core training. A multifaceted protocol to core training with a battery of exercises that attends to the three planes of motion is as follows: frontal movements that entail lateral flexion or bending to the left and right side, sagittal movements that engage flexion and extension of the trunk in forward and backward movement, and transverse movements, which involve rotary motion or twisting to the left and right (Voight and Cook, 1996). Strengthening abdominal muscles requires forcing more work than usual through overloading and also working from a variety of angles so that all the muscle fibers are used. A significant body of work demonstrates the importance of the deep abdominal musculature in providing trunk stabilization, particularly the transverse abdominals and obliques (Faries, 2007; Fredericson, 2005; Wilson, 2005).

The mesocycle sequencing of exercises begins with stability work in the general preparation phase, hypertrophy methods in the specific preparation phase, progressing into strength-building methods in the pre-competitive phase, followed by neural activation methods in the competitive phase, and finally speed-strength methods in the peaking phase (Poliquin, 1989; Schmidtbleicher, 1992). The key is to sequence the training modalities for developing core stability and strength during the different phases of training as a part of the total training program (Cissik, 2002). In the preparation phase, athletes begin building a strong base by performing the exercises using their body weight. When working the abdominals, work from the inside out. The main purposes of basic core strength training (training the local system) are to increase stability and to gain coordination and timing of the deep abdominal wall musculature, as well as to reduce and prevent injury (Faries, 2007; Fredericson, 2005; Wilson, 2005). The local musculature contains the diaphragm, medial fibers of external oblique, internal oblique, multifidus, pelvic floor muscles, quadratus lumborum, and transversus abdominis (TrA) (Faries, 2007; Stanford, 2002; Whitaker, 2004). These muscles have shorter muscle lengths, attach straight to the vertebrae, and are largely responsible to generate adequate force for segmental stability of the vertebrae (Briggs, 2004; Fredericson, 2005; Stanford, 2002). One programming option is to begin with local system exercises (Table 5-7) that involve little to no motion through the spine and pelvis to isolate local, stabilizing muscles (Faries, 2007). It is sometime difficult to isolate the lower abdominal muscles. Another programming option for the local system is to begin with the lower abdominals and work your way up through the external obliques and upper abdominals. Since most upper abdominal and oblique exercises work both the upper and lower abdominals, the lower abdominals must be worked first to isolate them.

Figure 5-3. The side crunch works the frontal plane.

Selected abdominal exercises that concentrate on one of the three planes of motion are programmed into the training regime during the specific preparation, pre-competitive, and competitive phases—including three-position crunches, V-ups, V-ups with a twist, seated twists with a dumbbell, plate walks, weighted side crunches, side bends with dumbbells, wavings, dumbbell leg raises, back hyperextensions, Russian twists, and delivery lifts with dumbbells (Table 5-5).

Many of these exercises work the global as well as the local system. All exercises should be performed with body weight first. Add resistance as fitness improves. Start with 10 repetitions, and continue with the same weight until the athlete can perform 15 to 20 reps, then increase resistance.

Frontal Movements
Entail lateral flexion or bending to the left and right side.
• Standing dumbbell side bends
• Wavings
• Lying side crunch

Sagittal Movements
Engage flexion and extension of the trunk in forward and backward movement.
• Three-position crunch
• V-up
• Lying dumbbell leg raise
• Lying Swiss ball leg raise
• Hanging straight leg raise
• Hanging bent leg raise
• Incline sit-up
• Back hyperextension

Transverse Movements
Involve rotary motion or twisting to the left and right.
• V-up twist
• Seated twist with dumbbell
• Seated twist with barbell
• Plate walk
• Standing twist
• Twist behind the back
• Russian twist
• Swiss ball twist

Multi-plane Movements
• Delivery lift with dumbbell
• Incline sit-up with twist
• Walking chop with medicine ball
• Cable chop

Table 5-5. Abdominal exercises

Figure 5-4. Back hyperextension

Symmetry of movement has also been identified in the literature as a very important aspect of spinal stabilization. Research by Grabiner has indicated that strength alone does not necessarily correlate with normal function. Subjects with LBP have consistently shown a lack of symmetry in paraspinal contraction during trunk extension (Grabiner, 1992). A programming option is to incorporate a dynamic flexibility series as part of the warm-up; leg swings, trail-leg windmills, lunge exchanges, side bends, donkey kicks, and leg whips aid the maintenance of symmetry of movement. Hurdle drills, such as walkovers with a constant lead leg, walkovers with an alternating lead leg, and multidirectional walkovers, where athletes walk over two hurdles forward and then one backward, can aid in mobility and symmetry of movement.

General strength circuits (Table 5-6) and pedestal exercises (Table 5-7) in the general preparation phase strengthen the core while also fostering coordination and body awareness (Judge, 2006). Stability balls (Swiss balls or physioballs) can be added to many of the general strength exercises in later mesocycles to put additional demands on the core musculature as the athlete adapts. The research of Saal and Grabiner help substantiate stability ball use in spine rehabilitation and conditioning (Saal, 1988; Grabiner, 1992). Cusi and colleagues (Cusi, 2001) used stability-ball exercises as an intervention to prevent lower-back and groin injuries in Rugby players. In this study, players experienced fewer injuries when utilizing a stability-ball training routine.

Following are two sample general-strength circuits used to strengthen the core. The first circuit is designed for use in open areas, while the second uses weight-room exercises. A Swiss ball can be added to many of the exercises to increase the difficulty for more advanced athletes.

Cowboy (outside circuit)
Crunches x 30
Clap push-ups x 10
Leg toss x 20
Push-ups x 15
V-ups x 20
Leg scissors x 20 in and x 20 out
Push-up toe walk x 10
Side crunch x 10 each side
Decline push-ups x 10
Wrestler's bridge x 5
Single-leg squats x 10 each leg

Cowgirl (weight-room circuit)
Hanging leg raise x 30
Chin-ups x 10
Roman-chair sit-up x 20
Dips x 15
Russian twists x 20
Lunge walk 10 steps

Table 5-6. General strength circuits

The core-training program begins with pedestal exercises that maximize trunk stability in the local system. Beginning athletes should start by holding each position in perfect alignment for 10 seconds. Once that is accomplished, athletes should progress to doing 10 reps of 10 seconds for each position. A Swiss ball can be added for the advanced athlete.

Six pack (pedestal work)
Prone elbow stand, single-leg raise
Supine elbow stand, single-leg raise
Prone hand stand, single-leg raise
Supine hand stand, single-leg raise
Lateral elbow stand, single-leg raise
Lateral hand stand, single-leg raise
Prone flexed knee, elbow stand, hip lift
Supine flexed knee, hip lift
Crunch, low reach (slow)
Crunch, low reach with twist (slow)

Table 5-7. Pedestal exercises

On the other hand, in a recent study by Nuzzo et al., it was concluded that stability-ball exercises may not provide a sufficient stimulus for increasing muscular strength or hypertrophy in the back extensor muscles. Thus, the role of stability-ball exercises for increasing muscular strength and/or hypertrophy in strength and conditioning programs is questionable (Nuzzo et al., 2008). The inability to increase the intensity of the stability-ball exercises through external loading may limit muscular adaptations over a continuous period. Therefore, it is recommended that strength and conditioning programs limit the use of stability-ball exercises (2008).

Figure 5-5. Stability-ball movements do not provide enough stimulus for increasing muscular strength or hypertrophy and therefore should not be used as primary core exercises for the thrower. Exercises like the stability-ball leg raise can be used on low-intensity lifting days for additional stimulus to develop the local system.

Medicine-ball exercises (Table 5-8) can be utilized for a wide range of functional movements that strengthen the core (Judge, 2006). In the general preparation phase, begin with some very general non-ballistic medicine-ball exercises for conditioning and progress to more sport-specific exercises as the athlete advances in the training cycle. Use a heavy medicine ball to develop power and a lighter ball to develop speed. Make sure that good technique is used at all times.

The hip and back muscles are developed by maximum strength-building exercises such as squats, dead lifts, and Olympic weightlifting exercises: clean,

Albert is a short in-season set of medicine-ball exercises. Alberta is a more extensive set used during the pre-competitive phase. Athletes should complete 10 reps of each exercise, starting with a 3 kg (6.6 lb) ball and increasing the weight once they can finish each rep under complete control.

Albert (in-season workout)
Catch-and-throw
Back-to-back partner pass
Over-and-under pass
Sit-ups
Seat-side throw

Alberta (pre-competitive phase workout)
Hip catch-and-toss
Medicine-ball good morning
Medicine-ball V-sit
Catch-and-throw
Hurdle reach
Partner-exchange hip
Prone catch-and-toss
Knee toss
Seated roll
Arms-adductors-abominals

Table 5-8. Medicine-ball exercises

snatch, and their derivatives (Judge, 2006). These exercises are an integral part of the year-round training program but are emphasized more in the specific preparation and pre-competitive phases. Back squats, front squats, quarter squats, overhead squats, step-ups, overhead step-ups, lunges, and one-legged squats are very effective in building core strength as well as leg strength. The squat and its derivatives will require the activation of the core musculature, both local and global systems, to ensure proper spinal stability during the movement (Faries, 2007). In a recent investigation by Nuzzo et al., it was determined, utilizing integrated electromyography, that muscle activity of the trunk muscles during squats and dead lifts is greater or equal to that which is produced during the stability-ball exercises. Further, squats and dead lifts at intensities as low as 50 percent 1 RM were more challenging to the neuromuscular system than the stability-ball exercises assessed in this investigation. Therefore, structural multi-joint exercises like squats and dead lifts are recommended for increasing strength and hypertrophy of the back extensors (Nuzzo et al., 2008) as the intensities of these exercises can be changed through external loading. Because of the tremendous training effect received from these multi-joint exercises, core training does not need additional emphasis on heavy lifting days. For the most part, core-isolation exercises should be done at the end of a workout; the torso muscles play an important role in helping to stabilize the spine during key strength-training movements (Voight and Cook, 1996). To allow for sufficient recovery of the torso musculature and to help prevent injuries, core isolation work should be incorporated primarily on light-lifting days.

Once the stability of the local and global core musculatures has been properly trained in the preparation and pre-competitive phases, then a progressive protocol may be added to develop the enhanced capabilities of the limb musculature in sport-specific training (Faries, 2007). Tippett and Voight indicate that determining sport-specific function requires addressing the athlete's sport-specific skills (Tippett and Voight, 1995). When developing a sport-specific program in the pre-competitive and competitive phases of training, it is important to combine sport-specific movements with resistance through appropriate ranges of motion (Axler, 1997). Voight and Cook (1996) indicate that multiplanar exercise can be used as a progression from uniplanar exercise by combining the PNF chop and lift patterns. Weight shifting, coordination, acceleration, and deceleration must be addressed not individually but in a harmonious blend (Gambetta, 1991; Voight and Cook, 1996).

Figure 5-6. The weighted lunge and weighted lunge jump are examples of sport-specific movements for the hammer thrower.

Various core exercises, including derivatives of weight-lifting movements, can be performed with dumbbells and grouped into complexes or mini-circuits (Javorek, 1993). Many of the exercises in the dumbbell complexes are combination lifts involving pushing, pulling, and squatting movements (Armstrong, 1994). Properly designed dumbbell complexes involve multi-joint activity, greatly enhancing overall coordination, timing, and the all-important element of ground reaction force (Armstrong, 1994). Dumbbell complexes are a great way to build core strength, while also providing sport-specific conditioning for your athletes during the different phases of training. Exercises with dumbbells provide excellent mobility/flexibility and coordination training and are very efficient since they can be done almost anywhere, even when the athlete is traveling for games and events (Javorek, 1993). Dumbbells are also less intimidating than other free weights and are great for training through injuries.

Seven dumbbell complexes are presented that are cycled throughout the training program (Table 5-9). Each dumbbell complex is designed with a specific purpose and uses multi-joint exercises that combine external resistance with bodyweight (Javorek, 1998). The complexes include Olympic-style lifts and their derivatives, which are the best movements for developing speed and power (Armstrong, 1994). They also offer an opportunity for unilateral training, which is important in many sports activities (Javorek, 1993). Typically, athletes can perform from one to four complexes every other day and perform 6 to 10 repetitions on each exercise. The complexes and number of repetitions performed on each exercise should change every three to four weeks as the athletes adapt. The weights of the dumbbells and number of repetitions should be adjusted for each complex based on where the athlete is in his training cycle or season (Javorek, 1993). Keep in mind that this type of training should be periodized and correlated with the other types of training.

Each of the following dumbbell complexes is designed for a specific purpose and is rotated through the training program. Sets of six repetitions are generally recommended. Weights and reps will vary, based on the athlete's training schedule.

Coffee (warm-up)
Bent rows
Twists behind the back
High pulls
Seated twists
Squat presses
Plate walks
One-arm snatches
Jerks
Side bends
Cleans

Nirvana (nervous system)
Shrugs
High pulls
Jump shrugs
Squat presses
Snatches
Clean-and-jerks
One-arm snatches
One-arm jerks
Step ups
Push jerks

Abzilla (abdominals)
Seated twists
Twists behind the back
Wavings
Antennas
Releases
Plate walks
Swings
Good mornings

Pre-Olympic
   (Olympic weightlifting warm-up)
Squat press
High pull
Jerk
Seated twist
Delivery lift

London (functional strength)
Squat punch
Side snatch
Side bend
Around the world
One-arm jerk

Beijing (functional strength)
Lunge press
High pull
Dumbbell snatch
Wavings
V-up twist
Squat jumps

Osaka (functional strength)
Overhead squat
One-arm snatch
Antennas
Swings
Jerk

Arnold (body building)
Bent rows
Curls
Upward rows
Triceps extensions
Squats
Standing calf extensions
Shrugs
Side bends

Table 5-9. Dumbbell complexes

The first complex, named Coffee, is designed to be a morning conditioning circuit or part of a warm-up prior to other activities. The Nirvana complex is designed to stimulate the nervous system while working the core. Included in this circuit are some ballistic movements that build speed. The Abzilla workout is a specialized complex for abdominal emphasis. Arnold is a body-building complex used for general conditioning and fitness. Pre-Olympic is a great warm-up for a weight-lifting workout as it contains pulling, pressing, squatting, twisting, and lifting exercises. London, Beijing, and Osaka are designed for developing functional strength. It is important to simulate the movements and posture encountered in the chosen activity while increasing the speed and efficiency of those movements, as the training program should contain exercises that address the concept of mechanical specificity (Stone, 2007). The benefit of exercises with mechanical specificity is not limited to movement pattern or velocity considerations but also includes peak rate of force, peak force, and positional characteristic development (Stone, 2007). Also, a training exercise similar to the actual physical performance increases the probability of transfer from the weight room to the playing field. Optimum performance can be achieved when muscles are used to complement each other to create integrated movements (McCarrol, 1982).

Figure 5-7. Overhead movements like the dumbbell jerk include positional characteristics transferable to the shot put. Dumbbell jerks can be used as part of a dumbbell complex or can be used as a stand-alone exercise to develop speed strength.

Core-Training Program Design

The integration of selected exercises into the training program requires careful planning. For optimal results, training programs generally follow a periodized method (Bartonietz, 1987; Bielik, 1984; Bompa, 1994; Fry, 1992; Stone, 2002; Stone, 2006). Periodization can be further explained as the division of the training year to meet specific objectives to produce high levels of performance at designated times and consist of periodic changes of training objectives as well as task workload and content (Gambetta, 1991; Haff, 2004; Schmidt, 2000). The periodization of training in the core musculature focuses on optimizing the function of the local system before emphasizing movements that utilize the global system (Faries, 2007). Functional progression is the most important aspect of the core-strengthening program, which includes performance goals, a thorough history of functional activities, varied assessments, and training in all three planes of motion (Akuthota, 2004; Kroll, 2000). Training progresses through several phases, which are progressive in nature, in a systematic fashion, and specific to the event or sport (Cissik, 2002). The prescription of the training program will be influenced by the athlete's skill level and training goals, as well as many other factors (Bompa, 1994; Bondarchouk, 1994; Haff, 2004).

The core-training program is organized in phases which progress from high volume of general conditioning exercises to more sport-specific exercises performed at a higher intensity and lower volume. The first phase of the core-training program (general preparation phase) is designed to build endurance through static sustained contractions in the local system (Robinson, 1992) and serves as the foundation for later postural strength and speed training. Because the literature supports the notion that endurance may be more important than strength, local muscular endurance will lay the core-training foundation (Faries, 2007). You can start with pedestal work as part of the warm-up (Figure 5-8). These exercises are very similar to Pilates.

Figure 5-8. Pedestal exercise (prone handstand)

The mid-torso musculature consists of postural muscles with a high percentage of slow-twitch muscle fibers (Norris, 1999). Part of their function is to maximize trunk stability by holding contractions for extended periods, so you should first focus on training these muscles. With reference to fiber typing, the local system comprises mainly type I fibers, whereas the global system mainly consists of type II fibers (Richardson, 1992; Stanford, 2002). The type I fibers of the local stabilization system have a susceptibility to grow weaker by sagging (Faries, 2007; Norris, 1999). Specificity, then, would necessitate local system exercises that involve diminutive to no motion through the spine and pelvis to isolate local, stabilizing muscles. Technically, the coach should emphasize the importance of keeping the body in perfect alignment while holding each position. The local system is activated with low resistances and slow movements that prolong the low-intensity isometric contraction of these specific stabilizing muscles (Norris, 1999; Stanton, 2002). Examples of these local system exercises are listed in Table 5-7.

After an athlete has developed the ability to maintain efficient postures while performing very simple motor tasks, they are able to develop more advanced skills at a quicker rate. This assessment agrees with Schmidt's schema theory. Schmidt proposes through the schema theory that skill learning is a process of recall and recognition. Schema learning occurs as the motor program stores information such as body position, skill parameters, accuracy, and sensory input (Schmidt, 1975). At the same time, the risk of long-term repetitive injury patterns—many of which result from improper posture—is reduced (Faries, 2007).

The second stage is the pre-competitive stage, when the focus turns to building strength. Strength is often a limiting factor in developing optimal technique required for the sport. Indeed, the stronger athletes are able to develop technique faster and refine technique to a greater extent than weaker athletes (Stone, 2002). Various approaches to core-strength development have arisen from the coaching, scientific, and physiotherapy communities (Faries, 2007). It is interesting to note, a recent review by Warren Young demonstrated little transfer between pure strength gains and athletic performance; combination training is necessary to fully develop power and performance (Young, 2006).

Once the athlete can perform acceptable slow isotonic mid-torso exercises, additional exercises that demand balance, utilizing the global system, can be introduced (Faries, 2007). Global muscles (sometimes classified as "slings") have long levers and large movement arms, making them capable of producing high outputs of torque, while countering external loads for transfer to the local musculature (Faries, 2007; Fredericson, 2005; Stanford, 2002). These muscles include the erector spinae, lateral fibers of the external oblique, psoas major, and the rectus abdominis (Faries, 2007). A wide repertoire of activities can be used to enhance functional postural integrity and as a result latent power resources. The global system, consisting of more type II fibers that generate movement of the spine, may be emphasized through exercises that engage more dynamic, eccentric, and concentric movement of the spine through a full range of motion (Faries, 2007). Conditioning regimens using body-weight exercises, medicine-ball throws, sprint drills, and low-level jumps are progressively integrated into the pre-competitive phase program. For the beginner, it is recommended to start the transition with body-weight exercises and movements. Traditional exercises, such as the sit-up, focus on enhancing the capacity of this global musculature (Faries, 2007). Keep in mind that these exercises *emphasize* the global systems rather than *isolate* the global systems, because both global and local systems theoretically work in synergism (Cholewicki, 2002). Global exercises also create an environment for the local system to begin to stabilize the spine in varying, multiplanar movements. Rapid movement and higher resistances also will recruit these global muscles, especially the rectus abdominus (Norris, 1999).

Following mastery, resistance can be added to each exercise and should be increased in a controlled progression as the athlete adapts to the resistance. Exercising the core for an emphasis in strength would consist of high-load, low-repetition tasks, while endurance development requires general, less technically challenging exercises at higher volumes and lower intensities (McGill, 1998). A simple method to outline a progression for the global musculature of the core is to have the athletes begin by selecting a weight they can handle for 10 reps and then increase the number of repetitions until they are able to use that same weight to complete 20 reps. The resistance is then increased to a weight that the athletes again can only comfortably complete 10 reps. The core-training program is conceptually based on the stimulus-fatigue-recovery-adaptation model, in which an appropriate stimulus can result in fatigue-

Figure 5-9. The weighted sit-up is a great exercise to work the rectus abdominis and global system.

recovery, an adaptation, and performance enhancement (i.e., supercompensation) (Behm, 1995; Haff and Potteiger, 2001; Leetun, 2004).

Explosive speed strength training is the final ingredient in the core-development program and coincides with the beginning of the competitive stage. Various training schemes using multi-throws, plyometrics, and sprint drills are implemented with different volumes and intensities; rest-to-work ratios are influenced by training age, time of the season, and skill parameters (Bompa, 1994; Pedemonte, 1986). The sprint drills emphasize horizontal movements through space, where limbs are worked through various ranges of movement under varying thresholds of velocities and force. Multiple-throw and multiple-jump exercises involve various rotations, flexion/extension factors, and both intra- and inter-muscular coordination (Table 5-10).

Sycamore (multi-throw circuit)
Overhead back
Between-the-legs forward
Toe-board chest-pass explosion
Releases right-handed and left-handed

Table 5-10. Multiple throw series

Exercises With a Release

All exercises are performed with a weight that the athlete can handle. Start with six reps and work up to 10. When the athlete can perform 10 reps, increase the weight.

Perform two to three sets of three exercises per session:
• Plate release (right and left side)
• Crossover release (right and left)
• Overhead back throw with pud (kettlebells)
• Between-the-legs forward throw with pud (kettlebells)
• Push press release into sand
• Snatch and release into sand
• One-arm pud (kettlebells) throws for height

Table 5-11. High-velocity release exercises

Even as progression aims to challenge the core musculature in environments similar to those of competition, it may be wise to begin slowly. Always consider this possibility: sufficiently train the local musculature. The types of explosive exercises in this phase can potentially create a situation where force is being produced by the global muscles that in some cases cannot be controlled and handled by the local musculature (Faries, 2007). It is imperative to maintain correct technique regardless of training load, for both safety and performance purposes. Winchester et al. was able to demonstrate that at the same training load, power output can be significantly improved through improved technique in the power clean exercise (Winchester, 2005). If fatigue compromises form, it is time to reduce the load or terminate the exercise.

In addition to the sprint drills, throws, and jumps, the workout contains sport-specific release movements that force core stabilization of high-velocity activities. For example, to work on acceleration, athletes perform different types of releases with one and two arms. Sport-specific medicine-ball exercises that mirror sport-specific release parameters are an effective way to build speed strength. Heavy weights (20 or 25 pounds) are used for power and lighter weights for speed. These exercises are designed to emulate key sport-specific positions. In addition to the speed-strength gains, these types of exercises may offer a challenge to postural integrity. Keep in mind physiological adaptations and skill acquisitions occur in multiple areas and are for the most part unrelated (Jensen, 2005). These special exercises must be combined with ongoing sport-specific technical work.

Conclusion

As its name implies, the core is at the center of the throwing events in track and field. Whether it's transferring energy from one area of the body to another or maintaining stability and balance while using the extremities, the core is under nearly constant stress in athletics. Coaches in all sports must include core training as part of their daily training regimen. A multifaceted approach that addresses the three planes of movement combining medicine-ball work, body-weight circuits, controlled movements, abdominal exercises, dumbbell complexes, and Olympic weightlifting exercises can provide physiological and biomechanical core advantages that enhance performance in most every sport. Because of the core's global importance in throwing, coaches must devise training programs that address core training and formulate a periodized core-training perscription. Above all, coaches must ground core-training philosophies in research. The next section will address designing the training cycles for the thrower.

Figure 5-10. The seated dumbbell twist works the transverse plane. This exercise can be part of a multi-planer dumbbell complex or can be done as a stand-alone movement to work the core.

Resistance-Training Program Design

© Getty Images

Chapter 6

The Training Cycles

The calendar year in track and field is broken down into training phases. The number of repetitions performed reflects each phase of the year (Table 6-1). The chronic variables in resistance training are the three- to four-week phases. The program is broken up into two macrocycles for the indoor and outdoor season. These cycles are further broken into mesocycles, each lasting three to four weeks (which is the amount of time it usually takes for adaptation to occur). These phases have a specific theme, are designed to blend smoothly into each other, and indicate an evolutionary process.

Chronic Variables					
Phase	Month	Time	Number of Reps		Length
			Strength Lifts	Olympic Lifts	
General preparation	September	Pre-season	10	6	4 weeks
Special preparation	October	Pre-season	5	3	4 weeks
Specific preparation	November	Pre-season	8	5	4 weeks
Pre-competitive	December	Pre-season	6	4	4 weeks
Competitive	January	In-season	5	3	4 weeks
Peaking	February	Peak	3-2	2	3 weeks
Transition	March	Between seasons	10	6	1 week
Pre-competitive	April	In-season	6	4	4 weeks
Competitive	May	In-season	5	3	4 weeks
Peaking	June	Peak	3-2	2	3 weeks
Transition	July	Active rest			2 weeks
	August				

Table 6-1. Number of repetitions for a macrocycle

Throughout the training year, you should sequence exercises for your athletes from high volume to low volume and from less to more sport-specific. Following the preparation phase, alternate accumulation and intensification phases for increases in relative strength. The mesocycle sequencing begins with hypertrophy methods, followed by neural activation methods, and finally speed-strength methods (Table 6-2). This cycle can be repeated three times annually. Before elaborating these phases, it is important to emphasize again that each phase is a process, not just a period of time. For example, the first mesocycle (mid-August to early September) emphasizes strength-endurance, basic conditioning, and hypertrophy methods (up to eight weeks is permissible if the athlete requires muscle mass). The second mesocycle (late September to early October) emphasizes basic strength. The third mesocycle (late October to early November) emphasizes strength/power, using three to four weeks of neural-activation methods. The fourth mesocycle (late November to early December) emphasizes explosive power and speed development using time-controlled speed-strength methods. The sequence would then repeat, following a regeneration period.

Phase Potentiation Sequencing:
Strength/Endurance > Strength > Strength/Power > Speed/Strength
Meso/Block 1: Emphasis on strength, endurance/basic conditioning
Meso/Block 2: Emphasis on squat and bench-press strength
Meso/Block 3: Emphasis on pulling strength
Meso/Block 4: Emphasis on speed/strength development
Adapted from Stone (1997)

Table 6-2. Throws mesocycle sequencing

Specifically, the general preparation phase begins in September and continues through November. The year begins with low intensity and high volume. Building this general base is crucial to support more specific, higher intensity work to come later. Repetitions are 10 to 12 on the strength lifts and five to six on the Olympic lifts. The special preparation phase extends through November and December. Toward the end of the phase, the repetitions are lowered and the number of exercises is decreased. Repetitions are six to eight on the strength lifts and three to four on the Olympic lifts. As the reps slightly decrease, the training emphasis is on all-out power and strength development. During the early indoor season in January and February, athletes engage the pre-competitive phase with a focus on strength development with fewer repetitions. Athletes reengage in this phase in the early outdoor season. Repetitions drop to four to five on the strength lifts and two to three on the Olympic lifts. The indoor season climaxes at the end of February and the beginning of March with a three-week peaking and competitive phase. The in-season peaking phase is similar for the indoor and outdoor season. The phase is designed with a dual purpose in mind. Each week is designed for a mini-peak at the end of each week, with the major peak at the end or the phase. A typical week consists of the heavy weight lifting early in the week. The repetitions are low (one to three), the exercises are basic (bench, squat, clean), and the intensity is high (80 to 90 percent). The middle of the week consists of light lifting used mostly for nerve stimulation. The end of the week is comprised of mostly mental preparation and recovery. As important competitions draw near, the workload is decreased, and the quality is high. Two weeks prior to an important competition, heavy squats are discontinued and replaced with step-ups. The lifting during this phase is light and fast.

Another special preparation phase will occur in late March and early April. A pre-competitive phase will follow in May, and a peaking phase will wind up the indoor season in June. A transition phase will follow the last peaking phase. The primary objective of the periodized resistance-training program is to ensure peak performance at the key competitions indoors and outdoors.

Figure 6-1. The primary objective of the periodized resistance-training program is to ensure peak performance at the key competitions indoors and outdoors.

The individual training session is the foundation of the entire training plan. The individual strength-training session determines how the long-term plan is actually implemented. An annual plan is a succession of connected individual training sessions in pursuit of particular objectives. Bear in mind, no single workout can make an athlete, but one workout can break an athlete; for that reason, the focus should be on the cumulative training effect. Hence, it is imperative to vigilantly plan the sequence of training sessions from day to day and within the day, as well as to project the potential effect of training on subsequent days. With these factors in mind, always be aware of the residual and cumulative training effects. The critical aim is the cumulative training effect, the changes in an athlete over the long term. Where does the workout fit within the microcycle plan? The workout is only one module of the immense training picture.

Exercise Prescription

What are the optimal strength-training exercises, and how are they executed? Because lifting weights has been a mainstream form of exercise for a long time, variations of the bench press, squat, and other lifts can confuse a coach trying to choose the correct exercises and teach them properly. Divide the weight-training session into three distinct areas: focus exercises, ancillary exercises, and remedial exercises. Focus or primary exercises are defined as the exercise or exercises that are the essential, absolute, need-to-do exercises. These total-body lifts have high muscle demands and usually include two to three lifts per session. Ancillary or secondary exercises are an exercise or exercises that will enhance the quality of the focus exercises. One to three ancillary exercises are generally performed in a session. Remedial movements are fundamental exercises designed to address basic needs for joint stability, proprioception, or postural improvement. Three to five remedial exercises are included in a session, depending on the degree of remedial work necessary. In order to ensure these exercises are effective, they must be executed in good form. When doing a series of exercises, you'll generally want to have your athletes start with the larger muscle groups and compound movements and work toward the smaller muscle groups and isolation movements. Following is a brief overview of some of the important lifts for throwers.

Exercise Selection

The use of free weights as a means of developing physical capabilities for the throws has long been a common practice. The use of other types of resistance equipment and machines has become popular in recent years. While any form of resistance applied against working muscles can enhance the strength of that muscle group, when throwing is concerned, the use of free weights is superior to fixed-position machines.

Since athletic performance on the track and in the field requires the athlete to perform tasks in free space, balance becomes an essential facet of performing the task. Athletic movements require a chain of structural forces that involves balance and stabilization, as well as movement. In training for most events, you should be concerned not only with the application of force, but the rate of force development (i.e., explosive strength). Therefore, the use of free-standing resistance, barbells, dumbbells, and other free weights provides the best type of exercise to improve more than just the individual muscular strength. The emphasis in this weight program is placed upon the exercises that incorporate total-body lifts, the clean, snatch, and clean and jerk as the foundation of the overall program.

One type of exercise that is beneficial to the throwing regime is resistance training, i.e., exercises that involve external resistance, usually using traditional weight-training equipment. These exercises can be subdivided into three groups:

- *Olympic or weightlifting lifts* are competitive lifts such as the clean, snatch, jerk, and similar movements. Normally, multiple sets of one to five repetitions are used, and recoveries are long enough to guarantee quality of work. Olympic lifts develop absolute strength, power, and coordination.

Figure 6-2. Snatch

• *Strength or static lifts* are traditional weight-lifting exercises involving major muscle groups. They also have been referred to as strength lifts or competitively are part of the sport known as power lifting. Most squatting and pressing movements fit into this category. They involve high resistances and low speeds of movement. Necessarily, they normally involve lower repetitions and high numbers of sets. Normally, you want to see multiple sets of five to eight repetitions, and recoveries are long enough to guarantee quality of work. Static lifts are a primary tool for absolute strength development in more experienced athletes.

Figure 6-3. The squat is primarily a strength lift, but derivatives like the jump can develop speed strength.

- *Body-building lifts* are traditional weight-lifting exercises performed in high-repetition, low-resistance, short-recovery formats. An example is the cable curl. These exercises can be used to improve body composition, strength endurance, and energy-system fitness. Typically, you want to see 18 to 24 total sets of 10 to 12 repetitions in a session, with recoveries ranging from one to two minutes.

It can be argued that to most effectively enhance strength or power attributes for a specific sports activity like throwing in track and field, the training program should contain exercises that address the concept of mechanical specificity. Mechanical specificity is not limited to movement pattern or velocity considerations but also is concerned with peak rate of force development, peak force, and positional characteristics. The closer a training exercise is to the actual physical performance, the greater the probabilities of transfer. Although the training for the throwing events is very similar, special exercises can be employed to enhance event-specific qualities. For the javelin, the pull-over is a primary exercise. This exercise can be performed with a barbell or dumbbell. Advanced throwers have utilized heavy weights on this exercise. The snatch is a great exercise to develop speed/strength for the javelin. Shot-putters employ various upper-body exercises like the bench press and the incline press. The close-grip bench press is an exercise that can help improve triceps strength for the shot-putter. Jerks and derivatives of the jerk closely resemble the shot put and are the best exercise for developing power. Discus throwers use various fly movements to develop special strength and flexibility in the upper body. Hammer throwers perform a lot of torso and back exercises.

Figure 6-4. Cable curls are one of many exercise choices for working the biceps muscle.

Numerous studies and review articles have reported evidence and logical arguments for the use of explosive exercises for throwers. This result is no surprise because of the fiery nature of all throwing events. Explosive exercises are marked by high-force and high-velocity movements. The snatch and clean and their derivatives have potential for power outputs higher than the so-called "power" or more appropriately termed strength lifts (squat, bench press, dead lift). However, many different kinds of exercise types are also important to developing the total package of a successful thrower.

Strength-building exercises are reduced as the year progresses, but exercises like the quarter squat and bench press are employed during the in-season competitive phase to complement the explosive exercises and set up the final mesocycle. The jerk out of the rack is an excellent lift during the in-season competitive/peaking phase as the development of speed strength is the top priority. The exercise is performed with spotters helping with the downward phase of the movement following the press. The jerk has the potential to produce the highest power output of the Olympic lifts. Another great sport-specific exercise for throwers that meets the criteria of mechanical specificity is the mid-thigh high pull. It is a derivative of the power clean, where the athlete performs an explosive shrug from the mid-thigh position in the power rack, allowing for maximum power development. Heavy weights can be handled in training without the wear and tear of the full movement. In terms of force and rate of force development, the pulling movements can be used as an example of integrating movement patterns and overload like those in the shot put. According to Lanka and Shalmanov (1982), the shot put and high-pull movements share common time frames and similar ground reaction forces, and they largely use the same muscles. Using an explosive performance such as the shot put as an example, comparisons indicate that pulling movements can provide a power overload. According to German coach, Klaus Bartonietz, elite throwers can generate approximately 54 W/kg during execution of the shot put. Using the optimum percentage of 1 RM for the pulling movements can produce power outputs up to 20 percent greater than the power generated in the shot put, thus providing an overload. Bartonietz (2000) suggests that power summation is a primary factor separating elite throwers from lesser throwers. Other exercises employed during the in-season training period, such as bench-press throws (using a Smith machine) and multiple repetition jump squats, may provide an excellent alternative or supplement to the traditional Olympic weightlifting style movements for the development of speed strength and for athletes of lower strength levels. The power produced during jump squats or bench-press throws can actually exceed that of the Olympic lifts, if done properly.

When performing timed exercises, the athlete should complete as many repetitions as possible in 10 seconds at 60 percent intensity for the development of explosive strength. Typically, you want to use the bench, clean, and squat in the timed regime. Jump squats are another excellent way to build explosive power. With 30 percent intensity, the athlete performs as many jump squats possible in 10 seconds. To build speed strength, simple jump-ups are performed. The athlete performs as many repetition jumps in 10 seconds without any load. Smith machine bench-press throws utilize what is termed the time-controlled speed-strength methods (TCSSM). The TCSSM controls the duration of the rest intervals between the sets and between the repetitions. This method is used to build upper-body speed strength during the competition period. The duration of rest between sets should be five minutes. Taking, for example, the Smith machine bench-press throw for upper-body speed-strength development, it is desirable to work in an intensity zone between 50 and 60 percent. Each rep is conducted with a certain amount of time in between. Spotting partners watch the clock and signal the athlete when the next repetition should commence. After the first repetition, it is important that the second, third, and subsequent reps are executed with a speed reduction of below 5 percent of the first rep in the competition period. The lift must be done with speed and without deceleration (the reason for bench-press throws). If the speed reductions are too great, the exercise does not effectively train speed and instead trains other variables not designated for the lift. Other specific training methods to increase force at high rates of muscular contraction include medicine-ball and power-ball drills and other high-speed, low-intensity resistance training such as snatch-and-release and press-and-release lifts in a sand pit.

Exercise Technique

Every throws coach should have an advanced understanding of the technique and the teaching progressions of the basic weight-lifting exercises. Weight lifting is a very important part of training in the throwing events. The technical execution of each lift is the key to any successful strength and conditioning program. What takes place between the first and last repetition of each exercise is what produces results. It's not the type of equipment that produces results—although good equipment helps. It is the proper execution of each exercise. It is possible to produce increases in strength by doing almost anything that places a demand on your musculature. Good technique must be used to progress in a consistent manner over a long period of time without injury. Basic exercises are:

- Power clean
- Bench press
- Squat
- Jerk
- Power snatch

The following section will provide a detailed description of the technique involved in the "big four" exercises for throwers: the bench press, the squat, the power clean, and the jerk. This section will also address common problems that may occur when performing each movement.

The Bench Press

The bench press is the fundamental exercise for developing upper-body strength for throwers. The multi-joint bench press is the pillar of strength exercises for the upper body. It hits the chest, frontal shoulders, and rear-arm muscles.

Figure 6-5. The bench press is the fundamental exercise for developing upper body strength.

The bench press also activates the long head of the biceps, which crosses both the shoulder and elbow joints. Since all activities in sports require some degree of upper-body strength, each athlete can benefit from using the bench-press exercise in his training program. Unfortunately, the bench press does little to train the core or educate the neuromuscular system about its role during upper-extremity patterns in a standing or functional posture.

Proper technique is important when using the bench press to supplement upper-body strength for throwers. Teach all of your athletes to bench with a fairly narrow grip, and to keep the elbows in while performing the exercise. While the bench press is the primary lift for upper-body strength development, have them perform incline bench press and close grip bench press as secondary lifts. In prescribing exercise, always try to vary the angle of pressing activities. The athletes should perform specific shoulder exercises like military press and lateral and front raises with dumbbells. Have them work the jerk from the rack. Make sure that their shoulders are worked only twice a week in order to allow for proper recovery. A lot of your remedial shoulder work can be done in your conditioning circuits. Have the athletes perform bench press and incline presses with dumbbells as secondary exercises. The shoulder stabilizers should be worked after the major lifts are performed, with remedial shoulder exercises. All of these upper-body exercises intertwine to maximize general upper-body strength. Together with the squat, the bench press is the cornerstone of sound weight-training programs. This section will examine the technical components of the bench press and will discuss some of the problems that can occur in each lift.

Two Types of Bench Press

Two basic types of technique can be employed in the bench press: wide grip and narrow grip ("power lifting").

Wide-Grip Bench Press

- This style emphasizes the outer pectoralis muscles.
- The bar touches the chest just above the xiphoid process.
- The athlete concentrates on keeping the elbows out, and the bar moves in a straight line. This type of bench press would be excellent for a discus thrower.

Narrow-Grip or "Power Lifting" Bench Press

- This exercise is not to be confused with the close-grip bench that is used as an auxiliary exercise.
- The athlete grips the bar a thumb's grip away from the smooth part of the knurling of the bar.
- The athlete tries to keep the elbows in and touch the bar just below the xiphoid process as the bar travels in an inward arc.

This style of bench pressing puts great stress on the triceps and front deltoids. A shot-putter would benefit from this style of bench press. Coaches should experiment with the grip of the athletes. Each individual is built differently; therefore, the grip and style of each athlete may vary.

Basic Fundamentals of the Bench Press

Preliminary Position

- The athlete's initial position in the bench press is that of lying on the bench in a supine position with the bar directly over the eyes.
- The key is to place the uprights of the bench (if they are adjustable) so that the athlete does as little work as possible to assume the starting position.
- The shoulders, back, and hips maintain contact with the bench.
- Keep the feet flat on the floor, equal distance from the leg supports.

• A slight arch should be kept in the back, but the hips should always maintain contact with the bench.

Hand Position

• The hand position on the bar is important for developing strength in the desired muscle groups.
• The hands must be equal distance from a constant point, either the center knurling or the outer grip line. Each athlete should measure his grip before each set.
• The grip should be shoulder-width or slightly wider and comfortable to the athlete or it can be narrower. The grip can vary from athlete to athlete. Remember the purpose of the exercise when selecting a grip.
• A wide grip concentrates on the outer pectoral muscles and the deltoids.
• A close grip concentrates on the inner pectoral muscles and triceps.
• Chalk can be used on the hands to ensure a strong grip.

Descent Phase

• Success of the lift depends on a proper eccentric contraction or descent of the bar.
• When removing the bar from the rack, the lifter should keep it in a comfortable position based on the path the bar will take in the descent with arms locked.
• After the bar is removed from the rack, the lifter should inhale and start the descent.
• The lifter should control the bar's descent with the elbows under it. A properly executed descent prepares the muscles to press the bar to the original starting position and protects the sternum from injury.

Power lifters use an inward arc pattern during the descent phase. This pattern stresses the latissimus dorsi eccentrically for stabilization. This pattern is excellent for athletes who must handle heavy weights. Another descent taken is an "s" pattern. This technique stresses the pectoralis major and minor.

At the end of the descent, the bar must contact the chest. This placement stretches the front deltoids and pectorals, resulting in a stronger contraction. Because the exercise is designed to develop specific muscles, it is important to control the bar and work throughout the full range of motion. This technique reduces the tendency to bounce the bar off the chest and thereby reduces the possibility of rib cage or sternum injury.

The location of bar contact on the chest is important. Some coaches suggest touching just above the xiphoid process, while others propose contact at the origin of the pectoralis major just below the anterior border of the clavicle, or 6 to 8 inches (15 to 20 cm) below the glenohumeral joint.

Inconsistent bar contact can result in altered mechanics. If the bar contacts the chest too high, the triceps and deltoids perform more of the action, and the pectoralis muscles develop less. Conversely, if the bar contacts the chest too low, the deltoids and triceps will be at a mechanical disadvantage for the next phase.

Ascent Phase

- In the bench press, the ascent phase begins when the bar touches the chest, and it ends when the arms are locked in the starting position.
- The bar should trace the same arc as the descent and must be pushed in a level fashion with the hands staying even both vertically and horizontally.
- A slow, deliberate push in necessary to decrease upward momentum of the bar and to maximally stress the muscle groups involved. Breathing is very important both for physiological reasons and for aiding in the completion of the lift.
- The athlete should inhale before starting the descent phase. Inhaling creates a stable thoracic pressure from which the muscles of the chest, shoulders, and triceps can push.
- Exhale as soon as the bar leaves the chest at the start of the ascent.

Teach your athletes to lock the bar out in a smooth, controlled fashion. Some athletes hyperextend the elbows at the conclusion of a repetition, which may lead to shoulder and elbow problems.

Spotting

Spotters should assist the person performing an exercise. The assistance may be before, during, or after the completion of an exercise. A spotter has two primary responsibilities:

- Prevent injuries to the lifter and anyone in the adjacent vicinity.
- Assist the lifter in such a way as to facilitate the proper execution of the exercise (for example, bring a heavy weight to the starting position in an exercise).

In the bench press, the spotter will stand behind the bench and will normally provide a lift off for the athlete. The spotter will then closely observe the lifter and, following the lift, help guide the bar into the uprights on the bench.

Common Errors in Executing the Bench Press

The bench press, which is the most common exercise performed in the weight room, is the simplest exercise in which poor technique is used. Technical errors in the bench press occur because the bench press is an "ego" lift, and people get overly concerned with big numbers. Athletes will cheat in order to try to lift more weight than they can with good technique.

Figure 6-6. Example of a correct spot in the bench press. Notice the spotter is not touching the bar but is ready in case he is needed.

Error #1: Arching the Back

This error is the most common. Arching the back occurs when the athlete attempts to lift a heavier weight than he can with proper technique.

When arching, the athlete pushes his feet to raise his buttocks off the bench. The arch assists the muscles by providing momentum to push the bar from the chest. By arching, a change results in the arm-chest angle at the sticking point of the exercise. It is an artificially induced, mechanically advantageous position.

Besides reducing the strength development of the desired muscles, great stress is placed on the lumbar spine when the athlete arches, which may result in injuries to the lower back, such as herniated discs and strained muscles. To prevent arching, the athlete should practice the technique properly with lighter weight or place the feet flat on the bench with knees bent.

Error #2: Bouncing the Bar Off the Chest

The consequences of this common error include:
- Possible injury to the sternum
- Damage to the integrity of the shoulder joint
- Soft tissue damage to the involved muscles

Bouncing the bar off the chest also may remove stress intended for the primary muscles and place it on the accessory muscle groups. By bouncing the bar off the chest, the athlete requires the rib cage to absorb the impact of the bar. This technique suggests that the athlete is trying to make up for a lack of strength or that the weight is too heavy. The amount of work done by the muscles is markedly reduced when this technique is used.

Some coaches use what is termed as a "plyometric bench" to overload the system. In this type of lift, the athlete uses a bounce pad on his chest to use heavier weight and bounces the bar off the pad. The best way to prevent this poor technique is to emphasize a slower descent and to remove the importance of the amount of weight lifted.

Many coaches use the legal competition bench to eliminate the poor technique involved with bouncing the bar off the chest. Use of the legal bench requires that:

- Shoulders and hips maintain contact with the bench.
- Feet are always flat on the floor.
- The bar is level during ascent.
- The bar must contact the chest for a minimum of a one-thousand-one count.
- Importance of the amount of weight lifted is removed.

The legal bench also has a slower descent phase. This slower phase has two main effects:

- The slower phase decreases the chance of trauma to the chest and shoulder region.
- Muscles have a 40 percent greater capacity to sustain eccentric loading compared to concentric contraction. This greater capacity results in greater tension developed by the muscle fibers.

Error #3: Young Lifters Being Too Close to the Upright Supports When Lying on the Bench

This common error will manifest itself by the bar contacting the supports in the ascent. This error can be easily corrected by having the bar positioned over the eyes and having the spotter lift the bar out to the athlete.

Error #4: Inconsistent Bar-Chest Contact

Athletes who bounce the bar off of their chest and arch the back when lifting will have a problem with maintaining technical consistency when performing the bench press exercise. Athletes should be taught to lift in a slow and controlled manner. This error can be corrected by chalking the contact area, thereby giving the lifter a kinesthetic clue of bar contact.

Error #5: Holding Breath

An error common to all lifters is the holding of breath. The more experienced lifters are typically not affected by this problem. The novice, however, may become disoriented or experience a blackout, which is obviously dangerous. Teach your lifters how to breathe. All lifters should inhale prior to the descent phase and exhale on the ascent phase.

Error #6: Locking the Bar Out Unevenly

Another error athletes often make is locking the bar out unevenly. This move is sometimes combined with a bounce off the chest and an arch in the back. Uneven bar movement is a problem seen in novices. The error is potentially dangerous if the weights slide off the bar. It increases the potential of a shoulder injury. This problem can occur when athletes use heavy weights and struggle to make a repetition.

Athletes often lock out one side and then the other as a way of using additional resistance. Athletes such as shot-putters sometimes lock out unevenly because the throwing arm becomes stronger than the non-throwing arm.

The best way to correct this problem is to use a very slow, deliberate descent phase. To correct this, have the athlete focus on the side that is lagging behind. Doing so forces the athlete to concentrate on that side and will level the bar.

Error #7: Lifting the Head When Performing the Bench Press

Novice athletes sometimes lift their heads when performing the bench press. This problem often occurs because athletes may lack flexibility or raise their heads to look at the bar. Great stress is placed on the lumbar spine when the athlete raises his head, which may result in injuries to the neck or lower back, such as herniated discs and strained muscles. Coaches should teach their lifters to keep their heads down when lifting.

Auxiliary Exercises

The incline bench press and the close-grip bench press are excellent supplementary exercises to improve power in the bench press. The incline bench press strengthens the deltoids and upper chest, while the close-grip bench press strengthens the all-important triceps muscles.

In the close-grip bench, the athlete grips the bar with the index finger on the smooth part of the knurling. This auxiliary lift closely resembles the power lifting bench press, but it has a much narrower grip. The combination of these two lifts following the bench press will provide an excellent upper-body workout for any athlete.

The bench press can be extremely beneficial to track and field athletes involved in resistance training. The combination of explosive exercises (cleans, jerks, snatches) and slow-velocity, high-force movements, such as the bench press, can produce better results than either method alone.

The Squat

The squat is probably the best total-body exercise for strength development. The squat is known as the "king of exercises" because it is a quick and efficient way of strengthening the legs and lower back. Due to its multi-joint action and nature, the squat is an excellent way to promote overall body growth. Table 6-4 lists the muscles used in the squat. The squat provides two primary benefits. First, it develops the lower back, hips, gluteals, and quadriceps by using a hip thrust. Second, the squat is sport-transferable. In other words, any sport that requires a powerful hip thrust can benefit from the squat exercise. The squat is especially applicable to the throwing events. Biomechanically, the squat maximizes dynamic strength development, while at the same time minimizing joint stress.

Flat bench press
Flat bench press with dumbbells
Flat bench dumbbell fly
Incline bench press
Incline dumbbell press
Parallel bar dips
Decline dumbbell bench press
Incline dumbbell fly
Dumbbell pullover

Table 6-3. Exercises for upper-body development

Gluteal group
Medial thigh
Anterior thigh (quadriceps)
Erector spinae
Posterior thigh (hamstrings)

Table 6-4. Muscles utilized in the squat

Figure 6-7. The parallel squat is a fundamental exercise for the thrower.

Squat Techniques

Wide Stance or "Power" Squat (Low Bar)

- This squat emphasizes the hamstrings and gluteals.
- The athlete carries the bar low on his back and sets up in a stance that is wider than shoulder-width.
- His feet are flared out at a 45-degree angle.
- This type of squat is excellent for a heavy strength/power phase. The athlete can handle a great amount of weight because of the excellent leverage position the power squat provides.

Figure 6-8. The position of the bar in the low-bar squat. Notice that the elbows are high to help balance the bar on the scapula.

- The athlete carries the bar high on his back and sets up in a stance that is shoulder-width. The athlete can put a board under his heels.
- This type of squat emphasizes the quadriceps and is excellent for a pre-season preparation phase.

Figure 6-9. In the high-bar squat, the bar is placed high on the trapezius and the elbows are low and underneath the bar.

In both types of squats, the athlete should perform the exercise in front of a mirror. Squatting in front of a mirror enables the athlete to perfect his technique because of the visual feedback the mirror provides.

Basic Fundamentals of the Squat

Execution of the Squat

- Coaches should always check to see that the athlete is wearing a weight belt before he approaches the bar. Athletes can lift without a belt during warm-up sets and on light days to build up the core.
- When the athlete approaches the bar, he should step forward with one leg then walk under the bar with the other leg
- Once under the bar, the athlete should flex his knees, extend his chest, and straighten his back with just a slight lordosis (inward curve of the spine)
- The athlete should keep his head neutral with eyes looking forward.
- Have the athlete position the bar above the scapula in the trapezius muscle if in the Olympic Squat, or position the bar below the trapezius on the scapula if in the power squat.
- The athlete should use the chalk on his hands and back to prevent the bar from slipping.
- Have the athlete position the hips under the bar before lifting it off the rack.

The Grip

- The grip in the squat is very important for even bar placement across the back of the athlete. Some authorities suggest a wide grip, while others promote a narrow grip.
- The athlete should grasp the bar with the hands equally spaced from the middle knurling.
- Comfort for the individual athlete is key when gripping the bar.

The Stance

- Getting into a comfortable stance is another important key to a successful lift in the squat.
- The athlete should raise the bar off the rack by driving with his hips and quadriceps, not by extending the lower back.
- The athlete should take his time when setting up. A poor set-up can lead to injury. The height of the uprights is an important consideration.
- The athlete should place the bar at a height so that he can remove it by performing a quarter squat.
- The athlete should take only one step backwards in preparation for the descent phase, unless using a stair rack (more than one step may be needed to get outside the frame of the rack). Walking back more than one step wastes energy and increases chance of injury.
- The athlete should keep his feet flat on the floor, approximately shoulder-width apart and parallel, with his toes pointed slightly outward.
- The athlete should keep his back straight with a slight lordotic curvature, his head and eyes up (straight ahead), and his elbows under the bar. He should be consistent with this position.

Setting the Back

- Setting the back helps remind the athlete to keep his back tight and in a good position.
- Prior to the descent phase, the athlete should take a deep breath and isometrically contract the muscles of the upper thigh and torso. Doing so stimulates the stretch reflex, resulting in a strong eccentric contraction of the flexor muscles used in the descent phase.

Descent Phase

- Coaches should teach their athletes to sit back on their heels when doing this exercise. The athlete should reach the parallel position to achieve maximal benefits. Parallel position is achieved when the knee joint is in line with the hip joint.
- Athletes should remember to begin the descent phase with a deep inhalation.

- Initially, the athlete should flex at the hips rather than the knees. Flexing the knees causes the majority of the stress to be placed on the knees and increases the potential for injury.
- After the initial hip flexion, the athlete should flex the knees while keeping the toes directly under the knee joint. Then, he should sit back slowly and maintain control in the eccentric phase of the lift until the parallel position is reached.
- During the descent, the athlete should keep his eyes and head up and his back straight with a slight lordosis (inward curvature of the spine).
- The athlete should keep his hips under the bar at all times.
- The athlete should descend in a controlled manner, using a strong eccentric contraction of his hips and quadriceps.
- This strong eccentric contraction is important to maintain proper vertical bar velocity and to store the kinetic energy that is critical in the transition to the ascent phase. The path of the bar during the descent depends on the position of the bar on the shoulders.
- If the athlete should use a high bar position, with the bar above the scapula, a perpendicular path is preferred.
- If the athlete uses a low bar position, with the bar two inches below the top if the shoulder, the bar will follow an arc, with the hips remaining under the bar as long as possible.

Ascent Phase

- Each athlete will develop a kinesthetic feel to determine the correct depth. Coaches should teach their athletes to lock the bar out in a smooth controlled fashion. This technique prevents the bar from bouncing off the shoulders at the top of the ascent. Some athletes hyperextend their knees at the conclusion of a repetition. This hyperextension will lead to knee and lower-back problems.
- Athletes should begin the ascent or concentric phase after reaching a parallel position and momentarily stopping at the low position.
- The athlete should initiate the ascent phase by driving with his legs and extending his hips under the bar.
- The athlete should extend his head to counteract the contraction of the trapezius.
- The athlete should maintain a tight torso throughout the entire ascent.
- After the sticking point (approximately 30 degrees above parallel), the athlete should slowly exhale and slow the velocity of the bar.
- The athlete should keep the torso rigid until the bar is racked.

Racking the Bar

- Spotters should help the athlete guide the bar to the rack.
- The athlete should walk to the rack in a controlled manner.

- The athlete should lower the bar by bending at the hips with his head up and body straight.
- He should not bend at the waist and drop the bar onto the rack.

Spotting

- In the squat, the athlete who is lifting must always use a spotter.
- The spotter should be positioned behind the athlete, ready to give support around the torso and hips.
- Two additional spotters should be positioned on either side of the lifting athlete. The spotters should be ready to grab either side of the bar if the athlete needs assistance completing the lift or putting the bar on the rack.

Training Equipment

- The use of training aids (e.g., belts, wraps, etc.) can enhance the amount of weight lifted and sometimes prevent injuries.
- Belts have been designed with a wide front especially for the squat. This type of belt usually has two or three layers of leather and provides extra support in the abdominal area. The use of these belts can be very beneficial.
- Knee wraps can also enhance the amount of weight an athlete can handle in training. Often termed "super wraps," these training aids support the knees and provide "recoil" at the bottom. Knee wraps should only be used when the effort is more than 90 percent of the athlete's perceived maximum.
- Power lifters also use what is termed a lifting suit. Similar to a wrestling suit, these tight-fitting garments provide extra support in the thigh and gluteal

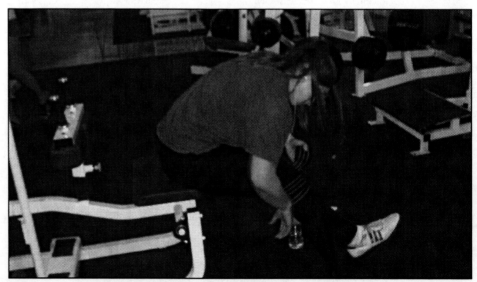

Figure 6-10. Knee wraps can enhance the amount of weight an athlete can handle in the squat. The use of wraps on the heavy lifting days will help increase the amount of overload on the lower body.

area. A lifting suit is available from any power-lifting magazine and will likely add extra pounds to an athlete's lift. Again, these garments are only needed on heavy days, if at all.

- Weight-lifting shoes are hard-soled leather shoes with raised heels. These shoes give the athlete an excellent base for lifting, adding extra support for those heavy days. Olympic lifters primarily use lifting shoes.

- Many training aids are available for the squat. These aids are certainly not a necessity for all lifters, but when used properly, they can add extra overload to the system.

Common Errors in Executing the Squat

Squat exercise errors can be corrected with technique alignment by the strength and conditioning coach. Coaches should use extra caution when supervising athletes performing the squat and should look for the following errors.

- Excessive forward lean places a dangerous amount of stress on the knees, which can result in injury to the capsular ligament and patellar tendon. This error is related to failing to lead with the chest and not thrusting the head back during the ascent. Bending over in this way will place too much stress on the lower back because the back, rather than the hips and legs, will initiate the ascent. To correct these mistakes, the coach should place a spot on the ceiling a foot in front of the athlete's head. The athlete then should keep his eyes focused on the spot. Doing so should reduce the tendency to lean forward and/or to lead with the back.

- Another common technique error is allowing flexibility in the torso during the lift. This error is closely associated with the forward lean. When these errors occur, it is difficult to keep the hips under the bar. An isometric contraction of the upper torso during the exercise will help to correct this error.

- Bouncing at the parallel position is another common fault. This error is usually caused by a rapid descent. Athletes sometimes bounce to get some rebound at the bottom. Olympic lifters are often guilty of bouncing. To correct this error, slow the descent, possibly decrease the weight, and remove emphasis on the amount of weight lifted. Bouncing at the parallel position places a dangerous amount of stress on the knees, which could result in injury to the capsular ligament and patellar tendon.

- Not descending to an adequate depth in the parallel position is another critical error in the squat exercise. Maximal benefits throughout the full range of motion are achieved only if the exercise is performed to parallel position prior to the ascent. Young, inexperienced lifters tend to pile on the weight and cut the depth a little short. To correct this error, the athlete should practice proper technique with light resistance before advancing to heavier weight.

- A problem many young lifters experience is lifting the heels and bending forward. This error occurs when the young athlete lacks flexibility in the ankle and lower leg. One possible solution is to place plates under the heels.

• Athletes are sometimes careless when setting up for the squat. They will take the bar off the rack, rush the set-up, and not have both feet parallel. This approach can cause the athlete to lean to one side during the repetition. Leaning to one side can lead to lower-back problems and is a hard habit to break. Getting set up in a comfortable stance is an important key to a successful lift. Athletes should take their time when setting up. A poor set-up can lead to injury.

Narrow stance (high-bar) squat
Wide stance (power) squat
Half squats
Quarter squats
Front squat
Overhead squat
Dumbbell squat
Leg press
Leg extensions
Leg curls
Hack squats
Dumbbell lunges
Step-ups

Table 6-5. Exercises for leg development

Figure 6-11. Leg extensions help develop the quadriceps muscle.

The Power Clean

When performed properly, the power clean is a very useful exercise for track and field. However, due to its technical nature, many coaches perceive the clean as potentially dangerous, and they do not include it in athletes' training programs. While the squat and bench press are classified as strength exercises, the power clean is the most effective total-body explosive exercise. Great throwers are able to accelerate their implement at forceful speeds from an effective power position. The power clean and its derivatives are so similar to throwing that it is an essential exercise in any throws coach's training plan. In a derivative of the power clean, the hang clean, the athlete grips the bar, lowers it to a power position, and explodes. The athlete catches the bar and adds more weight to develop the crucial explosive power necessary to throw far. When performed correctly, the power clean can be a safe and tremendously effective strength-training exercise. The power clean is the safest of the Olympic lifts because no overhead component is involved. Quick and explosive movements using the hips, legs, traps, and lower back are required to perform the power clean; therefore, training in this exercise generally results in power increases. The hips, legs, traps, and lower back are the primary movers in all field events as well as in sprints and hurdles. This section discusses the proper mechanics for the power clean and the advantages it has for track and field athletes.

Figure 6-12. This athlete is beginning the second pull in the power clean.

The power clean has many distinct advantages for all competitors in track and field. It is an excellent exercise to use as general warm-up: it is a total-body lift that provides the active warm-up for which many athletes are looking. The power clean is an exercise that develops explosive power and muscular strength. Explosive power is the application of force in a very brief time span and is one of the main attributes of a successful athlete in any sport. Muscular strength refers to the maximum amount of tension a muscle group can apply in a single effort. A successful track and field athlete possesses muscular power and explosive strength. The power clean can also be used as a total-body strengthening exercise.

The power clean also has characteristics contained by many track and field events and that no other resistance-training exercise possesses:
- During completion of the power clean, a pre-stretch occurs in the hips and quadriceps. This pre-stretch component allows for quick explosive power development.
- The power clean can also help improve coordination and balance. The development of coordination and balance is essential to technical development in the throwing events.
- Motor coordination, as well as static and dynamic balance, can be enhanced by working in a multi-joint pattern.

The improvement in each and all of these areas would be beneficial to the emerging athlete in the throwing events. The power clean movements are transferable to many of the field events in track and field:
- The pull and hip thrust in the power clean helps strengthen the muscles involved in the throwing and jumping events.
- This hip thrust helps strengthen the muscles needed to run and jump. The drop in the catch helps strengthen the quadriceps.

The power clean can also be an efficient timesaver because it is a multi-joint and multi-muscle exercise. Training with the power clean allows an athlete to work more muscle groups in a shorter period of time. Since virtually all events in track and field involve the coordination of the total body, the power clean has excellent transferability.

Execution of the Power Clean

Five basic components are involved in the execution of the power clean:
- Starting position
- First pull
- Second pull
- Catch
- Return to the starting position

When teaching the power clean, the phases should be taught separately. It is important for the athlete to master each phase prior to advancing to the next phase. After the parts are introduced, they should be combined so the athlete will understand the rhythm involved in the movement (Table 6-6).

Starting Position or Stance

- The feet should be flat and about shoulder-width apart.
- The bar should be directly over the first eyelet of the shoe, and the body weight should be on the balls of the feet.
- The hands are positioned outside the knees about one or two inches or thumbs' distance from the smooth part of the bar with the wrists flexed and forearms touching the outside of the thighs.

Technical Checkpoints in the Power Clean	
Grip	Thumb from the middle of the bar Wrists curled
Stance	Feet shoulder-width apart Bar at the middle of the shoes
First pull	Bar lifted just below the knees Shoulders over the bar
Second pull	Bar lifted above the knees in preparation for an explosive shrug
Explosive jump shrug	Arms are straight Traps to the ears Extended at the hip Finish on the toes
Recovery	Preparing to catch the bar Feet will be slightly turned out Knees will bend Core will stay firm
Rack	Bar will rest on the front delts Elbows will be up
Back to starting position	Bar will descend to the upper thigh Hips will drop Back will stay straight

Table 6-6. Power clean technical checklist

- The arms are extended in a straight line with the elbows pointing out.
- The back should be at a 45-degree angle to the floor and remain straight and tight.
- The hips should be slightly higher than the knees.
- The head is up, and the eyes are focused about 10 feet in front of the athlete.

The First Pull

The first pull is the second component and first phase of the actual power clean. The first pull is simply a mini-dead lift. The goal of this phase is to bring the bar into the proper pulling position and prepare the athlete for the second pull. The athlete should work for proper positions in this phase.

- Initially, in the first pull, the legs straighten and the hips should drive upward to lift the bar off the floor. The athlete should feel as if he is driving his feet into the floor.
- The center of gravity will change from being on the toes to the middle of the foot as the bar moves closer to the shins and then toward the knees.
- The shoulders must be in front of the bar, allowing the bar to remain close to the body.
- Throughout this phase, the arms must remain locked out with the elbows pointing outward.
- At the end of the first pull, the bar is slightly below the knees.

Figure 6-13. In the first pull, the athlete is over the bar as the bar is just below the knees.

The Second Pull

The second pull is the second phase and third component of the power clean. The athlete starts to accelerate the bar in this phase of the lift. Following the first and second pull, this slight hesitation is the point where the bar is beginning to accelerate and is unnoticeable in most experienced lifters. At the end of the transition, the athlete is in the power position.

- The bar is slightly above the knees.
- The lower back is arched.
- The wrists are flexed.
- The body weight is on the heels.
- The arms are straight.
- The trapezius is extended.

As the athlete begins the second pull, the knees will bend under the bar as a result of moving the hips down and forward.

- The back is almost vertical.
- The shoulders are in front of the bar.
- The wrists are flexed.

The knees are rebent at this point. The re-bending of the knees causes an eccentric contraction of the quadriceps. This contraction results in stored elastic energy that will be critical for the explosion of the second pull. Next, the athlete performs a movement similar to an explosive vertical jump.

- It is important to concentrate on driving the hips upward and toward the bar, while extending the knees and ankles.
- At the end of the lower-body extension, the trapezius contracts forcefully upward.

Figure 6-14. The arms begin to bend in the second pull after the athlete finishes extending the hips and the trapezius.

The final part of the second pull is performed after the shoulder shrug is complete. This step involves an abduction and medial rotation of the shoulder and flexing of the elbows. Upon completion of the second pull, the elbows will be facing sideways. The transferability to the track and field is especially evident in this phase.

The Catch

The catch is the final phase of the power clean. Foot quickness and flexibility in the shoulders and triceps is the key to catching and racking the bar.

- When the bar is at its highest point, the athlete should move under the bar by flexing the knees and hips. This flexion of the knees and hips will help absorb the force of the weight.

Remember, the athlete is performing a power clean and not a squat clean; therefore, it is not necessary to have the athlete drop extremely low when catching the bar. When moving under the bar:

- The torso is kept in a vertical position.
- The elbows move from their outward position of under the bar and then upward.
- The parallel position of the elbow, in relation to the floor, causes the chest to be up, creating a ledge along the clavicles for the bar to rest upon.
- The athlete should hold the bar in the racked position for a second or two as he regains his balance.

Figure 6-15. The elbows are high as the bar rests on the deltoids in the receiving position or catch in the power clean.

The Return

Following a completed repetition, the athlete must return to the starting position to perform the next repetition. If this return is done improperly, the result can be not only a poor anatomical position for the next repetition, but it can make the lower back susceptible to injury. Following the catch:

- The athlete lowers the bar from the shoulders to the upper thigh.
- The bar rests on the upper thigh as the athlete lowers the hips and gradually slides the bar down the quadriceps to the original starting position. This move is done in a slow and controlled manner.

A proper return will keep the athlete in a good power position and will prepare him for the next repetition. The athlete should not bounce the plates off the floor between repetitions.

Common Technical Flaws in the Power Clean

As in many events in track and field, the power clean is a very technical movement that demands the watchful eye of a trained professional. When correcting technical flaws in the power clean, the coach should check the different phases to see if the athlete is in proper position. A technical flaw in one phase will result in a technical problem with another phase.

The Starting Position

The coach should check the starting position or stance. While in the stance, the most common error is the bar being too far away from the body. This error can be corrected by moving the bar to a position over the first eyelet of the shoe.

- The athlete should be cautioned not to get the bar too close to the body because the athlete will have to move the bar away from the body to clear the knees as he begins the second pull. Getting the bar too close will create an inefficient swinging motion.
- Another technical error occurs when the shoulders are positioned behind the bar. The correct stance should have the shoulders positioned in front of the bar.
- A third error in the stance is having the back rounded and relaxed. The athlete must learn to stay tight. A relaxed and rounded back is a weak position. By keeping the hips low, the back will stay tight and straight.

The First Pull

In the first pull, the most common mistake is jerking the bar off the floor. Athletes will try to be too aggressive at the start instead of just getting in the position for the second pull. Jerking the bar off the floor will cause too much separation of the bar from the body.

- To correct this error, the athlete should maintain a shoulder position in front of the bar, refrain from jerking the bar off the floor, isometrically contract the latissimus dorsi, and squeeze the bar off the floor.

- Additionally, the hips should elevate at the same speed as the shoulders. If the athlete is performing a multiple-rep set, caution the athlete not to bounce the bar off the floor, as it will cause a poor anatomical position for the next repetition.

The Second Pull

During the second pull, the most common error is not achieving a solid pull.
- Many athletes forget to pull the bar because they are too concerned with getting under it and racking it. This error leads to a lack of total-body extension prior to flexing the elbows. Athletes will often cut the second pull phase short. Proper total-body extension will come after many repetitions with proper supervision. Having the athlete feel the pull by performing partial movements from the hand position is helpful.
- Another common fault is not using the trapezius muscles to their maximum potential. This error is evidenced by an extension of the head and retraction of the shoulders. To prevent this error, the supervisor needs to continue to instruct the athlete to use the trapezius muscle in an upward shrugging motion. Again, hang cleans would be a helpful teaching tool.

The Catch

The most common error when catching the bar is not getting the elbows up and losing the repetition because of a poor rack. Flexibility exercises that stress the triceps as well as forcing your athletes to practice a proper rack on each repetition will help.
- Allowing the bar to crash on the shoulders is another problem athletes face in the catch. To correct this timing error, the athlete needs to work on the timing by practicing the movement.
- Another problem that occurs in the catch is the athlete sometimes catches the bar while on the toes rather than being flat-footed. This error usually occurs because the bar is too far away from the body and should be corrected by bringing the bar closer during the lift.
- Athletes also lean back in the catch. This error occurs because the athlete does not drop under the bar.

The Return

The most common mistake following a successful repetition is a sloppy return or recovery phase. Because of muscular fatigue, athletes will often let the bar drop very quickly from the shoulders and will not let it rest on the upper thigh and slide down the quadriceps. This movement places great stress on the lower back and will lead to overuse injuries. Athletes must always use a slow and controlled return. Doing so will save wear and tear on the athlete's body and on the equipment. Another common mistake is bouncing the plates off the floor between each repetition. An inconsistent starting position is the result.

Teaching Progression for the Power Clean

Four-Stage Pull

This step teaches important phases and positions of the lift. Have the athlete complete the following repetition:
- Pull to below knee, and then back to the floor.
- Pull to above the knee, and then back to the floor.
- Pull to above the knee, shrug, and then back to the floor.
- Perform one full repetition of a clean pull from the floor.

Hang Clean

The athlete should start the movement from mid-thigh. When coaching a clean from the floor, progress to the full movement when the athlete understands the pull.

Figure 6-16. The starting position in the hang clean is a very athletic position. The hang clean is an excellent exercise to work during the peaking phase.

Clean Pull

Instruct the athlete to never bend the arms when performing clean pulls. Performing pulls from the following levels will help different parts of the lift:
- From the floor
- From just below the knee
- From mid-thigh (the most explosive of the pulls—best for peaking)

Figure 6-17. In the starting position of the mid-thigh clean pull, the athlete's shoulders are over the bar. At the finish of the exercise, the athlete is in a position similar to a vertical jump. This exercise has excellent transfer to the release in the throwing events that require a forceful hip extension.

The Jerk

While the squat and bench are the best strength-building exercises, the jerk, power clean, and snatch are the most effective total-body explosive exercises. The jerk out of the rack is an excellent lift during the in-season competitive peaking phase as the development of speed strength is the top priority. The exercise is performed out of a power rack with spotters helping with the downward phase of the movement following the recovery. The spotters help ease the stress on the wrists and the deltoids and reduce the risk of injury. This exercise can be performed from the traditional bar position or behind the neck. The behind-the-neck jerk is sometimes preferred by throwers who have mobility issues in the deltoids, wrists, and triceps. The jerk has the potential to produce the highest power output of the Olympic lifts.

Technical Description of the Jerk

The athlete should place a barbell on his shoulders (on the deltoids or upper chest or behind the neck high on the traps) and grip the bar at a comfortable width. He should relax the hands. Make sure his hips are over his feet, and that his shoulders are over his hips.

The athlete should tighten his chin by moving it backward a fraction of an inch. He should feel his full feet on the floor. He should then shift back slightly

Figure 6-18. The jerk with spotters

to feel pressure on his heels (raising his toes off of the platform may help him do this move).

Maintaining the pressure on his heels, the athlete lowers his body a few inches; he should immediately and quickly push his heels into the floor. Doing so will move the barbell off of his shoulders (or chest) directly up, not forward. For this moment, he has no weight on his body and he is in perfect vertical balance.

The athlete should immediately move his hips (and shoulders) directly under the bar while splitting his legs (one forward, and one backward). Make sure to have him step well forward (maybe aim to have the front heel contact the floor first).

As his hips reach their lowest position, instruct the athlete to tighten his hips and lower back and stretch up with his shoulders. He should keep pressure on the floor with his front foot. At this point, he is in a split-legs position, with the torso vertical from butt to barbell.

As soon as the bar feels balanced over his shoulders and hips, the athlete should push his front foot and take a step or two backward. When his front foot is about halfway straightened, he should step forward with his rear foot to bring both feet in line, and maintain upward pressure on the barbell over his hips and shoulders. The spotters should then help ease the bar down to the starting position for the next repetition.

Derivatives of the Jerk

- Push press
- Push jerk
- Split jerk
- Behind-the-neck jerk
- Jerks with dumbbells

Auxiliary Exercises

- Military press
- Behind-the-neck press

Figure 6-19. The dumbbell jerk can be performed heavy for power development or light for speed. One-arm dumbbell jerks are an excellent alternative for injured athletes.

Detection, Prevention, and Treatment of Injuries

© Victah Sailer@www.photorun.NET

Throwers train far differently than athletes in traditional sports. As mentioned previously, the majority of training is not actually throwing. General conditioning has the charge of accumulating morphological and functional changes. In simple terms, it is building the engine. On the basis of these accumulated changes, sport-specific exercises can be done in which efforts are much more intensive. The athlete is getting stronger and more powerful. The sport-specific exercises can be so intensive that while causing performance to improve, they eventually weaken some of the links in the movement chain. To put it another way, structures of the body might not adapt to intensive sport-specific exercises at the same rate as the athletes capabilities. What this means is that coaches need to program some general exercises during the same workouts or at least during the same microcycles as sport-specific exercises to prevent injuries.

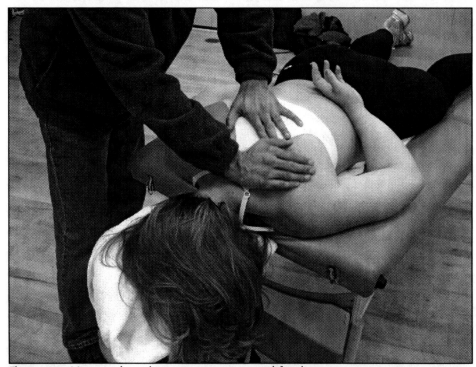

Figure 7-1. Massage is an important recovery tool for throwers.

Training for the Throwing Events

Supplementary strength and conditioning exercises usually make up two-thirds of a thrower's workout. Because of the extreme stress placed on a thrower's arms, shoulders, lower back, and lower body during the throw, workouts outside the throwing arena must serve a dual purpose: producing force and preventing injury. A motivated thrower is almost always training on the edge. As injuries are an almost inevitable consequence of training and competition, a successful coach must be able to deal with them effectively. One of the least-stressed, but certainly most fundamental principles of coaching is athlete health and fitness awareness. Coaches have a duty to monitor health and to prevent injury, making sure that if illness or injury does occur, they are managed promptly and correctly returning the athlete to full health as soon as possible. An understanding of injuries and recovery processes must be part of the coach's approach to the development and implementation of an athlete's strength and conditioning program. This basic overview of throwing injuries includes the role of the throws coach in injury prevention, identification of the principle areas of injury risk for throwing athletes (table 7-1), the classification of typical throwing injuries, the immediate treatment of soft-tissue injuries, and an understanding of the recovery and rehabilitation process. This essential component of the strength and conditioning and training process is often overlooked.

Figure 7-2. The javelin puts a lot of stress on the musculature of the shoulder and arm. This event requires careful planning of the training regimen and attention to detail following a workout. Throwing workouts should be performed only twice a week. Following a throwing workout or competition in the javelin, the thrower must ice and rehab similar to a pitcher in baseball.

Injuries

Enhanced muscle mass has been documented in muscle cross-sectional areas, and individual muscle-fiber size is much greater in throwers than in other individuals. Although injuries are not common in the field events compared to the running events, they do occur (Table 7-1). Watson and DiMartino (1987) found 82 percent of the injuries that occurred during participation in a track or field activity were in running events and 18 percent in field events. Only five to six percent of injuries occurring in track and field need treatment. Most injuries will get better with some simple first aid and appropriate rest and recovery. Overuse symptoms in the lower back, shoulders, elbow joint, and knees appear to be the most common injuries associated with the type of strength/power training performed with the throwing events. Increased curvature of the spine (hyperlordosis) can gradually develop over years of continual training and competition in the throwing events. With this increase, lumbar degeneration usually occurs and the onset of lower-back pain follows.

The cause of the many injuries can usually be attributed to erroneous technique or a sudden load progression or increased volume. Overuse symptoms from the lower back are the number-one injury in throwers, especially

Event	Potential Areas for Overuse Injuries	Specific Injuries That Can Occur
Shot put	Elbow, wrist, hand, lower back, hip flexor, iliopsoas, lower leg	Sprain/strain of the fingers/hand/wrist, carpal tunnel syndrome, sprained Achilles tendon, sprained iliotibial band, strained tensor fasciae latae, sprained sacroiliac
Discus	Pectorals, shoulder, lower back, knees	Strained adductor, strained anterior deltoid and pectorals minor, infrapatellar tendonitis in the knees, ruptured callus on the index finger
Hammer/Weight	Hands, trapezius, upper/middle/lower back, knees, ankles, feet	Tarsal spur, heel spur, tendonitis in the knees, lumbosacral sprain, shoulder impingement syndrome, rye neck syndrome, ruptured callus on the hands
Javelin	Shoulder, rotator cuff, elbow, lower back, knees, feet	Ulnar collateral ligament tears, ulnar neuritis, medial epicondylitis, olecranon bursitis, strained rotator cuff muscles, sprained lateral collateral ligament, sprained anterior cruciate ligament, sprained sacroiliac, plantar fasciitis

Adapted from Santino (1997) USATF Level III Presentation, Colorado Springs, Colorado

Table 7-1. Throwing events and potential areas for overuse injuries

in the hammer throw. Chronic overuse injuries in the shoulder, mainly the acromioclavicular (A/C) joint and muscle or tendon insertions around the shoulder, and inflammation of the subacromialis are frequent as well. The reason for shoulder problems may be due to the fact that the shoulders are excessively used and heavily involved in almost all upper-body exercises performed by throwers. Along with the A/C joint overuse, all the muscles that make up the "rotator cuff" suffer from the continual punishment from practice and competition. The subscapularis, supraspinatus, infraspinaus, and teres minor may cause pain and discomfort with loss of normal range of motion from microtrauma sustained over the years. Maintaining flexibility of these muscle groups is of paramount concern in training the thrower. The third-most prevalent injury is the overuse of the triceps insertion at the olecranon, which is stressed during shot-putting and many of the elbow-extensor exercises. Other overuse injuries in the knees have been reported but are not prevalent.

Almost daily, you hear or read about young athletes dropping out because of injuries and elite athletes struggling with injuries that have occurred during training or competition. Of course, this scenario is not limited to elite athletes. Over 50 percent of injuries occur during the final phase of the preparatory period. More than 30 percent of all injuries occur during the introductory portion of the workout. Also, a lot of injuries occur during the introductory portion of the warm-up.

The coach is not a doctor or sports-medicine professional, but he should:
- Have sufficient knowledge and understanding of the nature of athletics injuries.
- Be able to deal immediately with injuries.
- Know where to obtain early and reliable professional diagnosis.
- Know where to obtain early and reliable rehabilitation services.
- Know how to design training programs to minimize the chance of injury.
- Know how to design training programs to gradually return the athlete to full activity.

Screening for Injuries

Screening for muscle imbalances or weaknesses is the answer to injury prevention in the throws. Start each year with a comprehensive testing program, including assessment tools like the functional movement screen. The rationale behind this approach is that detectable and correctable abnormalities of muscle strength and length are fundamental to the development of almost all musculoskeletal pain and dysfunction. Detection of these abnormalities and correction before injury has occurred should be part of any injury-prevention strategy. This assessment should be part of the pre-season testing and screening program that was discussed previously and should be an ongoing process. Muscle imbalances are an ongoing part of training and competing in the throwing events. Assessment of muscle strength should be part of the continuing screening process and can be conducted by a massage therapist or athletic trainer.

Classification of Injuries

No matter how diligent you are in your assessment of injuries, the construction of your training plan, or how safety-conscious you are, injuries will occur. As a coach, you should prepare for this eventuality by developing your own emergency action plan. It is very important to know what actions to take when you feel an injury calls for an emergency response. Injuries, particularly soft-tissue injuries, require a basic first-aid knowledge, which can be used until a more thorough examination by a physician, athletic trainer, or physiotherapist can diagnose and treat the injury. Importantly, when dealing with injuries in emergency situations, know the limits of your knowledge and work within these limits. The key is rapid action when the injury first appears and a lot of psychological support to back up the remedial treatment.

A previous injury predisposes an athlete to a recurrence or further injury. To prevent this situation, all injuries should receive appropriate treatment and rehabilitation, with a planned, progressive return to full activity. The coach should confer with athletic trainers, chiropractors, physiotherapists, and doctors on the timing and manner of an individual's return to participation in athletics. Depending on the injury mechanism, tissues can be disrupted or inflamed. In soft tissues, disruption is known as a tear, and in the hard tissues, it is a fracture or break. In general, disruptions are acute traumatic injuries, and inflammation is the result of overuse. Tears can involve part of a soft tissue (a partial tear), or all of it (a complete tear or rupture). Inflammation is the body's reaction to an injury. In the acute stages, this process involves the local blood vessels, blood cells, chemicals, and proteins in attempts to limit damage and commence healing. However, if healing is not complete, the inflammation can become chronic. In this case, inappropriate and/or inadequate scar tissue may form, and the patient may have long-term symptoms or signs, and reduction of muscular and performance levels.

Chronic Injuries

Most chronic injuries are overuse injuries and are caused because the body cannot cope with the constant orthopedic stress placed on it. This stress can be caused by a sudden increase in training duration and/or intensity, persistent high-intensity training (e.g., plyometric) excessive hill training, training on "unfamiliar" surfaces (e.g., sand, snow, etc.), a single severe training session or competition, or a sudden return from a layoff. Chronic injuries are often caused by physical limitations in a part of the locomotive system as well. These types of injuries are effectively treated or managed by addressing the relevant causes.

Agonist and antagonist muscles need to be trained equally to establish balances in muscle strength. Chronic injuries are a dominant element in athletics. The reason injuries become chronic is because the injury is diagnosed and treated without looking into the underlying cause. Pelvic stabilization exercises are commonly ignored and can help prevent lower-back injuries (Table 5-7).

Tissue Damage

As explained previously, tissue damage can be the result of the overstrain of a muscle. This strain results in the inflammation of the cells and muscles, which in turn causes pain. Continued activity with this condition will result in more tissue damage or at best a slow healing of the damaged tissue, which will lead to more inflammation, which leads to more pain. The only way to break this cycle is through rest and recovery. Pain is a signal indicating tissue damage. When tissue damage occurs, "pain nerves" generate impulses transmitted to the spinal column to the brain for transformation into sensation of pain. Pain is increased by inflammation, direct stimulation, and the release of prostaglandins. To briefly review the terminology, athletic trainers will classify soft tissue injuries as:

- Mild
- Moderate
- Severe
- Avulsion

Treating Soft-Tissue Injuries

As mentioned, managing sporting injuries in the throws involves obtaining an accurate diagnosis from a medical professional, appropriate treatment, and finally, a specific rehabilitation process that allows full return to throwing. However, a delay often results between the time of injury and obtaining a diagnosis from a sports-medicine professional. It is important to begin treatment during this time to limit the amount of damage done before starting a more specific treatment regime.

The initial treatment program for a soft-tissue injury documented in many sports-medicine manuals can be best summarized by the acronym RICE, standing for rest, ice, compression, and elevation.

Rest

The amount of bleeding and swelling around an injury increases if the area continues to be moved or used. It is maximal during the first 48 hours and imperative that an athlete rests the affected area.

Ice

Cooling an injured tissue contracts blood vessels so that less bleeding and swelling occurs and the healing process starts earlier. It also provides local pain relief. Several methods can be used for cooling an injured area. These methods include crushed ice in a plastic bag or wrapped in a damp towel or cloth, reuseable gel ice packs, or immersion in an ice-water filled bucket. Cold water or cold sprays may be used if ice is not available, but they do not penetrate as effectively to deeper tissues. The amount of time to apply ice depends on the size and depth of the injury. Applying it for 15 minutes every 60 to 90 minutes is usually appropriate in the first three to six hours. The icing frequency reduces to three or four applications daily for the next two days.

Compression

A compression bandage provides counter pressure to the bleeding around an injury. Compression reduces swelling, and therefore pain, and allows a more effective start for the healing process. Apply an elastic-type bandage firmly, but not too tightly, as it will cut the blood supply beyond the injury and cause pain. The bandage can be applied both while icing and, more importantly, between ice applications. The bandage should extend a couple of centimeters (about an inch) beyond the upper and lower limits of the injured area.

Elevation

Elevating an injured limb reduces the blood flow to the injury and encourages fluid that has leaked out into the tissues back into the blood or lymphatic systems and away from the injury. Use a sling to elevate an arm and cushions or pillows for lower limbs. Elevation should occur throughout the day and at night, if possible. Elevate the injured part so that it rests above the level of the heart. As with all other aspects of the RICE program, elevation should continue for at least 48 hours after the injury.

Priced

The emphasis for the coach is injury prevention. Prevention is the combination of diagnosis and programming. You can use this particular emergency action plan, coined "PRICED," as you coach. However, when injuries cannot be prevented, they must be properly taken care of.
- *Prevention*
- *Rest* (injured area should be immobilized)
- *Ice* (ice or cold should be applied to control swelling and bleeding)
- *Compression* (usually done by wrapping with elastic bandage)
- *Elevation* (placing the injured part, when possible, slightly above the heart)
- *Diagnosis* (the injury should be assessed by a doctor or physiotherapist as soon as possible)

The Healing Process

The time taken for an injury to heal depends on the tissue(s) injured and the severity of the injury. As a general guide, the healing for various tissues is:
- Muscle: 6 weeks,
- Tendons and ligaments:12 weeks
- Bones and joints: 6 to 12 weeks

This timeline is only a basic guide for coaches to understand what to expect. Some injuries may take much longer to regain enough strength to return to practice. A doctor and sports-medicine professional should make all decisions concerning a thrower's return to activity. Healing of an injury follows a uniform pattern. It can be divided into three phases.

Acute Phase: The First 72 Hours

Bleeding and swelling make the area red, hot, and painful. Various cells, including white blood cells and scavenger cells, are attracted to the region to begin the process of cleaning up debris. These cells also release chemicals that encourage fibroblasts to multiply. Fibroblasts are the cells that produce the proteins of repair, especially collagen.

Proliferation (Repair) Phase: Three Days to Six Weeks

Many new blood vessels and fibroblasts grow into the damaged area, and a matrix of scar tissue is formed. New protein fibers are laid down in a haphazard manner, especially if the injured part is immobilized. Once laid down, the scar tissue begins to contract.

Remodelling/Maturing Phase: Six Weeks to Several Months

The protein fibres of the scar orient themselves in the direction in which pressure is applied, especially in ligaments. The protein matures, and the number of cells in the tissue decreases. It may take several months for the scar to fully mature and achieve its full strength.

Rehabilitation

During the acute phase, athletes are forced to temporarily discontinue training but want to return to action as soon as possible. Avoiding certain activities will accelerate the healing process. Heat causes blood vessels to dilate (open up), increasing the blood flow to an injured part and increasing bleeding, swelling, and pain. Do not apply heat to an injury for at least 48 hours. Drinking alcohol when injured also causes blood vessels to dilate and therefore has a similar effect to heat. In addition, alcohol decreases pain and falsely increases a person's confidence, thereby increasing the risk of further injury. Massage also increases blood flow to an area and prevents damaged blood vessels from healing adequately. Again, massage should be avoided in the first 48 hours. Pain relief can usually be achieved with the RICE regime. The use of other pain relievers can mask the signs of injury and should be avoided until appropriate diagnosis is obtained. If pain is very severe, diagnosis should be sought as soon as possible. It is important when modifying the training program to look at some of the underlying causes of the injury. Remediation may include correcting muscle and flexibility imbalances and attention to appropriate footwear.

If you follow the advice of a medical professional and the general principles of PRICED, the rehabilitation acronym previously discussed, then most throws injuries can, if treated conservatively, be rehabilitated to their former state. However, it does take time, and the coach can help play an active role by monitoring and following up to make sure the athlete completes all treatments and rehab. With active rest and a well-designed rehabilitation program, most athletes will often recover and return to competition. One word of caution: it is not useful to keep trying to test the injured area's fitness as it will almost certainly result in a further breakdown.

Preventing Injuries in the Throws

The old saying that "an ounce of prevention is worth a pound of cure" is particularly relevant. Athletes and their coaches can help reduce the incidence of injury if they follow the listed factors. Functional warm-up and cool-down procedures are vital. An athlete and coach must be aware of areas predisposed to injury and warm them up properly. For example, a shot-putter with a stiff wrist may take extra "snap-downs" or warm-up strikes to make sure the wrist will be in working condition. Other factors—like sufficient skill development, fitness status, obeying rules and regulations, sound nutrition, safe training and competition environments, proper clothing and equipment, an accurate appraisal of the level of fatigue, and appropriate training loads and recovery—can make the difference between success and being sidelined. Changing equipment is common knowledge (if something is broken, fix it), but if an athlete appears to be tired or overtrained, don't be afraid to make these types of changes:

- Modify training loads.
- Reduce structural stress through SDWR (suspended deep-water running) or move activities to a soft surface like grass.
- Reinforce a problem through first-aid activities like taping and wrapping.
- Make sure the athlete has the proper footwear.
- Suspend training and take a recovery day.

Figure 7-3. Recovery activities have to be programmed just like the training stimulus. A daily 10-minute cold plunge following training will help speed up the recovery process and help prepare the athlete for the next day's activities.

Nutrition and Ergogenic Aids

Chapter 8

© Michael Steele/Getty Images

Controlling the diet is the final part of complete track and field conditioning for the throws. Eating is one of the most elementary human activities and, at the same time, one of the most complex. Recent studies have shown that the diet of an athlete is a very important factor in his performance in training and competition. The diet of the throws athlete has two purposes: first, to cover caloric and nutrient needs, and second, to maintain fluid balance in the body. Situations and conditions specific to sport training and sport participation often make meeting these objectives difficult. Busy schedules that accompany the rigors of being a student-athlete often make suitable nutrition a challenge. Proper nutrition consists of the ingestion of all kinds of foods, minerals, and vitamins, plus water in the proportions that the body needs to function correctly. Eating for performance means eating food from all of the food groups and maintaining the caloric level needed for the body to do the work an elite athlete wishes or needs to do. The basic forms of food are carbohydrates, protein, and fat. Traditionally, the basic food groups include meats, dairy products, fruits, vegetables, and grains. The competitive athlete is looking for the proper dietary mix that will not only provide the proper nutrition necessary but the added edge that may mean that extra inch or even a centimeter improvement in a throw or an increased level of mental alertness that may make the difference for concentration during a practice session.

A Sound Nutritional Plan: One of the Keys to Superior Performance

The present level of elite sport performance requires intense research on the part of the athlete and the coach to find the correct recipe for improvement in

Figure 8-1. Recent studies have shown that the diet of an athlete is a very important factor in his performance in training and competition.

sport training. Throughout the history of sport, numerous attempts at altering an athlete's diet in a variety of ways have been made to improve performance in all events in sport. These attempts have ranged from fasting for a number of days to changing carbohydrate intake through loading techniques to changing protein intake through amino-acid supplementation. All of these principles can be applied to athletes in the throwing events. Most of the studies for sport nutrition have been conducted on subjects participating in aerobic activities of long duration. Since throwing is an anaerobic activity and requires sudden bursts of effort separated by periods of relative rest, the widely published and often repeated guidelines may not be the best recommendations for athletes participating and training for the throws.

An athlete's physical preparation and overall physical health can be aided by following some basic nutritional guidelines as a part of the daily routine. If judiciously chosen, a proper diet can bring about improvements in mobility, strength, and power, and also lead to a healthy, more productive lifestyle. Choosing a well-balanced diet can be beneficial physiologically and psychologically. The athlete who maintains the proper diet concentrates better, operates more efficiently, and sustains longer than the athlete who does not change his diet. What type of dietary habits do your athletes have? The question can be answered with some tests. Nutritional status assessments conducted can include: three-day dietary recalls, recalls of dietary intake during training and/or competition, clinical body-composition measurements, and biochemical analyses of blood samples. These types of measures are a great starting point, and should be part of the pre-season testing program. This chapter will focus in on some simple dietary ideas to help the competitive thrower.

Energy Requirements

Energy requirements for a thrower will depend on body mass, period of training, training environment, age, and non-training activity level, with body size being the primary determinant. You will find a wide range of energy intakes when comparing athletes participating in the same activity because the intake depends on body weight. Bear in mind, the nutritional requirements for a thrower are going to be much different than the RDA. The thrower's diet should contain a relative balance of carbohydrate, fat, and protein. Although all foods can ultimately be broken down to carbohydrate, fat, or protein, these nutrients are not all that the body needs. Of the total calories consumed, the generally recommended balance for most athletes is:

- Carbohydrate: 40 to 50 percent
- Fat: no more than 30 percent (less than 10 percent saturated)
- Protein: 20 to 30 percent

Strength-power athletes have higher protein requirements than athletes in more aerobically based sports. Consult organizations like the American College of Sports Medicine (ACSM) and the National Strength and Conditioning Association (NSCA) for their dietary recommendations for strength-power athletes. Read all of the available books and research on the subject, and stay away from fad diets. In recent years, a suggested nutritional balance that is very popular and has been effective with athletes in more anaerobic activities is the "Zone" or 40-30-30 diet. In the Zone diet formulated by Barry Sears, carbohydrates would comprise 40 percent of the diet with fats and protein making up the rest. Keep in mind that there are a variety of protocols for the fat, protein, carbohydrate balance. Finding the right balance is very athlete specific and dependent on each thrower's body chemistry and other genetic factors. Table 8-1 lists a basic guideline for choosing daily servings.

Meats, poultry, fish, eggs, nuts, beans	3-4 servings
Dairy products (milk, yogurt, cheese)	2-3 servings
Fruits and vegetables	5-9 servings
Grains (bread, cereal, rice, pasta)	5-10 servings
Water	8-10 glasses

Table 8-1. Basic daily servings guideline

Common questions for many athletes include: What are the caloric requirements of a thrower? Coach, how many calories should I be eating? A practical rule to determine the requirements is to start by checking the body weight of the athlete. Be cautioned: body weight is sometimes a sensitive issue with female athletes. It is sometimes better to have a dietician, trainer, or strength coach conduct the measurement to avoid making the athlete uncomfortable. If the body weight is stable, the athlete's energy intake is equal to the energy output. It is desirable to have the athlete record everything consumed for three consecutive days in a dietary recall. The results of this record should give an estimate of energy requirements in the presence of a stable body weight. A simple rule to determine energy needs (i.e., caloric requirements) is to multiply the athlete's body weight in pounds by the number shown in Table 8-2 for the athlete's gender and dietary goal.

The numbers provided in Table 8-2 are only a guideline and can be adjusted based on the athlete's energy output, metabolism, chronological age, and nutritional goals. The caloric requirements are going to be affected by the athlete's activity level. If an athlete is training very hard, he may have to use the caloric intake listed in the third row of Table 8-2 just to maintain weight. The metabolism will vary from athlete to athlete, so adjustments will have to be made to this general guideline.

Goal	Multiply the athlete's body weight in pounds by:	
	Male	Female
Maintain or lose mass (body fat)	10	8
Maintain or gain mass (lean muscle)	12-14	10-12
Gain significant body mass (lean muscle)	18-20	13-15

Table 8-2. Estimating caloric requirements

Understanding the Basics of Important Macronutrients and Hydration

Carbohydrates

Recent diet trends call for low carbohydrates, but it is important to not deny the use of this macronutrient. Carbohydrates play a critical role in all types of exercise, even elite throws training. During exercise, the body draws on carbohydrate storage for energy. This storage, however, is limited in the form of muscle glycogen (300 to 400 g, or 10 to 14 oz), liver glycogen (75 to 100 g, or 2.6 to 3.5 oz), and blood glucose (25 g, or 0.88 oz). Maintaining carbohydrate stores at optimal levels for exercise means specific attention to sustaining sufficient carbohydrate in the diet. Timing carbohydrate intake with exercise can work to an athlete's advantage. A designated amount of carbohydrates planned before training can "top off" carbohydrate stores. Carbohydrates planned during exercise may aid in maintaining blood glucose levels and carbohydrate oxidation. Carbohydrates immediately after exercise replenish used glycogen. Carbohydrates with respect to elite throws training will be discussed in further detail in the recommendation section (Coleman, 2006).

The Glycemic Index

The glycemic index is the rate at which a carbohydrate breaks down to be released as glucose into the bloodstream. Glucose itself is set as the standard and rated at 100 on the glycemic index. All other carbohydrates are rated in relationship to glucose. The glycemic rating does not entirely depend on whether a food is a simple or complex carbohydrate. Factors that affect the glycemic rating include: quantity of fiber, quantity of specific sugars, and the form in which the food is eaten (cooked versus raw). This system shows the difference between foods that offer a consistent level of endurance and those that cause a fast burnout. Foods with a high glycemic index are foods that release glucose into the bloodstream quickly. One way to slow down this quick glucose release is to eat a high-glycemic-index carbohydrate with a more slowly digested food, which has a leveling action on the glucose release. A food like chicken, which is high in protein, spurs the production of glucagon, which helps the athlete mobilize stored body fat. Carbohydrates are a prime source of energy, as well as fiber, vitamins, and minerals. Variety, moderation, and balance are the key nutritional watchwords. Thus, the glycemic index helps the individual choose appropriate carbohydrates to support consistent blood-sugar levels.

Protein

Contrary to popular belief, protein is not the most important energy source in exercise. Protein does, however, play very important physiological roles (Gibala, 2006). Twenty important amino acids are critical in physiological processes such as "protein synthesis and breakdown, intermediary metabolism, membrane transport, acid-base regulation, and immune function" (Rennie, 1996

p. 996). When considering protein's role in exercise, coaches and athletes must take a different vantage point than with carbohydrates. The question is not how does protein intake affect exercise, the question is how does exercise affect whole-body and skeletal-muscle-protein turnover (Gibala, 2006)? Answering this question effectively is especially important to throwers wanting to gain lean muscle mass and keep lean muscle mass throughout the breakdown of exercise.

Even in sedentary individuals, the body experiences a continuous amino-acid turnover. Almost all protein is recycled, but small portions are utilized for energy or are lost. Whether a certain type of exercise forces a larger amount of protein utilization or loss is still debatable (Gibala, 2006). The American College of Sports Medicine, American Dietetic Association, and Dieticians of Canada released a position statement supporting the idea that exercise may cause a greater need for protein intake in athletes (ACSM, 2000). The other side of the debate maintains that athletes become more efficient with protein utilization and, therefore, do not necessarily need more protein in the diet (Gibala, 2006).

Fat

Lipids have a variety of functions in the body that either directly or indirectly relates to exercise. Fats provide energy for daily activities including rest, protect organs, and maintain body temperature. Not all fats are helpful to the body; excessive consumption of saturated fats and cholesterol can increase the risk of cardiovascular disease and other chronic diseases. Looking at the different kinds of lipids helps decipher these roles more specifically (Johnalagadda, 2006).

Lipids can be broken down into two categories: open-chained and closed-ring lipids. Open-chained lipids include fatty acids and other types, but fatty acids are especially important; they provide the most energy in dietary fat. Fatty acids are classified into three categories: saturated fats, monounsaturated fats, and polyunsaturated fats. Polyunsaturated fats include two very important essential fatty acids: linoleic and linolenic acid. These two essential fatty acids help synthesize eicosanoids, entities related to blood pressure maintenance, blood-flow regulation, blood clotting, inflammation, and bronchiole airflow. Obviously, these functions relate to exercise considerably. Closed-ring lipids include steroids, important to the synthesis of steroid hormones, bile acids, and Vitamin D (Johnalagadda, 2006).

In direct relation, like carbohydrates, fats can be oxidized to supply energy to the exercising muscle. Whether the body utilizes carbohydrates or fats depends on the intensity of exercise. At around 70 to 80 percent $\dot{V}O_{2max}$, the body shifts from fat use to carbohydrate use. Fatty-acid use yields more energy, but it requires more oxygen, leaving carbohydrates as the main energy source in exercise (Johnalagadda, 2006).

Hydration

The body relies on fluid homeostasis for all processes, not just those processes involved in exercise. But for athletes, fluid maintenance is a critical issue for performance; even a slight amount of dehydration, greater than 1 percent of bodyweight loss, can affect the athlete in numerous ways—even performance decrement, depending on the exercise and the athlete. Athletes can circumvent fluid and hydration problems by pre-hydrating, drinking during exercise, and replacing what is lost in sweat and urine throughout exercise and the day. How an athlete must attack a fluid-and-hydration plan depends sweat loss, practice duration, type of exercise, practices per day, and environmental conditions. Water is not the only consideration: athletes, trainers, and coaches must assess individual electrolyte needs as well (Murray, 2006).

Recommendations

Carbohydrates

How many carbohydrates do collegiate throwers actually need? Research shows that collegiate athletes in general may not be getting the carbohydrate necessary to sustain daily training (Van Erp-Baart, 1989). The importance of adequate carbohydrate intake is significant: strength-training exercise significantly decreases muscle glycogen (Roy, 1998) and a low-carbohydrate, high-protein diet may contribute to reduced muscular endurance (Walberg, 1989).

Carbohydrate intake to compensate daily training deficits ranges from 5 to 7 grams per kilogram bodyweight a day (Burke, 2001). The official practice manual for the American Dietetics Association recommends 5 to 8 g/kg/day for field athletes in track and field, jumpers, and throwers (Dunford, 2006). Five grams per kg of body weight per day is adequate to support training of throwers or athletes involved in intermittent, power, or sprint activities. The ideal ultimately depends on the athlete's needs. The carbohydrate requirements may be lower for some female athletes depending on their metabolism and sensitivity to carbohydrates. Some female athletes may be better served at 3 to 4 grams of carbohydrates per kg of body weight if they are concerned with improving their body composition and ultimately their fitness levels, including power.

Since throws training requires repeated practices, some back to back, replenishing depleted muscle glycogen stores with a carbohydrate solution or sports drink post-exercise is important for recovery (Roy, 1998). For athletes engaged in exercise longer than 90 minutes and especially when athletes are practicing in heat extremes, the athlete should drink 1.5 g/kg of bodyweight in carbohydrates post-exercise (Coleman, 2006).

Protein

The body is able to recycle protein and amino acids; however, some important amino acids are irreversible lost (Phillips, 2004). The traditional line of thinking in elite throws training is a mistake; extreme high diets in protein are not effective and, in fact, are detrimental. The body utilizes a certain amount of protein, and the rest is excess; unfortunately, this excess is stored as fat. Whether or not exercise—specifically, strength training—requires more protein intake than the normal recommended intake is a topic still up for debate.

On one hand, research has shown that a training effect of strength training increases the efficiency of protein use, suggesting reduced protein requirements (Phillips, 2004). Higher protein intakes have not been consistently effective for strength-training athletes. On top of that, higher protein diets may even be associated with some health risks (Lemon, 1991).

On the other hand, an increased requirement for protein in strength-trained athletes might arise to support muscle-protein growth through elevated protein synthesis caused by intense strength training. The increased loss of amino acids associated with strength-training activities might also require strength athletes to consume more protein in the diet (Phillips, 2004). But if more protein is needed, how much more is needed for strength athletes as opposed to the general population?

A hypoenergy diet, providing twice the Recommended Dietary Allowance (0.8 g/kg/day) for protein for the average population, was more effective in retaining body protein in weight lifters than a diet with higher carbohydrate and only the minimum RDA for protein (Walberg, 1988). In a study comparing the effectiveness of low-protein diets, moderate-protein diets, and high-protein diets for sedentary and strength-trained athletes, the moderate protein diet was most suitable for strength athletes. The low-protein diets (0.86 g/kg/day) were adequate for sedentary, but not for strength athletes. Medium-protein diets (1.4 g/kg/day) created a state of adaptation for strength athletes, but overload for sedentary individuals. High-protein diets (2.4 g/kg/day) were an overload for both groups (Tarnopolsky, 1992). A review of studies that have examined the protein requirements of strength-trained athletes, using nitrogen balance methodology, has shown a modest increase in requirements in this group (Phillips, 2004).

At present, no evidence is available to suggest that supplements are required for optimal muscle growth or strength gain (Phillips, 2004). Strength athletes should consume approximately 12 to 15 percent of their daily total energy/calorie intake as protein, 188 to 250 percent of the U.S. recommended dietary allowance (Lemon, 1991; Phillips, 2004). The throws athlete should consume from 1.2 g/kg/day to 1.7 g/kg/day, depending on the needs of the athlete (Dunford, 2006). A strength-power athlete may feel more comfortable ingesting as much as 2 grams of protein per kilogram of body weight, but it is not recommended to go any higher.

Post-resistance exercise consumption of a protein drink compared with a carbohydrate-electrolyte drink (without protein) caused similar adaptations to resistance training, but the milk drink tended to increase body weight and fat-free soft tissue compared to a pure carbohydrate solution over a 10-week period (Rankin, 2004). An easy suggestion for athletes is to include 20 grams of protein powder along with the Gatorade or carbohydrate drink post-workout. This drink should be consumed within 30 minutes of the completion of the workout.

Fat

Fat recommendations for throws training should be purely individual with appropriate attention to specific guidelines issued by credible organizations. In general, throwers will have a tendency toward high-fat and even worse, high-saturated-fat diets (Dunford, 2006). However, like in all sports, dieticians will encounter both ends of the spectrum; certain throwing athletes perhaps seeking a specific body composition may also fall victim to dangerous fat restriction. In general, throws athletes should fill the remainder of calories needed in the diet with fats after protein and carbohydrate intakes are considered (Dunford, 2006).

In response to athletes cutting fat, the American Dietetic Association has recommended an acceptable intake for athletes. An athlete should consume no less than 20 to 25 percent fat of the total calorie diet, what the ADA names a moderate-fat diet (ADA, 2000). Negative consequences and no performance benefits arise from lower fat diets (ADA, 2000).

More commonly, however, throws athletes will adopt high-fat diets (Dunford, 2006). Cardiovascular health is an issue when considering diets high in saturated fat; saturated fatty acids contribute to atherogenesis and coronary artery heart disease (Noseda, 2005). Responsible dieticians, coaches, trainers, and athletes should not just advise against high-saturated-fat diets, but should take a proactive approach to circumvent and reduce the issue.

Because heart health is of particular concern, many research studies have investigated how to replace saturated fats in the diet. Noseda proclaims that if the monounsaturated fat like in olive oil replaces saturated fats, and omega-3-fatty acids like those in fish oils are introduced into the diet, sudden cardiac death and myocardial infarctions will be reduced (Noseda, 2005). In another study, total cholesterol decreased by 4.7 percent and low-density lipoprotein cholesterol decreased 5.8 percent, replacing the typical American diet with the use of NuSun® sunflower oil to replace saturated fats.

Changing a diet high in saturated fat does not mean a strict one-way solution. A diet high in carbohydrate with dietary selections like fruits, vegetables, and low-fat dairy products with low fat (low in saturated fat and cholesterol as well) will significantly reduce blood pressure and low-density lipoprotein cholesterol. Replacing a portion of the carbohydrate intake instead with protein from both plant and animal sources or monounsaturated fats will have a positive effect on blood pressure and lipoprotein cholesterol (Miller, 2006). Your athletes have many ways to get on track with a heart healthy diet.

Hydration

Hypohydration, a body water and electrolyte deficit, can occur when the amount of sweat exceeds water intake. The problem complicates for throws athletes as they move outdoors in the spring season and conduct multiple practices in heat; the warmer the climate, the greater potential for performance decrement. Hypohydration may inhibit an athlete's ability to regulate cooler body temperatures and therefore making the athlete susceptible to heat strain (Sawka and Montain, 2000). Heavy sweating with heat exposure may result in 1 to 8 percent loss in bodyweight. The body relies on fluid homeostasis for all processes, not just those involved in exercise. But for athletes, fluid maintenance is a critical issue for performance; even a slight amount of dehydration, greater than 1 percent of body-weight loss, can affect the athlete in numerous ways, even performance decrement depending on the exercise and the athlete. Athletes can circumvent fluid and hydration problems by prehydrating, drinking during exercise, and replacing what is lost in sweat and urine throughout exercise and the day. How an athlete must attack a fluid and hydration plan is dependent on factors like sweat loss, practice duration, type of exercise, and practices per day and environmental conditions. Water is not the only consideration; athletes, trainers, and coaches must assess individual electrolyte needs as well. Greater than 1 percent loss can contribute to some kind of performance decrement (Murray, 2006). It is important to emphasize drinking during exercise as well as at meals (Sawka and Montain, 2000). At the end of a practice, the athlete should replace what is lost (Maughan, Leiper, and Shirreffs, 1997).

How important is electrolyte content in the replenishment drinks of elite throws training post-exercise to maintain fluid balance? Research support for inclusion of sodium and other electrolytes in recovery beverages certainly exists (Sharp, 2006; Maughan, Leiper, and Shirreffs, 1997). The inclusion of sodium chloride reduces urinary water loss, leading to a more rapid recovery from exercise and heat-induced sweat and urine losses (Sharp, 2006). This inclusion is important for throwers maintaining double practices in hot climates for outdoor track and field. Another researched opinion calls for the addition of potassium along with 50 to 60 mmol/L of sodium for effective rehydration. Ingesting a carbohydrate-electrolyte drink post-exercise is more effective than just plain water, and even ingesting large volumes of plain water will inhibit thirst and promote a diuretic response (Maughan, Leiper, and Shirreffs, 1997).

Fluid recommendations should be individual; fluid volume and the content of electrolytes should be tailored to each athlete. Because of varying sweat rates, electrolyte losses, and varying climates, one should assess individual sweat loss in a practice by measuring bodyweight before and after exercise. In general, prehydrating with beverages in addition to fluids at regular meals should begin several hours before a workout (American College of Sports Medicine, 2007). Drinking at scheduled breaks prevents excessive water loss (American College of Sports Medicine, 2007; Sawka and Montain, 2000). The volume of liquid ingested after a workout should exceed the water lost (American College of Sports Medicine, 2007; Maughan, Leiper, and Shirreffs, 1997; Sharp, 2006). How much fluid? A guideline is to ingest 150 percent of what is lost (Sharp, 2006).

In conclusion, the effects of dehydration and fluid imbalance have a strong effect on performance and health in the case of avoiding complications with heat strain. Athletes should maintain hydration using a system of rehydration that utilizes sufficient electrolytes (Maughan, Leiper, and Shirreffs, 1997).

Other Considerations

Vitamins and Minerals

Vitamins and minerals are involved in the complete regimen of metabolic processes in the body, and many of the reactions necessary in exercise. Vitamins play a role in carbohydrate, fat, and protein metabolism as well as oxygen transfer and delivery and even tissue repair. Do athletes need more vitamins and minerals, and if so, how much more? The answer depends on the type and length of exercise, and even the exercise environment will be a factor (Wardlaw, 1999).

Vitamins are categorized by their solubility. Water-soluble vitamins include B-6, B-12, folate, thiamin, riboflavin, niacin, pantothenic acid, biotin, vitamin C, and choline. Fat-soluble vitamins include A, D, E, and K. Minerals are separated into major or trace minerals. Major minerals include calcium, phosphorus, magnesium, sulfur, potassium, and chloride. Iron, zinc, copper, selenium, iodide, fluoride, chromium, manganese, molybdenum, boron, and vanadium fill the trace mineral category (Volpe, 2006).

Over the broad spectrum of vitamins and minerals, most athletes require the same amount as the general population (Volpe, 2006). Throws athletes, coaches, trainers, and dieticians should simply ensure that the throws athlete is receiving at least 70 percent of the Recommended Dietary Allowance (RDA), and no more than the tolerable upper limit (UL). Special cases and concerns for athletes do exist, however; following is a discussion of some important issues to consider for one of the most important minerals: calcium.

Calcium is categorized as a mineral and receives lots of attention in athletics, especially in female athletics. Athletes in training may experience a loss of menstrual cycles; this loss is accompanied by a loss in bone mass, to maintain serum calcium (Snow-Harter, 1994). Osteoporosis is a disease characterized by this low bone mass; the result is fragile bones and an increased fracture risk (American College of Sports Medicine, 1995). Training decrease combined with an increase in calcium intake (adding three glasses of skim milk per day) may help the condition. Throwers are at an advantage, however; resistance training, increased muscle strength, and body mass can improve the "skeletal profile" and protect against injury. Regardless, athletes should maintain record of their menstrual cycles (Snow-Harter, 1994).

Special conditions are not the only reason to increase dietary calcium. High-protein diets, typical of both male and female throws athletes, can increase urinary calcium (Kerstetter et al., 2006) and exercising for 90 minutes or more in the heat can also contribute to calcium loss (Bergeron, Volpe, and Gelinas, 2006).

Designing a Nutritional Plan

When designing a nutritional plan, it is always prudent to seek the advice of a medical professional or dietician. These trained professionals can help you construct a dietary regimen that fits the special needs of your athletes. Nearly all athletes are trying to either gain or lose weight. Frequently, male athletes are trying to gain weight and muscle because they just have not yet fully physically matured. They may have grown tall without yet filling out. Many of them have not yet acquired their full height by age 18, since many males often continue to grow until their early 20s.

There are really only two correct ways to gain weight: eat more than is burned as energy, or burn less as energy than is consumed. In other words, to gain weight, one must eat more or exercise less. Since it is highly unlikely that student-athletes will exercise less, the answer is to eat more. However, all weight gain is not equal. The desirable weight gain for student-athletes is in muscle, not in fat, so eating tremendous quantities of junk foods is not the answer. One way to achieve desirable weight gain is to eat more servings or increase the size of servings of foods outlined in Table 8-1. Another is to eat more meals a day: an athlete can eat five meals a day instead of the usual three or eat three meals with three snacks in between. It is also important to eat breakfast, a meal that many athletes tend to skip.

Losing weight presents another set of problems, but again only two methods will accomplish this goal: burn off more calories than are consumed, or consume fewer calories than are burned. In other words, eat less and/or exercise more. Most often, it is women who are trying to lose weight as freshmen. This may be because many women are physically mature and filled out at age 18, unlike many men. Female athletes also naturally tend to have a higher percentage of muscle while trying to lose their weight. This situation can be a problem because muscle weighs more than fat. Thus, a female student-athlete may reduce fat, increase muscle, and lose inches but gain pounds. Table 8-3 provides an example of the nutritional recommendations for weight loss for a typical female throws athlete who is 18 to 22 years old, 5'11", and 100 kg (220 pounds).

Carbohydrates	2.5 -5.0 grams per kg of body weight
Protein	1.7 -2.0 grams per kg of body weight
Fat	20-25% of total calorie intake with an emphasis on heart-healthy fats
Vitamins and Minerals	Recommended Dietary Allowances and no more than upper limits, taking into consideration special needs
Fluids and Hydration	Replace 150% of what is lost in body weight for each practice. In hot and humid conditions, assess the need for electrolyte balance.

Table 8-3. Nutritional recommendations for weight loss for a typical female throws athlete

Since most throwers exercise a great deal, more exercise is not usually the answer to healthy weight loss for them. What they need to do is to reduce their intake of calories. They can do this by decreasing the size or number of servings from the food groups, but they need to keep these in the proper proportions even if reduced. They also need to avoid high-fat and sugar extras like butter, creamy salad dressings, and desserts. They should not unconsciously clean their plates, eating food just because it is there; they should eat only until they are satisfied. Listed are some sample nutritional plans for the thrower.

Sample Nutritional Plan #1

This diet is a high-protein diet that aids in post-workout recovery. Most of the carbohydrates are consumed after training.

- 8 a.m. (breakfast): Six-egg-white omelet with 1 cup of vegetables and one piece of fat-free cheese, one half cup of oatmeal
- 10 a.m. (snack): Protein shake in water with added flaxseed oil or protein bar
- 12 p.m. (lunch): Three- to six-ounce chicken breast and large salad with fish oil capsules
- 2 p.m. (snack): Protein shake in water with added flaxseed oil
- 4 p.m.-6.p.m (practice): Protein bar and a glucose-electrolyte beverage such as Gatorade (mix with 50 percent water)
- 6 p.m. (post-workout): Recovery drink (e.g., liquid drink) containing 20 to 25 g (0.7 to 0.8 oz) fast-digesting protein such as whey and 40 to 50 g (1.4 to 1.8 oz) of simple carbohydrate such as Gatorade
- 8 p.m. (dinner): Six-ounce lean burger or chicken breast, large salad, medium-sized baked potato, fish-oil capsules
- 10 p.m. (snack before bed): Plain yogurt, two pieces of fresh fruit or a protein shake

Total Calories = 2,500 to 3,000 kcal

Sample Nutritional Plan #2

This diet will help an individual lose body fat and maintain lean muscle tissue.

Breakfast
1 cup of orange juice
4 egg whites
1/2 cup of oatmeal
1 slice of wheat toast, dry
1 glass of skim milk

Mid-Morning Snack
7 oz lean red meat
1 1/2 cups brown rice

Lunch
1 tuna fish sandwich
1 glass of skim milk
1 cup vegetables
1 cup of pasta

Mid-Afternoon Snack
1 Myoplex Plus® or meal replacement with water

Dinner
1 baked chicken breast
1 10-oz potato
1 cup of vegetables
1 salad with low-calorie dressing

Evening Snack
1 low-fat protein drink with water

Total Calories = 3,000 to 3,500 kcal

Sample Nutritional Plan #3

This diet will help an individual gain lean body mass.

Breakfast
1 cup of orange juice
1 cup of oatmeal
4 scrambled eggs
2 slices of toast
1 T jelly

Snack
2 peanut butter sandwiches
1 banana
1 cup of orange juice

Lunch
1 chicken sandwich
1 large bowl of pasta
1 large salad with dressing
1 bowl of yogurt
1 glass of milk

Snack
1 cup of fruit
1 large protein shake with milk

Dinner
1 bowl of chowder
2 chicken breasts or 8 ounces of lean red meat
1 baked potato
2 rolls
1 cup of vegetables
1 fruit drink

Snack
1 8 oz baked potato
Large protein shake with milk

Total Calories = 6,000 to 6,500 kcal

The Pre-Competition Meal

The main focus of a thrower's diet should be on meal planning. Planning meals throughout the day helps improve energy and aids in recovery. The pre-workout/competition and post-workout/competition meals are no doubt the two most important meals of the day and are often neglected in the planning process. The primary purpose of the pre-competition meal is to provide fluid and energy to the thrower during the competitions. Various recommendations on timing, amount, and types of food for pre-competition meals appear in magazines and sports nutrition publications. Many of the recommendations in these publications are not supported by scientific data and may not be appropriate for all athletes. A few basic guidelines are important to consider. In general, throwers should avoid eating fat in the pre-competition meal because fat slows gastric emptying. During competition, you do not want the digestive system to compete with the muscles for the available blood supply because it was still processing a high-fat meal. Eating a high-fat meal will make you feel very similar to eating a meal high in sugar and white flour. Energy levels will be compromised. Liquid meals can replace conventional foods, and while suitable in any situation, may be of particular value in situations of limited availability of food at a competitive venue. The rates at which food is digested and nutrients are absorbed into the body are quite individualized, so timing the pre-competition meal might depend on prior experience. Following are some basic guidelines. Foods such as healthy cereal (low in sugar), yogurt, juice, and toast are digested rather quickly and won't leave the athlete feeling full during competition. A chicken or turkey sandwich on whole-grain bread is another pre-competition alternative. Although the meal ingested a few hours before competition might contribute little to muscle glycogen stores, it can ensure a normal blood-glucose level and prevent hunger. This meal should contain only about 300 to 500 kcal and consist mostly of carbohydrate foods that are easily digested. This meal should be very individualized and should be fairly reflective of the day-to-day dietary habits of the individual. It is not a good time to make radical changes.

Post-Workout Nutrition

Most athletes don't realize that certain food choices before exercise can actually reduce their performance. Even more importantly, many athletes are unaware that post-workout nutrition can have a profound effect on recovery. The biggest mistake people are making is not doing anything at all about post-workout nutrition. Nutritionally, most people don't plan for success. The most comprehensive training plan will not succeed without a strategy for recovery. Research suggests ingesting a carbohydrate/protein drink immediately after training will increase the rate sugar is stored in the muscles. Many post-workout drinks are available on the market. A post-workout drink should be consumed within 30 minutes of training.

The protein/carbohydrate content of the post-workout recovery drink is critical. Most research studies are demonstrating that post-workout nutrition should contain protein and carbohydrates in a ratio of two parts carbohydrate to every one part of protein. Have your athletes consume a liquid recovery drink of 0.8 g/kg of carbs and 0.4 g/kg of protein immediately after training. It is a great way to begin the recovery process. After consuming the post-workout drink, it is advised to eat a well-balanced meal within an hour-and-a-half. Therefore, within an hour-and-a-half of lifting, running, or throwing, the athlete should eat carbohydrate-based foods that also have a balance of protein. The six hours after exercise are absolutely critical to recovery. Basically, the muscles are most efficient at carbohydrate- and energy-uptake during this time. Therefore, the bulk of an athlete's calories (especially carbohydrates) should come during this post-workout period. Since fat is burned at high rates during the post-exercise period, regardless of what food you eat, during this time most of the ingested energy (protein and carbohydrates) will go to replenish the depleted muscle energy stores and to enhance recovery. A good choice would be a well-balanced meal that includes fruit, fruit juice, pasta, or cereal. Remember, the post-workout carbohydrate and protein consumption can rapidly replenish muscle carbohydrate stores much more rapidly than trying to do so during the other meals of the day. The idea is for the thrower to be ready for more training by the next day.

Dietary Supplements and Ergogenic Aids

Dietary Supplements

The dietary-supplement industry is growing at a feverish pace in the United States. In 1996, consumers spent 2 billion dollars on supplements compared to 16.7 billion spent in 2001. A dietary supplement can be defined as a product intended to supplement the diet that bears or contains one or more of the following: vitamin, mineral, herb, botanical, amino acid, synthetic compound, or a concentrate, metabolite, constituent, extract, or combination of these. People take supplements for a variety of reasons, including aesthetics, to improve function (energy, performance), improve health status, and to prevent a negative condition or consequence. The Dietary Supplement and Health

Education Act (DSHEA) of 1994 caused a big increase in supplements on the market. This act allows supplement manufacturers more freedom in producing and marketing their products. This act requires no research on effectiveness of product or even its safety. Supplements are not subject to the same pre-market safety evaluations. Market monitoring required for foods and drugs and supplement company claims do not need to be proven. It makes the supplement industry an advertisement-driven force with the ability to impact society. Certain segments of the populations may be subject to undue influence from the media.

Dietary supplements are substances you eat or drink. The exploding supplement industry is a sign that individuals are experimenting. Coaches and trainers must stay knowledgeable as athletes use supplements. They can be vitamins, minerals, herbs or other plants, amino acids (the individual building blocks of protein), or parts of these substances. Vitamins are a group of unrelated organic compounds that perform specific functions to promote growth and maintain health. Minerals do a kind of a balancing act inside your body. They make sure that your blood and body fluids are balanced and healthy. And of course, minerals are what make up your bones. Throwers need vitamins in relatively small quantities, but without them they could not utilize the other nutrients the athletes ingest. Intakes above requirements have not been shown to improve performance in the absence of deficiency. The main thing to remember about vitamin/mineral supplements is that most people eating a properly balanced diet do not need them. Generally, vitamin and mineral supplements are not encouraged by dieticians, due to their low absorption and high cost. Real food is much cheaper and better absorbed than supplements. Unabsorbed nutrients from a supplement will be secreted in the urine; however, some nutrients, such as vitamin D, can be potentially dangerous. Many people believe that extra quantities of certain vitamins have beneficial qualities; for example, many people believe that large quantities of vitamin B will provide an extra energy boost or extra vitamin C helps protect from colds and similar viral infections. Similarly, some people, especially menstruating women, are somewhat prone to iron deficiencies, and so mineral supplements can be quite helpful to them. However, some beliefs held by athletes that taking certain supplements will provide an ergogenic effect appear to exist without documented support. In fact, many supplements (like amino acids, for example), which have not been FDA-regulated, can even be dangerous in the event of contamination.

The most popular supplement on the market today is creatine monohydrate. Creatine monohydrate is marketed as "nature's muscle builder," and it is the hottest sports supplement around. Creatine, or methylguanidine-acetic acid, is an amino acid that was first identified in 1835 by Chevreul. It is synthesized from arginine and glycine in the liver, pancreas, and kidneys and is also available in meats and fish. Creatine was first introduced as a potential ergogenic aid in 1993 as creatine monohydrate, and it is currently being used extensively by athletes throughout the United States and worldwide. Professional and amateur athletes alike are gobbling up this alleged ergogenic aid, hoping to increase their strength/power, speed, and performance. Creatine supplementation has claimed to increase muscle power by playing a role in the transfer of energy to help the muscle contract. Supplement labels state that "creatine is converted to phosphocreatine, which is important for short energy bursts such as throwing, sprinting, and weight lifting" and that "depletion of phosphocreatine can result in muscle fatigue and fading muscle power." Claims are also made that supplementation increases muscle body mass. Creatine supplements come in a wide variety of brand names and products and are available over the counter at health-food, drug and grocery stores and on the Internet.

Although people respond differently, taking creatine supplements may increase the amount of creatine in muscles. Muscles may be able to generate more energy or generate energy at a faster rate. Some people think taking creatine supplements along with training may improve performance for quick bursts of intense energy, such as sprinting, weight lifting, and of course throwing. The purported ergogenic benefits of creatine have been well-documented (Birch, 1994; Earnest, 1995; Kelley, 1999; Kuno, 1995). Several authors have suggested that the ergogenic mechanism of creatine is the ability to handle higher training volumes and intensities. Popular literature recommends the creatine as a way to increase muscle mass and strength. To date, very little data is available on creatine use in adolescents.

People who take creatine supplements may gain weight caused by muscles holding water. Other side effects of long-term use include muscle cramps, dehydration, diarrhea, and nausea. The research is still unclear on long-term side effects. Hydration is very important when using the product. Medical researchers are studying the safety and effectiveness of creatine supplements. They also are studying if creatine supplements may help to treat diseases that cause muscles to shrink and fail, such as heart failure/disease, muscular/neuromuscular diseases, and stroke.

Nutritional supplements are here to stay in this era of functional foods. I do not recommend or advocate the use of any ergogenic aids or nutritional supplements such as creatine. The media has a huge impact on the attitude and perceptions of society. The basic rule of thumb for the throws coach and the thrower is to be aware of what dietary supplements do and don't do. Careful attention to the diet will provide all the vitamins and minerals necessary. If the athlete is not eating a well-balanced diet, a multi-vitamin pack is a good insurance policy. Protein, weight gain, and meal-replacement drinks, bars, and powders should only be used as a supplement to a good diet. Lean meats and other natural sources of protein are much better for you. The manufactured products can help increase the daily caloric/protein intake, but they should not be used exclusively. They are helpful alternatives for the athlete with a busy schedule. Products like creatine, glutamine, and HMB have gained popularity in recent years, but the research is unclear on the effectiveness or the long-term side effects of these products.

Caffeine

Caffeine is a naturally occurring compound or alkaloid present in many foods and beverages such as coffee, tea, cola, and chocolate that people consume every day. Caffeine, the most widely used drug in Western society, is believed to have been used as a stimulant since the Stone Age. The United States Food and Drug Administration recommends that beverages contain less than 65 milligrams of caffeine per 12 ounces of liquid. Yet, because caffeine has the FDA's GRAS ("generally regarded as safe") status, the agency does not provide a daily recommended allowance. The FDA also does not make any special recommendations for kids, though some studies show that kids react differently to caffeine than adults. Soft drinks, such as Coke and Pepsi, both of which contain about 40 milligrams of caffeine per serving, fall within FDA guidelines. A 12-ounce cup of brewed coffee, however, has about 200 milligrams.

High-energy caffeine drinks are the newest craze sweeping across the national and international sports horizon. Promoted by extreme-sport athletes and pro wrestlers, energy drinks, containing high amounts of caffeine, have exploded on to the scene in recent years. Today, the $3.5 billion energy-beverage market is 6 percent of the nonalcoholic beverage industry, which includes soft drinks. That figure is up 75 percent since 2004 and is expected to top $10 billion by 2010, thanks to a vivacious consumer demand and profit margins that are three times that of soda. Although sales of energy drinks in the United States were $3.5 billion in 2005, according to Beverage Digest, the category was only recently created with the launch of the Red Bull® brand energy drink. Red Bull was created by Dietrich Mateschitz, an Austrian who adapted the energy drink from a Thai beverage called Krating Daeng™, a popular drink with rickshaw drivers in Thailand. Red Bull is a very popular drink worldwide.

Other than water, most of the products marketed as energy drinks contain carbohydrate, taurine, and caffeine as their principal ingredients—the carbohydrate to provide nutrient energy and the caffeine to stimulate the central nervous system, but they may also contain a wide variety of other ingredients. John Sicher, editor and publisher of Beverage Digest, attributes the drinks' tremendous growth to "consumers' growing interest in what is termed functional foods." Red Bull contains nearly 80 mg of caffeine per can, about the same amount of caffeine as a cup of brewed coffee and twice the caffeine as a cup of tea. Other energy drinks contain several times this amount. The amount of

Figure 8-2. Red Bull® contains nearly 80 mg of caffeine per can, about the same amount of caffeine as a cup of brewed coffee and twice the caffeine as a cup of tea.

caffeine in an energy drink isn't always indicated on the label, so it is difficult to gauge how much is being consumed. One of the biggest concerns is that we just don't know enough about the effect of the combination of ingredients in energy drinks. Many ingredients are believed to work synergistically with caffeine to boost its stimulant power. With the emergence of Red Bull and the term "energy drinks" in recent years, caffeine is now considered a dietary supplement and ergogenic aid and not just a food additive.

Caffeine is legally classified as a drug and has some powerful physiological side effects on the body. Is it okay for an athlete? Caffeine's popularity is due in part to its effects on the central nervous system. One of the things that caffeine does is stimulate organs in your body called the adrenals to release hormones, which cause the sudden release of sugar (glucose) from its stores in the liver. Caffeine increases psychomotor coordination, which results in decreased motor-reaction time and increased vigilance. This reaction to caffeine is similar to the "flight or fight" response when an individual is in danger or feels threatened. The body does not care whether the sudden rise of blood sugar comes from a candy bar or from the liver; it responds to that sudden rise in the same way and the same symptoms can be produced.

Caffeine is a central-nervous-system stimulant that will increase alertness and stimulate heart function, blood circulation, and the release of epinephrine from the adrenal gland. Caffeine has also been found to enhance skeletal-muscle contractility by many researchers. Weight event athletes often use caffeine to "get up" for a competition. A protocol of 200 mg of caffeine 45 minutes before competition may provide an ergogenic effect. A recent study was done that concluded a 300 mg ingestion of caffeine reported the fastest reaction times; the group that ingested twice that amount acted no faster than the group receiving no caffeine. Thus, although some caffeine may aid performance, too much may be ineffective.

Research differs on the amount of time caffeine takes to reach its highest levels in the blood, but the average is somewhere between 15 and 45 minutes after ingestion. The half-life, or the time it takes the body to eliminate half of the mount consumed is about five hours in most adults. However, one must keep in mind that although caffeine can have performance-enhancing effects, like all drugs, it has potentially dangerous side effects. In high dosages it may cause extreme nervousness and can act as a diuretic. Hypersensitivity to caffeine may also be of concern to athletes who rarely consume it and then use it prior to competition. People who regularly consume caffeine develop a tolerance to it, hence the severity of the effects of caffeine are, in part, dose-dependent and also is a function of a person's tolerance to the drug. Some of the side effects for the individual who rarely uses caffeine are unpleasant feelings, jitters, and nervousness. This individual may also experience insomnia. In extreme cases of hypersensitivity or with the ingestion of extremely high dosages; the rhythm of the heart can be upset and become irregular.

Caffeine is legal for use outside of competition, but caffeine appears on the banned substance list for competition. Note that caffeine at high concentration levels is banned by the NCAA and other national and international sport-governing bodies. It is unlikely for an athlete to reach prohibited levels through caffeine-containing sports drinks, but other beverages, dietary supplements, and medications contain caffeine and additional stimulants. The mixture of these products and caffeinated sports drinks could cause problematic caffeine levels. A positive test is a possibility if it is used in very high quantities prior to competition.

Conclusion

Individuals who compete athletically are always looking for a means to improve performance. Nutrition may be an important factor in improving both health and physical performance. The science of human nutrition has made a significant contribution to our knowledge of essential nutrients needed during heavy training. As a nutrition coach, you must monitor the diet and make sure your athletes are getting the proper nutrition needed to recover from heavy training. Physically active individuals are major targets for those who market and sell nutritional supplements. Magazines for active people are filled with advertisements extolling the virtues of various supplements. Throws coaches and nutrition professionals must dispel the myths and misconceptions associated with sports nutrition.

When designing a nutritional plan, it is always prudent to seek the advice of a medical professional or dietician. These trained professionals can help you construct a dietary regime that fits the special needs of your athletes. An athlete's physical preparation and overall physical health can be aided by following some basic nutritional guidelines as a part of the daily routine. If judiciously chosen, a proper diet can bring about improvements in mobility, strength, power, and also lead to a healthy, more productive lifestyle. Choosing a well-balanced diet can be beneficial physiologically and psychologically. When considering all the macronutrient, fluid, vitamin and mineral recommendations, it is important to keep an eye on the big picture: total calorie intake. If an athlete experiences a lack of energy, it may be due to too few calories. Counting calories, carbohydrates, and other elements of food may seem like a daunting task in the first few weeks, but once habit is formed, the athlete's understanding of the proper diet becomes automatic. It is also an understanding that lasts a lifetime; ensuring athletes understand how food can impact their lives is critical to a healthy adulthood.

Putting a Training Program Together

© Tim DeFrisco/Getty Images

Chapter 9

Ready to get started? Still not sure what to do? This section will present a simplified nine-step approach to putting a training plan together. While going through this section, please refer to the tables in the appendix for examples and further clarification. These steps do not encompass all the information needed to be an international-level coach and develop an Olympic champion; it is just a starting point. However, all coaches can take the general principles of periodization and identify the specific considerations needed to design an annual training plan. Again, periodization is the structuring of a training process, according to the laws of adaptation, with the aim of developing athletic form. The two types of periodization models are single and double (Tables 9-1 and 9-2). Discus and javelin throwers would use a single periodization model. Because of the indoor season, shot-putters and hammer/weight throwers might use the double periodization model.

This chapter is a simplified outline of how to design and implement a training schedule. Start here and use the outlined steps to develop your own training plan. Refer to the sample workouts and training inventory in the appendix as a guideline. Keep detailed training logs and records. Over time, you

Macro	PP	1st meso	6 weeks	General athletic training
		2nd meso	6 weeks	Maximal strength training or strength endurance
		3rd meso	6 weeks	
		4th meso	6 weeks	Special strength endurance
		5th meso	6 weeks	Special throwing training
		6th meso	6 weeks	
	PCP	7th meso	6 weeks	Competition series
		1st-7th Mesos	42 weeks	Adapted from Bompa (1994)

Table 9-1. Single periodization model

Macrocycle		Mesocycle	Length	Training Contents
1st macro	PP1	1st meso	6 weeks	General athletic training
		2nd meso	6 weeks	
		3rd meso	6 weeks	Strength preparation and special training
	CP1	4th meso	4 weeks	Competition
		1st-4th mesos	22 weeks	
2nd macro	PP2	5th meso	6 weeks	General training, strength preparation, special training
		6th meso	6 weeks	
	CP2	7th meso	5-7 weeks	Competition
		5th-7th mesos	17-19 weeks	
1st and 2nd macros		1st-7th mesos	39-41 weeks	Adapted from Bompa (1994)

Table 9-2. Double periodization model

will develop your own training/coaching theories supported not just by books, but by experience as well. Continue to study and learn. The more aware a coach becomes of scientific principles, the more effective a coach can be at adjusting a training program at crucial times. Years of experience, however, are just as crucial as well-rounded, detailed book knowledge. Coaches do not have to know and understand every last scientific principle to be effective as beginning coaches and to eventually become great coaches. Enthusiasm and work ethic can help balance lack of experience.

Important Time Frames

Coaches and strength trainers categorize training plans in time frames. Important competitions designate the training schedule for a particular time of year. At the collegiate level, fancy words describe important chunks of training time: the macrocycle, the mesocycle, and the microcycle. Think of them as just an annual, monthly, and weekly time frame. The annual plan is divided into the following time periods (listed from longest to shortest):

- Preparation period (general preparation phase and specific preparation phase)
- Competition period (pre-competitive phase, competitive phase, and peaking phase)
- Transition period (the length of time between the last competition and the next practice)

Important Training Terminology

Macrocycle: Annual plan
Phase: A season
Mesocycle: Monthly plan
Microcycle: Weekly plan
Training session: Daily or hourly plan
Training unit: One aspect of a training session

The Yearly Plan

The macrocycle, or the yearly plan, is a useful tool to layout different training-element emphasis at different times of the year. The macrocycle allows the coach to layout the year on a timeline to plan the appropriate training activities for the upcoming season. Questions like when it is appropriate for an athlete to condition and improve fitness, emphasize strength, improve speed, either gain or lose weight and when it is necessary for an athlete to rest for a tapering effect can be addressed by simply planning. In track and field, the preparation period is clearly longer than the competition or transition period. Overall, the yearly plan begins with high-volume, low-intensity general training exercises and progresses to specific high-intensity, low-volume training exercises. For example, during the general preparation phase, the workout may consist of throwing drills, medicine-ball/general-strength circuits, ground-level plyometrics, long sprints (5 x 80 m), high-repetition (sets of 10) resistance training, and extensive flexibility routines. In the weeks before a championship meet, the technical training and speed/strength development are the main emphasis, and a majority of the general conditioning may be cut to a bare minimum (once per week) and may be included in the warm-up. In the transition phase, the two weeks immediately following the last meet of the season may involve active rest and recreational sports like volleyball, soccer, basketball, and/or swimming. The remainder of the transition period may involve lifting, conditioning, and sprints, with a limited emphasis on the throw (two times per week). The yearly plan determines the chain link of monthly training plans in which different training variables are emphasized. The training year can be split up into the following:

- Preparation period (PP)
- Competition period (CP)
- Transition period (TP)

The Monthly Plan

Notable adaptations require at least six weeks of training. This time interval is called a mesocycle. The mesocycle, or monthly plan, is a one- to two-month (four- to six-week) period of training time. It is well known that 15 to 18 training weeks (i.e., the period of three mesocycles) are necessary to develop athletic form. In my training plan, I use this increment of time to observe an athlete's progress with the training variable that corresponds to the annual plan. I tend to use shorter mesocycles (three weeks) with my elite athletes. The more advanced the training age of an athlete, the quicker the athlete adapts to the training stimulus. Suppose in the fall, I designate a mesocycle to stress heavy-implement work to create a strength base for the upcoming season. At the end of the cycle, I hold an intrasquad competition with heavy implements to assess the effectiveness of that particular cycle. It is hard to judge progress in just one week. If a coach waits until the end of the year to assess an athlete's progress, it may be too late to adjust a training plan before a championship. By utilizing the mesocycle, a coach can test athlete's development periodically and make adjustments in subsequent mesocycles (Table 9-3)

Between mesocycles, you may have a whole new set of weekly activities. This period is often referred to as an "unload week." It keeps things fresh, prevents stagnation, and allows the athlete the opportunity to regenerate.

Macro	1st meso	6 weeks	Preparation period
	2nd meso	6 weeks	
	3rd meso	6 weeks	
	4th meso	6 weeks	Competition period

Adapted from Bompa (1994)

Table 9-3. Basic model of athletic form development

The Weekly Plan

The microcycle is approximately a week of training activities. The time between competitions usually determines the length of the microcycle. Microcycles can last between four to 10 days. Three to six microcycles combine to form one mesocycle. Therefore, microcycle training variables should reflect the goals of that particular mesocycle. For example, a mesocycle that focuses on special strength training, for a strong throwing base, will include microcycles with a high throwing volume (30+ throws) and heavier implements (10 to 20 percent above the standard implement).

The main factor to consider when planning microcycles is the action planned for that corresponding weekend. Will an athlete's Saturday include rest or a competition? If an athlete is in-season, is the competition early in the season or a championship meet? Planning microcycles during the season differs from out-of-season planning. In-season, a Sunday, the day after the meet, is a rest day. Most training is Monday through Thursday. Meet preparation is Friday, which involves an abbreviated session of a few quality (set-up) throws. During the week, throwing volume is dictated by mesocycle goals and goals for weekend competitions. Some extraneous conditioning training activities include exercises described previously in the book like pud (kettle-bell) throws, multi-throws with various weigh implements, plyometrics, running, and general strength work (agilities). Each of these elements should probably be done once a week during the season. The pud releases and plyometrics should be done earlier in the week when an upcoming competition is scheduled.

Figure 9-1. The overhead back (OHB) shot put throw is a great exercise for building power. To be effective, the OHB must be performed at maximum intensity. This exercise can be utilized as a testing exercise to gauge the training state of an athlete throughout the season.

The training sessions are combined to form a microcycle. Training sessions can occur once, twice, or up to three times per day. It is in the session planner that you should think of combining warm-up, the body of the workout or "load," and recovery activities into the microcycle. The sessions should vary in volume or load. A load activity is how much volume is required in that training session. Keep in mind that a certain intensity or training zone is necessary for each activity in the session planner. A training session that has a high training load often requires a subsequent recovery session the next day. A recovery activity is mentally and physically easy ("low-load") and actually helps the thrower recover faster. A warm-up activity prepares the athlete for a load activity. Total workload is volume and can be amplified by intensity. In designing the weekly schedule, you need to be mindful of not placing similar, high-load activities on consecutive days. Always think globally when you plan the volume and intensity of your weekly microcycles. The volume and intensity on the track, in the ring, and in the weight room should all be coordinated for recovery purposes. Remember that one microcycle sets up the next. The microcycle needs to be checked against the following principles, particularly when checking the content of a training session and from one training session to the next.

Microcycle Session Structure

- Warm-up
- Technical
- Speed, speed strength, maximum strength
- Speed endurance, strength endurance
- Conditioning
- Strength endurance

The Training Session

The training sessions are the individual workouts in the weight room and out at the field. The coach must first master the concept of designing a training session. Individual training sessions are comprised of training units that are listed on the training inventory. It is important to understand an athlete's physical capabilities when designing a training session. Training sessions that last too long may not be effective, and training sessions that are too short may not allow for the proper volume to make a physical adaptation.

Throwing can be done for conditioning or for speed. High-volume, high-intensity throwing can improve special strength. However, not all throwing sessions should involve going all-out for a long session. You can also have the athletes concentrate on correcting or modifying an element in the throw. Throwing drills can be done with or without implements. Workouts can include heavy and light implements or focus on throwing the standard implement. Each throwing session should probably involve some brief warm-up activities, such as agilities and running. The training session should always have a briefing session, where the coach explains to the athletes what they are going to do and what is expected of them (objectives). Similarly, a debriefing at the end of the session would compare what was achieved in terms of the objectives: what was good, and what was not so good. However, at least once a week, you should do some additional running or flexibility work at the end of the session. Each training session should be constructed in the following progression:

- Warm-up
- Brief
- Skills/technical unit
- Fitness unit
- Cool-down
- Debriefing

Training Units

This section will describe the different training units and provide some background for planning strength sessions throughout the year. All athletic action requires force production, rate of force development, speed and power, as well as specific endurance.

During the general preparation phase, strength endurance is emphasized. Strength endurance refers to the ability to produce higher forces over a longer period of time. This element is important in the beginning of the general preparation phase to help build the base for later maximum strength training. Performing strength-endurance work for the throwing events during the later phases of training has no relevance.

Following the strength-endurance phase, the emphasis shifts to maximum strength. Maximum strength represents the highest force production in a voluntary contraction. The basic dimension of strength is maximum strength because maximum strength is the quality that affects all other dimensions. Research has shown maximum strength and peak power have moderate to high correlations. Peak power is one of the major determinants in speed. Maximum strength measures are highly correlated with strength/power exercises like the power clean and snatch. Measures of maximum strength are also associated with elite sports performance. Stronger athletes are more powerful and, thus, better performers

Force is a major component of power as power = force x velocity. Following the development of maximum strength, the emphasis shifts to the development of power. Power (or speed strength) describes the potential of a muscle to produce high forces in a short time. Quite often, you will find the term "explosive strength." Explosive strength is the ability to overcome the maximum weight in the shortest time possible, which then determines how efficient strength is trained. Explosive strength boils down to efficient power and is very important in the throws.

The final mesocycle emphasis shifts to speed and reactive strength. Force production results in rate of force development (RFD) and duration. Reactive strength is also an important dimension of strength in the throws. For the moment, it is sufficient to say that reactive strength describes the potential of muscle to produce high forces in a stretch shortening cycle (combination of eccentric and concentric work) within less than 200 milliseconds (0.2 sec). An example specific to throwing is the right foot action at the beginning of the delivery phase. The following section lists the training units for a thrower with some guidelines for implementation.

Strength Endurance Training

When: During the general preparation phase (two times a year for the double periodization model)

How often: Two to three times per week in GPP

What: General strengthening, weight lifting (e.g., bench press, dead lift, and squat)

Maximum Strength Training

When: During the whole year

Build-up: General preparation, beginning of special preparation

Maintenance: Second half of special preparation, competition period

How often: Two to three times per week in GPP; one to two times per week in SPP and CP

What: General strengthening, weight lifting (e.g., bench press, dead lift, and squat)

Power Training

When: During the whole year

Build-up: Special preparation and pre-competitive phase

Maintenance: Second half of competitive period

How often: Two to three times per week in GPP; one to two times per week in SPP and CP

What: Weight lifting (power clean, power snatch, jerks, pulls), heavy-implement throws, medicine-ball throws

Plyometric Training

When: During the whole year (maybe except the first two to three weeks of GPP)

How often: One to two times per week in GPP and CP; two to three times per week in SPP

What: Hops and alternate bounding, hurdle jumps, depth jumps, medicine-ball throws

Speed Training

When: During the whole year (maybe except the first two to three weeks of GPP)

How often: One to two times per week in GPP and CP; two to three times per week in SPP

What: Running drills, maximal sprints (20 to 50m), throws with light weight implements

Technical Training

When: During the whole year

How often: Two to three times per week in GPP and CP; three to four times per week in SPP

What: Drills, imitations, power-position throws, full-technique throws

Getting Started: Planning a Training Session

- Set the overall goals and objectives. Decide how this practice fits into the big picture of the microcycle and the period of training.
- Set specific goals and objectives. Decide which skills, biomotor abilities, and energy systems will be developed.
- Build in the principles of effective practice sessions. Include aspects of variety and change. Make it fun.
- Design the training session. Decide what activities, and in what order, will achieve your goals and objectives.

Take an athlete inventory (testing).

It's the first day of practice for the new season, and you are the new throws coach. You ask yourself, "What do I do to get started?" Assuming that all the athletes have their physicals and are cleared to start, a great place to begin is with a battery of physical tests. How can a coach plan a practice without first knowing the physical capabilities of his athletes? No matter if it is a coach's first practice at a new institution or athletes are coming back after a summer, it is important to understand an athlete's physical condition before instituting the appropriate training plan. But first, even before the athletes step foot on the practice field, know the key athletic qualities needed for throwing events; power, speed, explosiveness, agility, and strength. Have them in mind. Once understanding what qualities to look for, the physical tests will help determine if the athletes have them. How do your athletes measure up to the qualities that the event requires?

When examining an athlete after a summer or for the first time, look at the following areas:
- Fitness, health and status of previous injuries
- Current strength and conditioning level
- Performance from last year/current level of performance
- Throwing technique

For the first practice, plan a testing day, including a number of competitions or tests. From overhead shot with various weight implements to standing broad jump into a sand pit to a timed 30-meter shuttle run, selected repetition maximums in the weight room, and throwing performance trials, numerous combinations of testing-day activities are available to help assess these qualities. These tests isolate qualities needed to become a great thrower. The overhead shot tests explosiveness and power. Standing broad jump tests explosiveness but also tests an athlete's ability to move quickly from a stationary position. A shuttle run tests agility and speed, and repetition maximums tests strength. As regular practice begins, the coach will have a better idea of an athlete's technical proficiency. By taking the time to look at an event and what is involved in its execution, you may accumulate information to help you make decisions about what qualities athletes need to train. By observing the athletes, it is possible to plan the qualities most needed to be successful.

Establish the goals and objectives, and develop an annual-plan template.

When setting season goals and objectives, it is important to determine a realistic level of expectation. For example, when looking at technical mastery of the athlete's event, you should consider two questions. First, how close is the athlete's actual technique to "ideal" technique? Second, how important is technical mastery for this particular athlete? Poor technique may hinder performance. Good technique is important to an athlete's performance. The ability to hold positions and execute is often hindered by biomotor weaknesses.

What you need to consider is how vital is superior technical mastery for a particular athlete, and how realistic is it given the athlete's physical capabilities? Age and development level can be guides. For example, is it important to coach all the finer points of technique to middle-school kids? What about to collegiate-level athletes? What about to Olympians? When is it appropriate to focus entirely on drill and position work? When in the training cycle should this type of training be discontinued or minimized?

The question that is asked most often is what type of training activities yield the best results. Table 9-4 lists a series of training activities and a correlation coefficient based on the level of the athlete for the men's hammer throw (Bondarchuck, 1994). This table illustrates the importance of changing the emphasis of the training program as the athlete advances, and serves as an example of what should be emphasized at the different stages of development. Notice the high correlation related to work with overweight implements.

Exercise	Correlation Coefficient						
	45-50 M	50-55 M	55-60 M	60-65 M	65-70 M	70-75 M	75-80 M
Hammer 5 kg	0.667	0.785	0.789	0.824	0.542	0.645	0.564
Hammer 6 kg	0.812	0.666	0.675	0.786	0.768	0.790	0.684
Hammer 8 kg	0.684	0.521	0.689	0.869	0.805	0.842	0.798
Hammer 9 kg	-	-	-	0.675	0.589	0.745	0.766
Hammer 10 kg	-	-	-	0.542	0.745	0.801	0.824
Hammer 16 kg (short)	-	-	-	0.452	0.586	0.677	0.609
Power snatch	0.580	0.487	0.559	0.451	0.245	0.198	0.245
Power clean	0.490	0.542	0.467	0.421	0.356	0.215	0.270
Full squat	0.620	0.546	0.524	0.437	0.225	0.147	0.196
Standing long jump	0.425	0.507	0.433	0.397	0.258	-0.214	-0.127
Standing triple jump	0.396	0.452	0.406	0.388	-0.266	-0.165	0.098
Vertical jump	0.425	0.390	0.422	0.380	-0.247	-0.200	0.124
Shot put BLF	0.455	0.424	0.398	0.245	0.167	-0.178	-0.168
Shot put OHB	0.540	0.425	0.478	-0.378	0.298	-0.245	0.256
30 m sprint	-0.178	0.387	0.330	-0.242	-0.197	-0.227	0.226

Adapted from Bondarchuk (1994)

Table 9-4. Training activities and performance correlation for the men's hammer

When forming an effective strength and conditioning program, you need to make a number of decisions:

- What physical characteristics are necessary for this event?
- What exercises will best develop those characteristics?
- How much time do you have to weight train and what equipment is available?
- What tests will best assess those characteristics throughout the year?
- What physical characteristics need to be developed to have success in key meets?

The answers to these questions become the goals and training variables for an annual plan. Without concrete goals, objectives, and priority meets, planning training becomes misguided, and the plan will lack controls over training outputs.

To help with organization, also have a general computerized template for the annual plan. You can design your plans using a spreadsheet program such as Microsoft Excel. An annual plan is something a coach will refer to throughout the year, so having a written or typed guide to keep is of utmost importance. The key to success is staying directed and organized with clear goals.

Ascertain the number of weeks available for training.

The annual plan is designated the yearly plan, but it is important to realize the training plan may not encompass a full calendar. Counting backwards in weeks from the last track and field meet working down to the first scheduled practice day determines the length of the annual plan. This number will vary depending on the level of the athlete. I usually end the season in late August and start practice the middle of October, a typical schedule of an international-level athlete. I typically have 35 to 37 weeks of practice in my annual plan. At the high-school level, the season usually ends in June and starts in February. The state high school association or the National Collegiate Athletic Association mandate starting dates and the number of practice days allowed for high school and collegiate practices. Take a look at the calendar, and make sure you factor in holidays and vacation periods. From this information, you can determine some of your recovery periods and the transition phase. The transition phase starts following the last competition and ends when practice resumes.

Grade the competitions as "developmental," "important," and "championship," and record these designations.

After tallying the weeks of the annual plan, the next step is to evaluate the most crucial part of the training year: the actual season. Designating each meet as either "developmental," "important," or "championship" will aid time-frame selection for the preparation and competitive training phases. The correct designations lead to proper physical peaking for championship meets. It also allows you to target a selected competition or competitions as important and back off for a mini-peak earlier in the season. It may be for your rival dual meet or a big invitational like the Mt. SAC or Penn Relays.

Developmental meets are the meets at the beginning of each season, indoor and outdoor, where coaches and athletes alike "iron" out the kinks in the competitive process. Training before these meets can still be heavier in the preparation phase in order to create a peak for the championship meets. Important meets later in the season are not quite the championship meet where performance makes or breaks the season, but it is still important for an athlete to throw far. The competitive training phase should start before these meets. Championship meets are the pinnacle meets of the year. For high school, the meets can be state meets, and for college, NCAA meets or conference meets. Most of these championship meets have performance standards. Coaches will have an idea of an athlete's chances at qualification for the championship season based on the year's previous performances and the current season progression. The peaking phase of training can be adjusted if an athlete performs that unexpected big throw that qualifies him for later meets.

Make sure to include every indoor and outdoor track and field meet. Not every competition can be classified as important and/or championship; doing so will lead to overtraining, mental staleness, and an ineffective peak phase. I only designate one competition in the indoor and outdoor seasons as a championship or focus competition. For athletes competing in the shot put and weight/hammer throw, my annual plan is designed for two peaking phases.

Make training-phase notes.

After assessing physical-training goals, technical-proficiency goals, and setting crucial time periods, the next step is to break the annual plan into training phases. The length of each phase will depend on the length of the annual plan, from start date to championship meets or season. Once again, it is easiest to start by counting backwards.

Three weeks out from the pinnacle championship meet, plan the peaking phase. Four weeks back from the beginning of the peak phase, plan the competitive phase. Four weeks from the beginning of the competitive phase, plan the pre-competitive phase. The special prep phase lasts about three weeks before the pre-competitive phase, and the general prep phase should be executed before that.

Every athlete has the potential for an exception to the rule. Some athletes play fall sports, the high school season has many meets during the week earlier in the year, and some athletes will compete longer than others. Be flexible with the athlete's schedule. The general prep phase may just be activity in another sport or participation in a weight-lifting class. The pre-competitive phase may extend into a long season with many meets, forcing athletes to "train through" the least important meets of the year to ensure a great peaking phase. Individualize these phases, making certain each athlete trains the way they need to.

Evaluate designation of volume, intensity, and training components.

Throughout the year, volume, intensity, and training components change. To further specify training, a coach must combine the number of mesocycles and microcycles in the annual plan with the training phases of the year and designate these training variables for the full annual plan calendar. Certain training components should be planned by mesocycle and some components by microcycle, but each component should reflect the elected training phase. Stay structured, and chart the following suggestions in a written document.

Each mesocycle will have a low, medium, or high volume and intensity and a specified number of strength-training and Olympic-lifting repetitions. Plan these cycles according to the training phase, keeping in mind that the number of repetitions has a large effect on athlete fatigue levels and ability to execute in a throwing practice. Repetitions in the ring will also impact an athlete's physical state. Throwing workouts must reflect the training period.

Figure 9-2. The shot put must be programmed using a double periodization model because championship competitions occur both indoors and outdoors.

A coach's direction for his athletes should be even more specific than just planning volumes, intensities, and repetition numbers for the mesocycle. Each individual athlete will react to training stimuli a little differently; therefore, individual modifications must be made. The physical or biomotor goals discussed previously come to fruition when planning the individual microcycles that compose the mesocycles. Each of the targeted physical qualities cannot be emphasized at the same time. To keep from overtraining your athletes with incompatible training elements, list the five biomotor qualities on your macrocycle planner, and rate their importance for that mesocycle with a number system: one through five. One is most important and highest emphasis, while five is least important with the lowest emphasis. Refer to the document often; look at your mesocycles, and make your training emphasis match your themes. The strength-training volume and intensity will be rated "low," "medium," or "high. The ratings change with each week within the mesocycle correspond to the training phase and mesocycle weight-room repetition numbers, volumes, and intensities.

Usually after a conducting a repetition max in the weight room and other testing to conclude a mesocycle, it is important to plan a microcycle that involves alternate activities, rest, and recovery. This "unload" microcycle is extremely important for tracking gains in training with testing and allowing for rest along with adaptation to training.

Transfer annual plan information into a four-week mesocycle training document/plan.

The annual plan serves as the blueprint of your training plan. It is time to put your plan into action. To further organize and include more detailed information, break the annual plan document into a series of monthly or mesocycle documents. The mesocycles are constructed to reflect the themes determined by the annual plan.

Start by producing a four-week mesocycle strength-training workout, general information is then taken from the annual plan and added. From your annual plan, transfer such things as: competition dates, mesocycle training dates, volume and intensity, training loads, training themes, and training phases. From there, other specific daily-training details can be included like plyometrics, medicine-ball throws, core work, and speed work. Make sure your training elements match your mesocycle period and theme and stay in line with your resistance training. From month to month and week to week, refer to your annual plan to make sure you stay on track with your chosen themes.

Complete the mesocycle with daily training activities and construct a training inventory.

The final step to completing the written guide for training is planning the daily activities, the actual exercises. Each day is different, with various training activities using different modalities corresponding to the mesocycle, training phase, and annual plan. Once again, in order to keep all the details straight, it is important to record all pre-planned daily activities to complete mesocycle training. On the mesocycle plan, use general terms to refer to a specific training workout.

For example, one training session of the mesocycle document will look like this: warm-up A, pedestal, throwing workout B, 6 x 60 m sprints. Do not include the specifics of different training activities like warm-up A in the mesocycle document. Too many details will make the mesocycle document too large and may confuse your athletes. Instead, create a training inventory that consists of all training activities and their specific exercises. To save even more time, give each athlete a training inventory. That way, when instructing a practice, a coach does not have to specify each exercise; the athlete will already have the complete list to follow. (Refer to the appendix for detailed lists of training activities.) The athletes will eventually memorize the activities listed in the training inventory.

The particular training inventory I hand to the athletes excludes weight lifting. I like to print a separate document including the full mesocycle of weight-training activities for the athletes. The athletes do not need to know the month's designations for simple warm-up drills, but it is important the athlete set monthly goals in the weight-training program. The first weight-training week for the month sets the pace for the last max week. Table 9-4 provides a brief strength-training exercise reminder.

Power clean
Snatch
Squat (back and front)
Bench press
Jerks
Mid-thigh high pulls

Table 9-4. Six key exercises that should be foundational to your training routine

At this point, daily training sessions can relate to the ideas and concepts of the annual plan. This method is beneficial to a coach in many ways. A coach can provide workouts for a four- to six-week period of time and be assured that it follows the annual plan. Knowing the workouts and having the training inventory at each workout becomes the athlete's daily responsibility. Nothing can replace planning ahead.

Implement the plan and evaluate.

The annual plan forces coaches to look ahead. Having a practice plan for each day of the year frees a coach for other daily time-consuming activities. The training plan serves as a constant reminder to inject variety and change into the practice routine as you follow the periodized model. As a collegiate coach, having a training plan ahead of time allowed me to recruit, talk to athletes, and complete paperwork without feeling unprepared for practice. The plan gave me a starting point to make daily adjustments for each individual athlete. I always had plan B and sometimes plan C in the back of my mind in case of weather or facility issues. Combining strength training and throwing in the proper volumes and intensities for success has developed into a complicated science. But, sometimes the science is the easy part.

With the plan in hand, the coach steps out to the field. Various personalities, team chemistries, motivations, and attitudes coalesce to create a series of variables to juggle. That gap between the science on paper and the performance on the field separates good coaches from great coaches. Implementing the plan may very well be the most important step. It does not matter what is on paper if the coach cannot relate to the athletes. Understanding each individual athlete and knowing what motivates him is the crucial stride to a great performance. Each athlete will have an optimal practice length, peak strength, and a different level of concentration; the list is infinite.

Figure 9-3. In the discus, a perfectly executed throw into a tailwind can turn into a disappointment for an athlete. Because of varying wind conditions, coaches have to adapt expectations to conditions.

Be persistent with learning what works for each athlete and for the team of throwers as a whole. It is important to sit back at the end of the season and evaluate the training program. Which athletes had their best performances at certain meets? Did all athletes peak at the designated times? Compare the program results with the projected goals. Did the training program train the qualities intended? Make the necessary changes, and it is time to start the cycle all over again. Remember last year's training plan will bring last year's results. A new set of indoor and outdoor seasons requires a new training plan.

Figure 9-4. Throwing the hammer is very similar to setting up a training program. A successful hammer throw is a series of perfect turns blended together and a training plan is a series of mesocycles with different themes that must be harmoniously blended for peak performance.

Psychological Preparation: Getting Into the "Flow"

© Victah Sailer@www.photorun.NET

Chapter 10

This book has been a thorough review of all types of physical training to help coaches take their athletes to their utmost potential. However, is physical and technical training enough to be successful? Dedicated and driven coaches seeking success cannot stop their knowledge base at just understanding the physical aspect of throws training. Sport psychology has emerged as the latest tool for helping coaches prepare athletes to edge out another competitor; however, few coaches take full advantage of psychological skill preparation. How can track and field throws coaches specifically take advantage of sport psychology to achieve optimal competitive mind states? Psychological training must be part of the periodized plan.

Track and field throwing events appear from the outside as simply a test of brute strength and aggression. Track and field throws coaches and athletes, however, understand the true nature of the event: a delicate balance between technical execution and explosiveness. An optimal arousal state is a commodity to throwers: too aroused and throws technique breaks down, not aroused

Figure 10-1. Encourage athletes to develop their own "flow" state in practice so they can begin to prepare for the mental challenges of competition.

enough and the dynamic physical qualities to accelerate the implement all of a sudden are missing from the throw. The optimal arousal state for a thrower can be referred to as controlled aggression or a throwing "flow" state—just enough explosion with the precise technique.

Throws coaches know how to train the physical qualities needed to propel the implement. What is missing in the literature is a system of psychological preparation that is thorough enough to match the physical preparation and help the athlete to achieve "flow" when it counts in big meet situations. Plenty of theoretical articles can be found on the psychological skills necessary for performance mastery, but the gap in the literature is how and when to apply these necessary skills into the training program. This chapter will discuss how to apply the science of sport psychology to achieve flow into the training and pre-competitive routine of a track and field thrower.

Flow Defined

Mihaly Csikszentmihalyi, a University of Chicago psychology professor, identified the source of human happiness in what he termed "flow." He described the state of consciousness as flow, "a state of concentration so focused that it amounts to absolute absorption in an activity." It is a universal experience that occurs whenever individuals set a goal for themselves and seek to overcome the obstacles in their way to enjoying it. People typically report feeling strong, alert, in effortless control, and at the peak of their abilities. Emotional problems and the sense of time seem to disappear (Csikszentmihalyi, 1990).

Csikszentmihalyi (1990) cites the case of a female schizophrenic patient in Holland who had failed to respond to conventional psychiatric treatment. Using an electronic beeper, psychiatrists interrupted the woman at different points in the day and asked her how she felt. After doing so a number of times, they discovered that she was invariably happiest when cutting her nails. Concluding that this activity was for her an optimal experience, they found her a job as a manicurist and successfully returned her to the community.

Csikszentmihalyi claims a set of conditions makes flow more likely to occur, although he does acknowledge the spontaneity of the state of consciousness. He proceeds to discuss flow in terms of qualities that facilitate flow; particular activities are more likely to produce flow and certain personal traits may help people achieve flow more easily. Flow-producing activities facilitate concentration and involvement by making the activity as different from everyday reality as possible (1990).

Each flow activity Csikszentmihalyi studied had the ability to: "provide a sense of discovery, a creative feeling of transporting the person into a new reality. It pushed the person to higher levels of performance, and led to undreamed-of states of consciousness" (1990, p. 74).

Within the state of flow is a delicate balance between skill level and challenge (Jackson, 1995). If the demands of an activity are greater than a person's skills, then a state of anxiety is a result. If skill level exceeds the situational challenges, boredom will result. A flow state includes the achievement of a positive state void of either of these states" (Csikszentmihalyi, 1990).

Role of the Flow State in Athletics

Where does this concept of a flow state fit into athletics? The body of research exploring the relationship between flow states and sports supports the notion that a flow state also acts as a peak performance state in athletics.

Jackson and Roberts (1992) found correlational support for flow and peak performance in sport. Aside from correlational data, qualitative studies have

211

also shown a flow-peak performance link. An in-depth investigation was conducted by Jackson (1996), in order to understand this optimal state experienced by elite athletes. Twenty-eight elite-level athletes, representing seven sports, were interviewed on their perceptions of flow state during performance of their sport. Csikszentmihlyi's model of the flow state has been examined for its applicability to elite athletes. Similarities were found between dimensions of flow, as described by Csikszentmihlyi (1990), and the athletes' descriptions of their experience of flow. Some dimensions received greater support through qualitative analysis of the athletes' descriptions than others. The experience of flow, total concentration on the task at hand, merging of action awareness, and the paradox of control were the dimensions of flow most represented across the group's data. The analysis provided a detailed, sport picture of flow state in elite athletes.

Fundamentals of Flow

Athletes often describe flow as being in the zone, on autopilot, or just feeling it. According to Reardon and Gordin (1999), three fundamental psychological skills are necessary to achieve a high level of performance or flow state in athletic tasks: concentration, composure, and confidence. These three items are generally defined as follows:

- Concentration: The act or process of directing ones attention to a single object.
- Composure: A calmness of mind, body, bearing and appearance.
- Confidence: A state of mind or consciousness marked by certainty of ones abilities and ease and freedom from doubt.

It is important to think of the three psychological skills as three psychological skill groups. Each one may embody one or more mental skills and can be affected by infinite competition variables. To be able to apply a mental training program including these skills to create the flow experience in athletic competition, a more extensive discussion of these three psychological skill groups is necessary.

Concentration is the ability to focus on one single object or task (Reardon and Gordin, 1995). Nideffer and Sagal (2001) identified four main areas of attention/concentration. These four main areas are broad external, narrow external, broad internal, and narrow internal. An example of broad external would be a javelin thrower attending to the wind direction and determining optimal placement of the throw in the sector. An example of narrow external would be noticing the presence of significant dust in the circle that would cause the circle to be too slick and asking the official to sweep out the ring. An example of broad internal attention would be the application of positive self-talk during warm-ups. An example of narrow internal focus would be the application of a pre-performance routine. All of these concentration or focusing areas are essential to successful competitive performances. It must be noted that during a practice or competition, numerous transitions are required between these four areas of attention and concentration. An athlete's concentration level can be enhanced by an athlete's motivation to compete, optimal physiological arousal, and can be affected by competition conditions like weather or other competitors (Jackson, 1995).

An athlete's ability to keep composure relates to a peace of mind and body (Reardon and Gordin, 1995). A significant body of literature in both clinical and counseling psychology, as well as sport psychology, documents the adverse effects of anxiety and tension on performance (Selye, 1974). In cases of these extreme feelings or mental states, the athlete has lost composure. Keeping composure in competition also has a physiological component. The ability to maintain a relaxed and composed state can also facilitate reduced energy consumption, and it may lower lactic-acid levels (Reardon, 1995). Composure can also be affected by the same variables that affect concentration and can also be affected by confidence (Jackson, 1995).

Confidence refers to an athlete's perceived ability to overcome a challenge (Reardon and Gordin, 1995). This crucial element to achieving flow in sport performance can mean and can be affected by different variables according to the individual athlete. Jackson (1995) identifies several variables related to confidence that can help an athlete into flow: pre-competitive plans and preparation, positive attitudes, and optimal physical preparation and readiness.

Concentration, composure and confidence are interwoven (Reardon and Gordin, 1995). A letdown in one area may affect another, and as a result, it may not only disrupt flow, but unfortunately cause performance breakdown in big meet situations. An upside to the psychological skills associated with flow is that Jackson (1995) reported that 19 out of 28 athletes responding to a questionnaire reported that flow was controllable. Preparation was one of the main factors that made the control of flow possible. Flow skills can be learned and applied in a systematic and progressive manner (Reardon and Gordin, 1995). As these skills are learned and practiced, they will ideally become integrated into the athlete's personality and manifested as the fundamental abilities of concentration, composure, and confidence. The discussion of the integration of these mental skills begins with skill training identification.

Flow Skill Training Examples

This section is designed with the everyday coach in mind to help apply the scientific concepts to the practice field. Following are some practical suggestions to enhance the three easily identifiable flow skills: concentration, composure, and confidence.

Concentration

Athletes having trouble staying focused during practice or competition can extend their concentration abilities by practicing concentration skill

Figure 10-2. It is important to formulate strategies for maintaining focus and to go over a concentration blueprint with your athletes.

development. One particular method calls for an athlete to focus on his breathing, air going in and out and the chest or stomach rising and falling. Instruct the athlete to count his breaths until he loses concentration on the breathing and starts to think of something else. The athlete can make it his goal to extend the amount of breaths each time before losing focus. An extension of this exercise involves an athlete, once he has begun to focus on something else, bringing the focus quickly back to the breathing. This exercise mimics situations in competition when an athlete may lose concentration and trains the skill to bring that concentration back to where it is needed. An athlete may also pick something to focus on and time himself, working to concentrate without interruption longer and longer each time (Hanton and Jones, 1999).

Composure

Sometimes, creating physical and mental composure means releasing tension. Utilizing relaxation techniques in practice and in meets may aid the athlete to keep composure when pressure and tension is high.

If an athlete experiences anxiety in competitive practice situations or big meet competitions, the optimal arousal state is disrupted, eliminating composure. A coach can take an athlete through the "systematic desensitization" process. An athlete relaxes his muscles with a process like the relaxation technique previously mentioned, followed by having the athlete imagine increasingly sensitive scenes that relate to the conditions that typically evoke anxiety or tension. The athlete relaxes, and then imagines competing in the opening meet of the year. Once the athlete is comfortable and relaxed again, the athlete imagines competing at a championship, also returning to a relaxed state. The process is designed to "desensitize" the athlete from the tight feelings and tension related to composure loss in big meet situations. This process has been proven to work for performance and speech anxiety (Wardle, 1975; Appel, 1976; Allen, Hunter, and Donahue, 1989), but may not necessarily extinguish performance anxiety (Steptoe and Fidler, 1987; Wesner et al., 1990).

The coach can take a very active role in minimizing the perceived effects of anxiety. Hanton and Jones (1999) found that successful elite swimmers viewed pre-competition anxiety as helpful to a far greater extent than non-elite swimmers. Convincing an athlete that his physiological responses are energy and not detriment can benefit an athlete's composure when feeling the pre-competition stress (Meichenbaum, 1985; Salmon, 1991).

Confidence

Cognitive psychology theory (Beck, 1979; Ellis, 1973) has taught us the relationship between our thoughts, feelings, physical states, and behavior. Too often, negative self-talk plagues an athlete's confidence, making a situation even more difficult than it might otherwise appear. Self-talk modification is one very effective way to correct thinking errors that hinder peak performance of an

Figure 10-3. Some athletes have trouble maintaining their composure during competition. The coach must stay relaxed and help desensitize the athlete from the feelings of tension associated with competing.

activity. Confident self-talk for athletic performance is characterized by the following.

According to Reardon (1992), positive self-talk includes a focus on process variables and technical aspects of training and competing, rather than product or outcome, winning or losing. A focus on the present moment time dimension ("What can/am I doing now to enhance performance?") rather than being distracted by future worrying ("Will I get a personal best?" "What if...?") or past failures ("I should have..." "If only I had..."). Composure and appropriate level of arousal, rather than tension, worried thoughts, and anxious overarousal, are important for success. Striving for that effortless state of mind instead of trying too hard is a coach's dream (Reardon, 1992).

Self-talk modification is one very effective way to correct the thinking errors that hinder both performance and "flow" enjoyment in athletic endeavors. If you are thinking about what you don't want, you vastly increase your chances of producing an undesirable outcome or overreacting (i.e., becoming very tentative). This "negative imagery rehearsal" results because it is impossible to "not imagine" something without having a clear picture in mind of what you don't want (Reardon, 1992).

Another type of positive reassurance can come in the form of mental rehearsal and imagery (Hanton and Jones, 1999; Orlick, 1990). Athletes will imagine as vividly as they can, going through their performance in the ideal way they would like it to go. In imagining, they can draw on all senses: sound, sight, touch, taste, smell, and kinesthetic with an external focus (watching themselves from the audience) or internal focus (imagining as if they are actually performing). The effect of mental rehearsal appears to be that it provides a form of neuromuscular programming so that the performer is more likely to automatically behave in the preferred way during the actual performance (Roland, 1997).

Application of Skill Training to Achieve Flow in the Throws Events

Sport psychologists can assist athlete control of the frequency of his flow state by facilitating the athlete's improvement of his psychological skills, but coaches without this school-hired asset to sport performance can take their own initiative and implement flow skill training into their physical-training programs. Each athlete is different; discovering the correct combination of exercises that work for each athlete may be a trial-and-error process discovered in practice.

According to Reardon and Gordin (1995), incorporating concentration, composure, and confidence into an athlete's training and competition regimen will maximize the opportunity for the athlete to achieve a peak and particularly achieve a peak performance when it counts. The process of skill acquisition begins with the concentration and composure skills, which encompass skills such as deep breathing and relaxation, focusing techniques, developing the skills of breathing control as well as arousal management. Also, skills such as attentional control and attentional endurance, as well as transitional flexibility, are necessary in the early stages of skill development. These fundamental and specific skills encompassed by concentration and composure provide the base for the development of higher-level skills such as visualization, imagery, and self-talk management. The concentration and composure skills seem less directly related to performance, but what becomes apparent when viewing high-level performance or performance breakdown is that breakdown occurs most often in the areas of concentration and composure (Reardon and Gordin, 1995).

The application of psychological skills to competitive situations requires developing an effective pre-competition routine (Table 10-1), a sound pre-performance routine, and a sound recovery/refocusing routine for use in the heat of competition (Reardon, 1992). All of these routines need to be developed, utilized, and applied in a practice situation in order to be able to effectively implement them in a competitive situation. The principle of specificity is very important to keep in mind when designing training programs, and it is equally important in the development of psychological skills. The biggest challenge that competitive athletes and their coaches face is how to put the continued development of psychological skills into the training program. How you practice is essentially how you will compete. A pre-competition routine may include a planned warm-up, positive self-talk, a focus on performance goals, a relaxation strategy, controlling the type and amount of interaction with others, a nap earlier in the day, and monitoring fluid and food intake. Ultimately, athletes need to experiment with the pre-competition routine in practice with the guidance of the coach, keeping the three skill areas of flow in mind to help the athlete evaluate the strategy.

Figure 10-4. In individual sports, the coach must formulate a pre-competition routine for the athletes to come together for a final debriefing prior to competition.

Coaches can include relaxation strategies in two ways: on a regular basis, or as part of a pre-performance routine. When performed regularly, relaxation techniques can reduce the physiological response to stress, prevent the cumulative effect of stress, improve memory and concentration, increase energy levels, and reduce muscle tension (Bourne, 1995).

Four hours prior to competition
- Watch video review.
- Visualize proper technique.

Two hours prior to competition
- Arrive at the competition site and set up camp.
- Walk over and examine throwing venue.
- Review technical cues worked on in the previous week of practice.
- Positive self-talk: review all reasons why he should do well that meet.
- Count breaths if he loses focus until concentration is once again reached.

One hour prior to competition
- Execute a series of planned jogs and skips to increase body temperature and begin to achieve physical arousal.
- Count breaths if he loses focus until concentration is once again reached.

30 minutes prior to competition
- Execute specific warm-up drills to set up the technique.
- Feel the desired body positions during the drills.

20 minutes prior to competition
- Execute predetermined number of warm-up throws.
- Count breaths in between throws to refocus for the next throw.
- Positive self-talk: no negative thoughts about or during throwing warm–up.

Competition
- Count breaths in between throws to refocus for next throw.

Post-competition
- Review competitive strategy.

Table 10-1. Sample pre-competition routine for a shot-putter

Conclusion

Psychological preparation for any athletic endeavor is a complex process that involves acquiring, practicing, and applying many different specific psychological skills. Everyone strives for the ability to perform in an uninhibited, relaxed, skillful manner. Competing at a high level in the throwing events in track and field requires a well-planned program of physical training and technical preparation. Many athletes and coaches utilize training programs that concentrate too heavily on physical training. Inadequate mental preparation can easily overcome and undermine an excellent physical technical preparation. Flow, or as many experts in the field term as "being in the zone," is the goal of athletes and coaches alike. Introducing a plan to train the psychological skills along with the physical skills will take the guessing game out of performing to the best of an athlete's ability when it counts in big meet situations.

Figure 10-5. Mental preparation can be a difficult and arduous process. Developing a strategy for psychological preparation will help your team realize its full potential and enjoy the post-event celebration on the awards stand. The hard work pays off!

© Victah Sailer@www.photorun.NET

Conclusion

Successful coaching in past decades may have had a lot to do with an athlete's physical capabilities. With the evolution of sports and society over the years, the concept of developing athletes to their full potential has developed into a soft science. The notion that only "talented" athletes achieve sports' greatest accolades may now only be a piece of the puzzle. The art of coaching has grown to accommodate athletes with many different physical-talent capabilities and varying levels of mental toughness. With the evolution of sports and all of the training information available to coaches and athletes alike, what is the separating factor between athletes? Is the difference still an athlete's level of talent, how important is the coaching aspect, or is it just plain luck?

Motivation. Successful athletes have it; everyone else wants it. Motivation is the vital component to success in sport—especially for the throwing events in track and field. Motivation must exist on all levels in order to create throwing success. For athletes, motivation is energy to focus, to train hard and to compete even harder. For coaches, motivation is the fire that allows the coach to raise an athlete's capabilities outside of his own expectations—and it is the one element that will allow athletes and coaches to get back up after repeated failures and still achieve goals. A motivated athlete and coach is a dangerous combination, sure to create success in the throws. How can a coach become a great motivator? Like anything else, being a good motivator takes work.

Good motivators are supreme salespeople. A coach must sell athletes on hard work and the pursuit of excellence. Athletes need to believe that their hard work, sacrifices, and sweat are worth the price of the goal. Even though the weight and endurance events are opposites as far as energy-system training, they are a lot alike as well; both require a lot of time, patience and commitment. Volume is a prerequisite for success. To accomplish the necessary rigorous training, the throws coach has to explain to the athletes the need of their efforts. Simply instructing an athlete to do something is nowhere near as effective as explaining to them how this exercise or drill will help them get closer to that big throw. Sometimes, the coach has to get in the ring or on the platform to demonstrate or even jump into the workout and perform a few reps to show the athlete the desired technique and intensity. Even professional athletes need outside motivation from their coach. Too many coaches wrongly presume that the athlete should already be totally motivated and that this incentive piece is up to the athlete. Ninety-five percent of the impact of motivation happens in practice from day one. The other 5 to 10 percent of motivation comes just before the big meet. Unless a coach is working every day at being a motivator, the gimmicks and talks pulled out on meet day will be ineffective. The message is: don't forget about the psychological aspect of preparing athletes for practice and competition. Even the best training plan will fall short if the psychological aspect of is left to chance.

To complete the circle of an athlete's training, a motivated athlete must be working hard and working smart to construct the engine necessary for success. Motivation combined with a poor training plan means countless hours of frustration, heartache, and the ultimate possibility of an injury. The steps outlined in *The Complete Track and Field Coaches Guide to Conditioning for the Throwing Events*, in the development of a periodized training plan, will provide a starting place and reference point for coaches. With the method presented in this book, the coach will be able to accurately plan an athlete's yearly training. The principal components that allow this transition from general to specific training throughout the year are the design of the annual plan, the use of a training inventory, and the development of the mesocycle. An annual plan is the foundation of the competitive season in the sport of track and field. The macrocycle planner organizes and outlines the training year to provide a visual reference. The training inventory organizes training components that will meet the different biomotor requirements. Finally, planning a mesocycle will have specific workout information for a three- to four-week time period. Pooled, these essential steps will allow you to make the transition from the annual plan to a meticulously organized daily training session.

The comprehensive approach presented in this book allows coaches to systemize and individualize training; it leaves less to chance and keeps training from becoming guesswork.

Good luck!

I contend that as a coach, you must practice what you preach. If you set an example for your athletes by living the lifestyle and utilizing the concepts and practices that you stress, you can motivate your athletes to aspire to fulfill their potential.

Sample Training Programs

© Victah Sailer@www.photorun.NET

Appendix

Sample Resistance Training Plan
Preparation Phase Microcycle
Week 1

Day 1

Lift	Reps/Weight	Reps/Weight	Reps/Weight
Bench press (90%)	10/	10/	10/
Incline press	10/	10/	10/
Push jerks (90%)	5/	5/	5/
Close grips	10/	10/	10/
Push downs	10/	10/	10/
French curl	10/	10/	10/
Russian twists	20/	20/	20/
Crunches	30/	30/	30/
V-ups	20/	20/	20/

Day 2

Lift	Reps/Weight	Reps/Weight	Reps/Weight
Four-stage pull	3	3	3
Cleans (90%)	5/	5/	5/
Squats (90%)	10/	10/	10/
Four-position squat	4/	4/	
Leg curls	10/	10/	10/
Leg extensions	10/	10/	10/
Calf raises	15/	15/	15/
Back hyperextensions	10/	10/	10/
Leg raises with dumbbell	20/	20/	20/
Plate walk			
Weighted crunch	20/	20/	20/

Day 3

Lift	Reps/Weight	Reps/Weight	Reps/Weight
Clean shrugs	10/	10/	10/
Mid-thigh clean pull	10/	10/	10/
Clean pull bent knee	10/		
Chin-ups	6/	6/	6/
Lat pulls	10/	10/	10/
Seated row	10/	10/	10/
Dumbbell row	8/	8/	8/
Preacher curl	10/	10/	10/
Dumbbell curl	8/	8/	8/
Roman sit-up	20/	20/	20/
Side bends	20/	20/	
Incline sit-up with twist	10/	10/	10/

Day 4

Lift	Reps/Weight	Reps/Weight	Reps/Weight
Bench press (75%)	10/	10/	10/
Dumbbell bench	10	10/	
Incline press	10/	10/	10/
Push jerks	5/	5/	5/
Close grips	10/	10/	10/
Push-downs	10/	10/	10/
Dips	10/	10/	10/
Russian twists	20/	20/	20/
Crunches	30/	30/	30/
V-ups	20/	20/	20/

Day 5

Lift	Reps/Weight	Reps/Weight	Reps/Weight	Reps/Weight	Reps/Weight
Four-stage pull	3/	3/	3/		
Clean (75%)	5/	5/	5/	5/	
Squats (75%)	10/	10/	10/	10/	10/
Four-position squat	4/	4/	4/		
Leg curls	10/	10/	10/		
Leg extensions	10/	10/	10/		
Calf raises	15/	15/	15/		
Back hyperextensions	10/	10/	10/		
Leg raises	20/	20/	20/		
Russian twist	10/	10/	10/		
Weighted crunch	20/	20/	20/		

Day 6

Lift	Reps/Weight	Reps/Weight	Reps/Weight
Snatch shrugs	10/	10/	
Mid-thigh snatch pull	10/	10/	10/
Snatch pull bent knee	10/		
Chin-ups	6/	6/	6/
Lat pulls	10/	10/	10/
Seated row	10/	10/	10/
Dumbbell row	8/	8/	8/
Preacher curl	10/	10/	10/
Dumbbell curl	8/	8/	8/
Roman sit-up	20/	20/	20/
Side bends	20/	20/	
Incline sit-up with twist	10/	10/	10/

Day 7

Rest

Sample Resistance Training Plan
Pre-Competitive Phase Microcycle
Week 1

Day 1

Lift	Reps/Weight	Reps/Weight	Reps/Weight	Reps/Weight	Reps/Weight
Bench (85%)	5/	5/	5/	5/	5/
Dead lift (85%)	5/	5/	5/	5/	5/
Squats (85%)	5/	5/	5/	5/	5/
Mid-thigh clean high pulls	5/	5/	5/		
Close grips	5/	5/	5/		
Concentric jumps	3/	3/	3/		
Russian twists	10/	10/	10/		
V-ups with weight	10/	10/	10/		
Weighted crunch	30/	30/	30/		

Day 2

Lift	Reps/Weight	Reps/Weight	Reps/Weight
Clean shrugs	10/	10/	10/
Narrow-grip lat pull	8/	8/	8/
Lat pulls	8/	8/	8/
Bench dips with weight	6/	6/	6/
Low row	8/	8/	8/
Dumbbell curls	8/	8/	8/
Dumbbell rows	8/	8/	
Dumbbell pullover	8/	8/	8/
Push-downs	8/	8/	8/
Preacher curls	8/	8/	8/
Leg extensions	8/	8/	8/
Calf raises	15/	15/	15/
Leg curls	8/	8/	8/
Lateral raise	8/	8/	8/
Plate walk		3x	
Leg raise with dumbbell	10/	10/	10/
Back hyperextensions with weight	10/	10/	10/
Sit-ups with weight	20/	20/	20/

Day 3

Lift	Reps/Weight	Reps/Weight	Reps/Weight	Reps/Weight	Reps/Weight
Incline (85%)	5/	5/	5/	5/	5/
Hang cleans (85%)	3/	3/	3/	3/	3/
Front squats (85%)	5/	5/	5/		
Jerks (85%)	3/	3/	3/		
Clean pulls	5/	5/	5/		
Dumbbell step-ups	6/	6/	6/		
Roman sit-ups	20/	20/	20/		
Side-ups with weight	20/	20/	20/		
Sit-ups with weight	20/	20/	20/		
Russian twist	10/	10/	10/		

Day 4

Lift	Reps/Weight	Reps/Weight	Reps/Weight
Clean shrugs	10/	10/	10/
Narrow-grip lat pull	8/	8/	8/
Lat pulls	8/	8/	8/
Bench dips with weight	6/	6/	6/
Low row	8/	8/	8/
Dumbbell curls	8/	8/	8/
Dumbbell rows	8/	8/	
Dumbbell pullover	8/	8/	8/
Push-downs	8/	8/	8/
Preacher curls	8/	8/	8/
Leg extensions	8/	8/	8/
Calf raises	15/	15/	15/
Leg curls	8/	8/	8/
Lateral raise	8/	8/	8/
Plate walk		3x	
Leg raise with dumbbell	10/	10/	10/
Back hyperextensions with weight	10/	10/	10/

Day 5

Lift	Reps/Weight	Reps/Weight	Reps/Weight	Reps/Weight	Reps/Weight
Band bench	3/	3/	3/	3/	3/
Bench (70%)	5/	5/	5/		
Band squat	3/	3/	3/	3/	3/
Squat (70%)	5/	5/	5/		
Hang snatch (85%)	3/	3/	3/	3/	3/
Snatch high pulls	5/	5/	5/		
Close grips	5/	5/	5/		
Russian twists	10/	10/	10/		
V-ups with weight	10/	10/	10/		
Weighted crunch	30/	30/	30/		

Day 6

Hammer Circuit	Reps/Weight	Reps/Weight	Reps/Weight
Narrow-grip snatch	10/		
Snatch beside body	10/		
Rotation with barbell	10/		
Rotation with weight	10/		
Large swings	10/		
Side lift	10/		
One-leg front squat	10/		
Hammer squat jump	10/		
Fast jump	10/		
Turns with plate	10/		
Medicine-ball sit-up with twist	10/	10/	10/

Day 7

Rest

Sample Resistance-Training Plan
Competitive Phase Microcycle

All percentages are based on repetition maximums.
Sets in parentheses are speed sets performed at 50 percent of maximum.

Day 1

Lift	Week 1 (90%)	Week 2 (95%)	Week 3 (100%)
Hang clean	3 x 3 1 x 2 (1 x 5)	3 x 3 1 x 2 (1 x 5)	3 x 3 1 x 2 (1 x 5)
Incline bench press	3 x 5 1 x 3 (1 x 5)	2 x 5 1 x 3 (1 x 5)	1 x 5 1 x 3 (1 x 5)
Back squat	3 x 5 1 x 3 (1 x 5)	3 x 5 1 x 3 (1 x 5)	3 x 5 1 x 3 (1 x 5)
Concentric jumps	3 x 5	3 x 5	3 x 5
Weighted V-up	5 x 10	5 x 10	5 x 10
Dumbbell twist	5 x 10	5 x 10	5 x 10

Day 2

Lift	Week 1 (90%)	Week 2 (95%)	Week 3 (100%)
Mid-thigh clean pull	3 x 5 1 x 3 (1 x 5)	3 x 5 1 x 3 (1 x 5)	3 x 5 1 x 3 (1 x 5)
Behind-the-neck jerks	3 x 3 1 x 2 (1 x 5)	3 x 3 1 x 2 (1 x 5)	3 x 3 1 x 2 (1 x 5)
Shrugs	3 x 5	3 x 5	3 x 5
Lat pulls	3 x 8	3 x 8	5 x 8
Dumbbell rows	3 x 8	3 x 8	3 x 8
Dumbbell curls	3 x 8	3 x 8	3 x 8
Triceps push-downs	3 x 8	3 x 8	3 x 8
Weighted tri-crunch	5 x 30	5 x 30	5 x 30
Standing plate twist	5 x 5	5 x 5	5 x 5

Day 3

Lift	Week 1 (75%)	Week 2 (75%)	Week 3 (70%)
Hang clean	3 x 3 (1 x 5)	3 x 3 (1 x 5)	3 x 3 (1 x 5)
Incline bench press	3 x 5 (1 x 5)	2 x 5 (1 x 5)	1 x 5 (1 x 5)
Back squat	3 x 5 (1 x 5)	3 x 5 (1 x 5)	3 x 5 (1 x 5)
Concentric jumps	3 x 5	3 x 5	3 x 5
Weighted V-up	5 x 10	5 x 10	5 x 10
Dumbbell twist	5 x 10	5 x 10	5 x 10

Day 4

Lift	Week 1 (75%)	Week 2 (75%)	Week 3 (70%)
Mid-thigh clean pull	3 x 5 (1 x 5)	3 x 5 (1 x 5)	3 x 5 (1 x 5)
Behind-the-neck jerks	3 x 3 (1 x 5)	3 x 3 (1 x 5)	3 x 3 (1 x 5)
Shrugs	3 x 5	3 x 5	3 x 5
Lat pulls	3 x 8	3 x 8	5 x 8
Dumbbell rows	3 x 8	3 x 8	3 x 8
Dumbbell curls	3 x 8	3 x 8	3 x 8
Triceps push-downs	3 x 8	3 x 8	3 x 8
Weighted tri-crunch	5 x 30	5 x 30	5 x 30
Standing plate twist	5 x 5	5 x 5	5 x 5

Sample Resistance Training Plan
Peaking Phase Microcycle

All percentages are based on repetition maximums.
Sets in parenthesis are speed sets performed at 50 percent of maximum.
The quarter squats and overhead back throws with the medicine ball are performed in a complex.

Day 1

Lift	Week 1	Week 2	Week 3
Snatch	90% (2) 95% (2) 97.5% (1) 95% (2) 90% (2)–increase each week		
Bench press	3 x 4 1 x 2	2 x 4 1 x 2	1 x 4 1 x 2
Bench-press throws	3 x 5	3 x 5	3 x 5
Quarter squat	3 x 3	3 x 3	3 x 3
Overhead back medicine ball	3 x 5	3 x 5	3 x 5
Weighted leg raise	5 x 10	5 x 10	5 x 10
Twist barbell	5 x 5	5 x 5	5 x 5

Day 2

Lift	Week 1	Week 2	Week 3
Shrugs	3 x 5	3 x 5	3 x 5
Clean pull	1 x 3 (3 x 5)	1 x 3 (3 x 5)	1 x 3 (1 x 5)
Behind-the-neck jerks	90% (2) 95% (2) 97.5% (1) 95% (2) 90% (2)–increase each week		
Lat pulls	3 x 8	3 x 8	5 x 8
Dumbbell rows	3 x 8	3 x 8	3 x 8
Dumbbell curls	3 x 8	3 x 8	3 x 8
Triceps push-downs	3 x 8	3 x 8	3 x 8
Weighted sit-ups	5 x 30	5 x 30	5 x 30
Standing plate twist	5 x 5	5 x 5	5 x 5

Day 3

Lift	Week 1 (75%)	Week 2 (75%)	Week 3 (70%)	
Snatch	5 x 2		5 x 2	5 x 2
Bench-press throws	3 x 5	3 x 5	3 x 5	
Jump squat	3 x 5	3 x 5	3 x 5	
Depth jumps	3 x 5	3 x 5	3 x 5	
Weighted leg raise	3 x 5	3 x 5	3 x 5	
Twist barbell	3 x 5	3 x 5	3 x 5	

Day 4

Lift	Week 1 (75%)	Week 2 (75%)	Week 3 (70%)
Shrugs	3 x 5	3 x 5	3 x 5
Clean pull	1 x 3 (3 x 5)	1 x 3 (3 x 5)	1 x 3 (1 x 5)
Behind-the-neck jerks	3 x 2	3 x 2	3 x 2
Lat pulls	3 x 8	3 x 8	3 x 8
Dumbbell rows	3 x 8	3 x 8	3 x 8
Dumbbell curls	3 x 8	3 x 8	3 x 8
Triceps push-downs	3 x 8	3 x 8	3 x 8
Weighted sit-ups	3 x 30	3 x 30	3 x 30
Standing plate twist	3 x 5	3 x 5	3 x 5

Sample Training Program for the Javelin

	General Javelin Preparation #1							
Mon	*Medicine Ball*	*Kilo M/F*	*Week 1*	*Week 2*	*Week 3*	*Week 4*	*Week 5*	*Time*
1	Feet together	5k / 3k	2 x 10	2 x 10	2 x 10	3 x 10	3 x 10	
2	Roll and throw	5k / 3k	2 x 10	2 x 10	2 x 10	2 x 10	2 x 10	
3	Kneeling throw	5k / 3k	3 x 10	4 x 10	5 x 10	5 x 10	5 x 10	
4	Stand throw	5k / 3k	2 x 10	2 x 10	2 x 10	3 x 10	3 x 10	
5	Swing throw	5k / 3k	2 x 10	2 x 10	2 x 10	2 x 10	2 x 10	
6	Three-step throw	5k / 3k	2 x 10	3 x 10	4 x 10	5 x 10	5 x 10	
	Total		130	150	170	200	200	60-75 min
Tue	*Rehab Drills*	*Time*	*Week 1*	*Week 2*	*Week 3*	*Week 4*	*Week 5*	
1	Partner stretch	10-15 min						
2	Crawl/walk							
3	Band drills							
4	Clock drill							
	Technique	60 min						
1	Three-step		10	10	10	10	10	
2	Five -step		10	10	10	10	10	
3	Half approach		10	10	10	10	10	
	Total		30	30	30	30	30	
	Runway Work	25-35 min						
1	Run with javelin		3 x 30m	3 x 40m	3 x 50m	3 x 60m	3 x 70m	
2	Repeat withdrawals		5 x 30m	5 x 40m	5 x 50m	5 x 60m	5 x 70m	
3	Cross steps		5 x 30m	5 x 40m	5 x 50m	5 x 60m	5 x 70m	
4	Hose drags		5 x 30m	5 x 40m	5 x 50m	5 x 60m	5 x 70m	
5	Full approach 110%		6 x	6 x	6 x	6 x	6 x	
	Weight Room							
1	Pull-overs		3 x 8	3 x 8	3 x 8	3 x 8	3 x 8	
2	Dumbbell pull-overs		3 x 8	3 x 8	3 x 8	3 x 8	3 x 8	
3	Hyper ball throw		3 x 10	3 x 10	3 x 10	3 x 10	3 x 10	
4	Three-way arch throw		3 x 10	3 x 10	3 x 10	3 x 10	3 x 10	

Wed	Medicine Ball	Kilo M/F	Week 1	Week 2	Week 3	Week 4	Week 5	Time
1	Feet together	5k / 3k	2 x 10	2 x 10	2 x 10	2 x 10	2 x 10	
2	Roll and throw	5k / 3k	2 x 10	2 x 10	2 x 10	2 x 10	2 x 10	
3	Kneeling throw	5k / 3k	2 x 10	3 x 10	3 x 10	3 x 10	3 x 10	
4	Stand throw	5k / 3k	2 x 10	2 x 10	2 x 10	2 x 10	2 x 10	
5	Swing throw	5k / 3k	2 x 10	2 x 10	2 x 10	2 x 10	2 x 10	
6	Three-step throw	5k / 3k	2 x 10	3 x 10	3 x 10	3 x 10	3 x 10	
	Total		120	140	140	140	140	45-60 min

Thur	Rehab Drills	Time	Week 1	Week 2	Week 3	Week 4	Week 5
1	Partner stretch	10-15 min					
2	Crawl/walk						
3	Band drills						
4	Clock drill						
	Technique	10 min					
	Easy walk and throw on grass						
	Runway Work	25-35 min					
1	Run with javelin		3 x 30m	3 x 40m	3 x 50m	3 x 60m	3 x 70m
2	Repeat withdrawals		5 x 30m	5 x 40m	5 x 50m	5 x 60m	5 x 70m
3	Cross steps		5 x 30m	5 x 40m	5 x 50m	5 x 60m	5 x 70m
4	Hose drags		5 x 30m	5 x 40m	5 x 50m	5 x 60m	5 x 70m
	Full approach						
5	110%		6 x	6 x	6 x	6 x	6 x
	Weight Room						
1	Pull-overs		3 x 8	3 x 8	3 x 8	3 x 8	3 x 8
2	Dumbbell pull-overs		3 x 8	3 x 8	3 x 8	3 x 8	3 x 8
3	Hyper ball throw		3 x 10	3 x 10	3 x 10	3 x 10	3 x 10
4	Three-way arch throw		3 x 10	3 x 10	3 x 10	3 x 10	3 x 10

Fri	Medicine Ball	Kilo M/F	Week 1	Week 2	Week 3	Week 4	Week 5	Time
1	Feet together	5k / 3k	2 x 10	2 x 10	2 x 10	3 x 10	3 x 10	
2	Roll and throw	5k / 3k	2 x 10	2 x 10	2 x 10	2 x 10	2 x 10	
3	Kneeling throw	5k / 3k	3 x 10	4 x 10	5 x 10	5 x 10	5 x 10	
4	Stand throw	5k / 3k	2 x 10	2 x 10	2 x 10	3 x 10	3 x 10	
5	Swing throw	5k / 3k	2 x 10	2 x 10	2 x 10	2 x 10	2 x 10	
6	Three-step throw	5k / 3k	2 x 10	3 x 10	4 x 10	5 x 10	5 x 10	
	Total		130	150	170	200	200	60-75 min

Training For The Discus

Preparation Phase

Activity	High School Female	High School Male	College Female	College Male
Line drills	5x	5x	5x	5x
Entry drill series	5x	5x	5x	5x
Standing throw #1	5 throws 1.4 kg	5 throws 1.8 kg	10 throws 1.5 kg	10 throws 2.5 kg
Standing throw #2	5 throws 1.4 kg	5 throws 1.8 kg	10 throws 1.5 kg	10 throws 2.5 kg
Wheel and throw	5 throws 1.4 kg	5 throws 1.8 kg	10 throws 1.5 kg	10 throws 2.5 kg
South African drill	5 throws 1.4 kg	5 throws 1.8 kg	10 throws 1.5 kg	10 throws 2.5 kg
Full turn	5 throws 1.4 kg	5 throws 1.8 kg	10 throws 1.5 kg	10 throws 2.5 kg
Full turn with reverse	5 throws 1.4 kg	5 throws 1.8 kg	10 throws 1.5 kg	10 throws 2.5 kg
Heavy standing throws	10x 3 kg shot put	10x 3.5 kg shot put	10x 3.5 kg shot put	10x 4 kg shot put

Pre-Competitive Phase

Activity	High School Female	High School Male	College Female	College Male
Line drills	3x	3x	3x	3x
Entry drill series	3x	3x	3x	3x
Standing throw #1	5 throws 1.4 kg	5 throws 1.8 kg	10 throws 1.5 kg	10 throws 2.5 kg
Wheel and throw	5 throws 1.4 kg	5 throws 1.8 kg	10 throws 1.5 kg	10 throws 2.5 kg
Full turn	5 throws 1.4 kg	5 throws 1.8 kg	10 throws 1.5 kg	10 throws 2.5 kg
Full turn with reverse	20 throws 1 kg	20 throws 1.6	30 throws 1 kg	30 throws 2 kg
Heavy standing throws	10x 3 kg shot put	10x 3.5 kg shot put	10x 3.5 kg shot put	10x 4 kg shot put

Competitive Phase

Activity	High School Female	High School Male	College Female	College Male
Line drills	3x	3x	3x	3x
Entry drill series	3x	3x	3x	3x
Standing throw #1	3 throws 1 kg	3 throws 1.6 kg	3 throws 1 kg	3 throws 1 kg
Wheel and throw	3 throws 1 kg	3 throws 1.6 kg	3 throws 1 kg	3 throws 1 kg
Full turn	3 throws 1 kg	3 throws 1.6 kg	3 throws 1 kg	3 throws 1 kg
Full turn with reverse	20 throws 1 kg	20 throws 1.6 kg	30 throws 1 kg	30 throws 2 kg
Full turn with reverse	5 throws 0.8 kg	5 throws 1.5 kg	5 throws 0.8 kg	5 throws 1.8 kg

Training for the Shot Put
(Pre-Season)

November/December / Monday and Wednesday

Order of Drills	High School Boys		High School Girls		Collegiate Men		Collegiate Women	
Drill	**Weight**	**#**	**Weight**	**#**	**Weight**	**#**	**Weight**	**#**
Wrist flip	16 lbs	3	12 lbs	3	20 lbs	3	12 lbs	3
Front push	16 lbs	3	12 lbs	3	20 lbs	3	12 lbs	3
Standing throw #1	16 lbs	5	12 lbs	5	20 lbs	5	12 lbs	5
Standing throw #2 (glide)	16 lbs	8	12 lbs	8	20 lbs	8	12 lbs	8
or								
Wheel-spin technique	16 lbs	5	12 lbs	5	20 lbs	5	12 lbs	5
or	14 lbs	6	10 lbs	6	18 lbs	6	10 lbs	6
Full-spin or glides	12 lbs	5	4 kg	5	18 lbs	5	4 kg	5
or								
Full spin or glide (with reverse)	12 lbs	15	4 kg	15	16 lbs	15	4 kg	15

*All drills are performed without the reverse unless indicated.

November/December / Tuesday and Friday

Order of Drills	High School Boys		High School Girls		Collegiate Men		Collegiate Women	
Drill	**Weight**	**#**	**Weight**	**#**	**Weight**	**#**	**Weight**	**#**
Wrist flip	15 lbs	3	5 kg	3	19 lbs	3	5 kg	3
Standing throw #1	15 lbs	5	5 kg	5	19 lbs	5	5 kg	5
Standing throw #2	15 lbs	8	5 kg	8	19 lbs	8	5 kg	8
or								
Wheel glide and stop	15 lbs	3	5 kg	3	19 lbs	3	5 kg	3
or								
South African glide (no reverse)	15 lbs	10	5 kg	10	19 lbs	10	5 kg	10
or								
Full-spin or glide (no reverse)	12 lbs	5	4 kg	5	16 lbs	5	4 kg	5
or								
Full-spin or glide (with reverse)	12 lbs	10	4 kg	10	16 lbs	10	4 kg	10

Training for the Shot Put Using a Ladder System (Pre-Season)

September/October / Monday and Thursday

Order of Drills	High School Boys		High School Girls		Collegiate Men		Collegiate Women	
Drill	Weight	#	Weight	#	Weight	#	Weight	#
Wrist flip	14 lbs	3	10 lbs	3	18 lbs	3	10 lbs	3
Front push	14 lbs	3	10 lbs	3	18 lbs	3	10 lbs	3
Standing throw #1	14 lbs	5	10 lbs	5	18 lbs	5	10 lbs	5
Standing throw #2	14 lbs	5	10 lbs	5	18 lbs	5	10 lbs	5
or								
Wheel standing throw #2	12 lbs	10	4 kg	10	16 lbs	0	4 kg	10
or								
Wheel (with reverse)	12 lbs	8	4 kg	8	16 lbs	8	4 kg	8

All drills are performed without the reverse unless indicated.

September/October / Tuesday and Friday

Order of Drills	High School Boys		High School Girls		Collegiate Men		Collegiate Women	
Drill	Weight	#	Weight	#	Weight	#	Weight	#
Wrist flip	15 lbs	3	5 kg	3	19 lbs	3	5 kg	3
Standing throw #1	15 lbs	5	5 kg	5	19 lbs	5	5 kg	5
Standing throw #2	15 lbs	8	5 kg	8	19 lbs	8	5 kg	8
or								
Wheel glide and stop	15 lbs	3	5 kg	3	19 lbs	3	5 kg	3
or								
South African glide (no reverse)	12 lbs	5	4 kg	5	16 lbs	5	4 kg	5
or								
Full-spin glide (with reverse)	12 lbs	10	4 kg	10	16 lbs	10	4 kg	10

Training for the Shot Put by Throwing Variable Weight Implements
(In Season)

Need	Light	Standard	Overweight
Speed	2	1	1
Timing	1	2	1
Power	1	1	2

Example of a Variable Weight Throwing Workout
Emphasis: Development of Power

Order of Drills	High School Boys		High School Girls		Collegiate Men		Collegiate Women	
Drill	Weight	#	Weight	#	Weight	#	Weight	#
Standing throw #2	10 lbs	1	3.5 kg	1	14 lbs	1	3.5 kg	1
or Wheel	12 lbs	1	4 kg	1	16 lbs	1	4 kg	1
(perform three sets)	14 lbs	2	10 lbs	2	18 lbs	2	10 lbs	2
Glide and stop	10 lbs	1	3.5 kg	1	14 lbs	1	3.5 kg	1
or South African	12 lbs	1	4 kg	1	16 lbs	1	4 kg	1
(perform one set)	14 lbs	2	10 lbs	2	18 lbs	2	10 lbs	2
Glide (no reverse)	10 lbs	1	3.5 kg	1	14 lbs	1	3.5 kg	1
or Full spin	12 lbs	1	4 kg	1	16 lbs	1	4 kg	1
(perform three sets)	14 lbs	2	10 lbs	2	18 lbs	2	10 lbs	2
Glide (reverse)	10 lbs	1	3.5 kg	1	14 lbs	1	3.5 kg	1
or Full spin (reverse)	12 lbs	1	4 kg	1	16 lbs	1	4 kg	1
(perform three sets)	14 lbs	2	10 lbs	2	18 lbs	2	10 lbs	2

Developing a Training Plan for the Hammer Thrower

Preparation Phase Training					
Day	Warm-Up	Number of of Throws	Men's Implement	Women's Implement	High School Boys' Implement
Monday	A series	15	16 lbs	4 kg	12 lbs
Tuesday	B series	15	18 lbs	10 lbs	14 lbs
Wednesday	Rest				
Thursday	A series	15	16 lbs	4 kg	12 lbs
Friday	B series	15	18 lbs	10 lbs	14 lbs
Saturday	No drills	10	16 lbs	4 kg	12 lbs
Sunday	Rest				

Pre-Competitive Phase Training					
Day	Warm-Up	Number of of Throws	Men's Implement	Women's Implement	High School Boys' Implement
Monday	A series x 3	30	15x 20 lbs 15x 16 lbs	15x 12 lbs 15x 4 kg	15x 16 lbs 15x 12 lbs
Tuesday	B series x 3	20	10x 18 lbs 10x 16 lbs	10x 10 lbs 10x 4 kg	10x 14 lbs 10x 12 lbs
Wednesday	Rest				
Thursday	A series x 3	30	15x 20 lbs 15x 6 lbs	15x 12 lbs 15x 4 kg	15x 16 lbs 15x 12 lbs
Friday	B series x 3	20	10x 18 lbs 10x 6 lbs	10x 10 lbs 10x 4 kg	10x 14 lbs 10x 12 lbs
Saturday	No drills	10	14 lbs	3.5 kg	10 lbs
Sunday	Rest				

Pre-Competitive Phase Training

Day	Warm-Up	Number of of Throws	Men's Implement	Women's Implement	High School Boys' Implement
Monday	C series	30	10x 20 lbs 10x 18 lbs 10x 16lbs	10x 12 lbs 10x 10 lbs 10x 4 kg	10x 16 lbs 10x 14 lbs 10x 12 lbs
Tuesday	D series	20	15x 14 lbs 15x 16 kg	15x 3.5 kg 15x 4 kg	15x 10 lbs 15x 12 lbs
Wednesday	Rest				
Thursday	C series	30	10x 20 lbs 10x 18 kg 10x 16 lbs	10x 12 lbs 10x 10 lbs 10x 4 kg	10x 16 lbs 10x 14 lbs 10x 12 lbs
Friday	D series	30	15x 14 lbs 15x 16 lbs	15x 3.5 kg 15x 4 kg	15x 10 lbs 15x 12 lbs
Saturday	No drills	Competition			
Sunday	Rest				

Peaking Phase

Day	Warm-Up	Number of of Throws	Men's Implement	Women's Implement	High School Boys' Implement
Monday	E series	25	8x 18 lbs 8x 16 lbs	8x 10 lbs 8x 4 kg	8x 14 lbs 8x 12 lbs
Tuesday	E series	20	10x 16 lbs 10x 14 lbs	10x 4 kg 10x 3.5 kg	10x 12 lbs 10x 10 lbs
Wednesday	Rest				
Thursday	E series	20	10x 16 lbs 10x 14 lbs	10x 4 lbs 10x 3.5 kg	10x 10 lbs 10x 10 lbs
Friday	E series	10	10x 16 lbs	10x 4 kg	10x 12 lbs
Saturday	No drills	Competition			
Sunday	Rest				

Hammer General Preparation Phase
Sample Workout

Day	A.M. Conditioning	A.M. Throwing	P.M. Conditioning	P.M. Throwing	Weight Lifting

Day 1 Monday	Skipping drills
	Prisoner squat
	One-leg squat
	Lunge
	Side lunge
		Position drills
		Left arm drill x 3
		4-4 turns x 5
		5x 30 lb
		5x 25 lb
		5x 20 lb
			Warm-up A
			General strength
			  circuit #1
			6 x 1 wind
			release with pud
			  (kettlebells)
			3x wavings
			Sprints 6 x 40m
				Position drill
				5x 360 winds
				5 x 1 wind 1 turn
				Walk the dog x 5
				6x comp tech 14
				  and 12 lb
				4x hard throws
				  12 lb
				6x comp tech 6 kg
				  and 12 lb
				6x 1 turn 20 lb
					After A.M. throwing

Day 2 Tuesday	Morning skip
	Prisoner squat
	One-leg squat
	Lunge
	Side lunge
		Position drills
		Right arm drill x 3
		1 wind 2 turn x 5
		8x 30 lb
		8x 25 lb
			Warm-up B
			Med Ball #1
			Jump circuit #1
			10 seconds for
			  each exercise
			  and then 20
			  seconds rest
			5 between-leg
			  forward 12 lbs
			6x one-arm
			  crossover
			  release
				Position drill
				2 x 5 narrow
				  stance wind
				5 x 1 wind 1 turn
				5 x 8 turns
				6x comp tech
				  6 and 6 kg
				4x hard throws
				  6 kg
				6x comp tech
				  14 and 6 kg
				6 x 1 turn 20 lb
					After A.M. throwing

Day 3 Wedsday	Rest Massage Chiropractor	No throwing		No throwing	Lift

Day	A.M. Conditioning	A.M. Throwing	P.M. Conditioning	P.M. Throwing	Weight Lifting

Day 4 Thursday	Morning skip
	Skipping drills
	Prisoner squat
	One-leg squat
	Lunge
	Side lunge
		Position drills
		Left arm drill x 3
		4-4 turns x 5
		8x 25 lb
		8x 20 lb
			Warm-up A
			General strength
			  circuit #2
			6x 40m
			3x wavings
			6x one-arm
			  crossover
			  release
				Position drill
				2 x 5 narrow
				  stance wind
				5 x 1 wind 1 turn
				5 x 8 turns
				6x comp tech 16
				  and 6 kg
				4x hard throws 6k
				6x comp tech
				  14 and 6 kg
				6 x 1 turn 20 lb
					After A.M. throwing

Day 5 Friday	Morning skip
	Prisoner squat
	One-leg squat
	Lunge
	Side lunge
		Right arm drill x 3
		1 wind 2 turn x 5
		5x 30 lb
		5x 25 lb
		5x 20 lb
			Warm-up C
			Med ball #2
			Jump circuit #2
			6x 1 wind release
			5 between leg
			  forward 12 lbs
				Position drill
				5 x 360 winds
				5 x 1 wind 1 turn
				5x walk the dog
				6x comp tech
				  14 and 12 lb
				4x hard throws
				  12lb
				6x comp tech 6 kg
				  and 12 lb
				6 x 1 turn 20 lb
					After A.M. throwing

Throws Training Terminology

© Victah Sailer@www.photorun.NET

Acceleration: The rate of change of velocity

Acyclic: A motor skill, such as throwing

Acyclic combined: A cyclic movement followed an acyclic activity; jumping

Aerobic: With oxygen

Anaerobic: Without oxygen

Annual plan: The length of a training period that usually embodies one to three mesocycles

Biological age: The physical maturity of an athlete

Burnout: A feeling of disinterest and lack of motivation toward an activity

Center of mass (COM): The point on a body where forces are applied

Chronological age: The athlete's age

Competition period: A period of event-specific training and important and crucial competition

Competition-specific training: Training involving complete rehearsal of the technical and metabolic demands of the competition. Competition-specific training is the period when technique and conditioning are specifically rehearsed.

Coordination: Refers to the timing and sequencing of movement

Cyclic: A repetitious act, such as walking or running

Density: The number of training units per unit of time

Displacement: The straight-line distance and direction an object travels from one point to another

Double periodization: An annual plan with two macrocycles and two target/peaks

Duration: How long a workout will last

Endurance: The limit of time over which work of a given intensity can be performed

Energy: The capacity to do work

Fitness: The degree of adaptation to training

Flexibility: The capacity to perform movement through a range of motion (ROM)

Force: Mass x acceleration

General training: General exercises that usually don't contain any specific element of the technical or metabolic demands of the event. General training helps improve non-specific work capacity of an athlete. Also referred to as foundation training.

Horsepower: A unit equal to 550 foot-pounds of work per second

Hypertrophy: To increase size

Inertia: A body's resistance to acceleration

Intensity: The strength of the stimulus or concentration of work per unit of time; the quality of effort

Law of overload: The principle stating that the nature of loading must challenge an athlete's present fitness status

Law of reversibility: The principle that states that when there is no training load, and consequently no need to adapt, the fitness level of the athlete will return to a level consistent with the demands of the training

Law of specificity: The principle that states that the training load must be specific to the individual athlete and the specific metabolic and technical demands of the event for which the athlete is training

Macrocycle: The largest division of the training year or season consisting of a preparation, competition and transition period

Main competition phase: The phase of training dedicated to the optimum achievement in competition

Mesocycle: A training period that typically consists of four to six microcycles

Microcycle: A group of training sessions usually performed over a seven-day period

Modeling: A training unit in which the requirements of competition are stimulated

Motivation: The intensity and direction of achievement behavior

Negative acceleration: Means deceleration, or decreasing the velocity slower and slower

Overtraining: A physical and mental state caused by too much exertion over a sustained period of time

Peaking: Tapering training for a major or championship event

Period: Consists of several phases of training grouped together. There are three periods within a seasonal cycle, preparation, competition and transition.

Periodization: The continuous cyclical structure of training to achieve optimal development of performance capacities

Phase: A collection of mesocycles in pursuit of a specific objective

Power: The rate of work, or work divided by time

Pre-competitive phase: A phase of training in which the vigorous development of a specific skill and fitness will occur. The training in the phase begins to address event-specific objectives.

Preparation period: A period of foundation training and developmental competitions

Preparation phase: A phase of training in which the objective of "training to train" dominates

Progressive overload: The methodical increase in the training load above that which the athlete is accustomed

Repetition: Number of intervals in a set

Single periodization: An annual plan with one macrocycle

Special preparation phase: A phase of training in which the primary objective is continual foundation development, but with a trend toward special training (event-specific training)

Special training: Exercises, which are similar to the sequence of movement or contain similar metabolic demands of the competition. Special training develops certain characteristics of technique and conditioning which are specific to the event.

Speed: The capacity to move the body or a body segment rapidly

Speed endurance: Any interval or run where an athlete must maintain near top speeds for a lengthened period of time

Staleness: A lethargic feeling (either mental or physical) caused by prolonged activity or training

Strength: The ability to apply force

Stress: Wear or tear on the body (can be either mental or physical)

Super compensation: Returning to a level of fitness beyond that of the original, following the fatigue resulting from training

Tapering: Modifying the intensity, volume, and density of training in preparation for a peak performance

Torque: Measurement of force to produce a rotation about an axis

Training: The process of acquiring fitness specific to an event

Training session: Individual workout

Training age: The number of years spent in training for an event

Training theory: The interpretation of relevant work, which provides a systematic and scientific program to mesh with practical coaching experience

Training ratio: The ratio between training and recovery

Training session: The combination of training units of a complimentary nature (typically referred to as a workout)

Training unit: The segment of a session that meets the objective of a single training component/biomotor ability

Transition period: The link between two macrocycles when the primary objective is restoration

Velocity: The rate of change of position in a given direction

Volume: The extent of training; the quantity of work performed

Weight: The force of attraction between an object and the earth

Work: Force times distance in the direction of the force

References

Aderson, B., Beauliue, J., Cornelius, W., Dominquez, R., Prentice, W., & Wallace, L. (1984). Roundtable: Flexibility. *National Strength Coaches Association Journal*, 10(22), 71-73.

Ajan, T. (1988). *Weightlifting*. Budapest, Hungary: Medicina Publishing.

Akuthota, V. (2004). Core strengthening. *Arch. Phys. Med. Rehab*, 85(3), 86-92.

Allen, M., Hunter, J. E., & Donahue, W. A. (1989). Meta-analysis of self-report data on the effectiveness of public speaking anxiety treatment techniques. *Communication Education*, 38, 54-76.

American Academy of Pediatrics Policy Statement. (1990). Strength, weight and power lifting, and body building. *Children and Adolescents Pediatrics*, 5, 801-803.

American College of Sports Medicine, American Dietetics Association, and Dieticians of Canada. (2000). Joint position statement: Nutrition and athletic performance. *Med Sci Sports Exerc.*, 32, 2130-2145.

American College of Sports Medicine; Sawka, M.N., Burke, L.M., Eichner, E.R., Maughan, R.J., Montain, S.J., & Stachenfeld, N.S. (2007). American College of Sports Medicine position stand: exercise and fluid replacement. *Med Sci Sports Exerc.*, 39(2): 377-390.

American College of Sports Medicine. (2000). *ACSM Guidelines for Exercise Testing and Prescription* (6th ed.). B.A. Franklin, M.H. Whaley, & E.T. Howley (Eds.) Baltimore, Maryland: Lippincott, Williams & Wilkins Publishers.

American College of Sports Medicine. (1995). American College of Sports Medicine position stand: osteoporosis and exercise. *Med Sci Sports Exerc.*, 27(4): i-vii.

American Dietetic Association. (2000). Position of the American Dietetic Association, Dieticians of Canada, and the American College of Sports Medicine: nutrition and athletic performance. *J Am Diet Assoc.*, 100: 1543-1556.

Anderson, B. (1980). Conditioning report: Stretching for football. *National Strength Coaches Association Journal*, 2, 14-18.

Anderson, S.A., & Raiten, D.J. (1992). *Safety of Amino Acids Used as Dietary Supplements*. Bethesda, Maryland: Life Sciences Research Office, Federation of American Societies for Experimental Biology.

Andrews, J. (1997). *On Field Evaluation and Treatment of Common Athletic Injuries*. St. Louis, Missouri: Mosby.

Appel, L.J., Sacks, F.M., Carey, V.J., Obarzanek, E., Swain, J F., Miller, E.R., Conlin, P.R., Erlinger, T.P, Rosner, B.A., Laranjo, N.M., Charleston, J., McCarron, P., & Bishop, L.M. (2006). Effects of protein, monounsaturated fat, and carbohydrate intake on blood pressure and serum lipids: Results of the Omni Heart randomized trial. *Current Atheroscler Rep*, 8(6), 445-447.

Appel, S.S. (1976). Modifying solo performance anxiety in solo patients. *Journal of Music Therapy*, 13, 2-16.

Applegate, L. (1987). Brewing controversy. *Runner's World,* 22, 20-22.

Armstrong, D.F. (1994). Combination lifts for in-season training. *Strength and Conditioning*, 16(4), 14-16.

Aronson, V. (1986). Protein and miscellaneous ergogenic aids. *The Physician and Sports Medicine*, 14(5), 199-202.

Axler, C.T. & McGill, S.M. (1997). Low back loads over a variety of abdominal exercises: Searching for the safest abdominal challenge. *Med. Sci. Sports Exerc.*, 29, 804-811.

Barr, K.P., Griggs, M., & Cadby, T. (2005). Lumbar stabilization: Core concepts and current literature, part one. *Am. J. Phys. Med Rehabil*, 84, 473-480.

Bartlett, R. (1992). The biomechanics of the discus throw: A review. *Journal of Sport Sciences*, 10, 467-510.

Bartonietz, K., et al. (1988). The view of the DvFL of the GDR on talent selection, technique, and training of throwers from teginner to top level athlete. *New Studies in Athletics*. 1:39-56.

Bartonietz, K.E. (1996). Biomechanics of the snatch: Toward a higher training efficiency. *Strength Cond. J*, 18, 24-31.

Bartonietz, K.E. (1987). Strength training for throwers. *The Throws*, 22-24.

Bartonietz, K.E. (2000). Strength training for throwers. In J. Jarver (Ed.) *The Throws* (pp. 22-26). Mountain View, California: Tafnews Press.

Bartonietz, K. (1994). Rotational shot technique: Biomechanical findings and recommendations for training. *Track and Field Quarterly Review*, 94(3), 18-29.

Beck, A. & Emery, G. (1985). *Anxiety disorders and phobias: A cognitive perspective*. New York, New York: Basic Books.

Behm, D.G. (1995). Neuromuscular implications and applications of resistance training. *J. Strength. Cond. Res*, 9(4), 264-274.

Bellet, S., Kershbaum, A., & Aspe, J. (1965). The effects of caffeine on free fatty acids. *Arch Intern Medicine*, 116, 750-752.

Bergeron, M.F., Volpe, S.L., & Gelinas, Y. (1998). Cutaneous calcium losses during exercise in the heat: A regional sweat patch estimation technique [abstract]. *Clin Chem*. (suppl): A167.

Bielik, E. (1984). Diagonal-rotational strength training for the trunk: A track and field throwers' program. *NSCA Journal*, 6(1), 36-37.

Bielik, E. (1988). Teaching technique #1: The power clean. *National Strength and Conditioning Journal*, 12(6), 52-54.

Biering-Sorensen, F. (1984). Physical measurements as risk indicators for low back trouble over a one-year period. *Spine*, 9, 106-119.

Binkoski, A.E., Kris-Etherton, P.M., Wilson, T.A., Mountain, M.L., & Nicolosi, R.J. (2005). Balance of unsaturated fatty acids is important to a cholesterol-lowering diet: Comparison of mid-oleic sunflower oil and olive oil on cardiovascular disease risk factors. *JADA*, 105(7), 1080-1086.

Bompa, T. (2000). *Total training for young champions*. Champaign, Illinois: Human Kinetics.

Bompa, T.O. (1994). *Theory and methodology of training: The key to athletic performance* (3rd ed.). Dubuque, Iowa: Kendall/Hunt Publishing Company.

Bondarchuck, A. (1994). *Long term training for throwers*. Brisbane/Sydney, Australia: Australian Track and Field Coaches Association/Rothmans Foundation.

Bondarchuk, A.P. (1999). Hints for beginning hammer throwers. Excerpts reprinted in *Modern Athlete and Coach from The Hammer Throw* by A.P. Bondarchuk.

Bourne, E. (1995). *The Anxiety and Phobia Workbook*. Oakland, California: New Harbinger.

Bottcher, J. & Kuhl, L. (1998). The technique of the best female javelin throwers in 1997. *New Studies in Athletics*, 13(1), 47-61.

Bosen, K.O. (1985). A comparative study between the conventional & rotational techniques of shot put. *Track & Field Quarterly Review*, 85(1), 7-11.

Briggs, A.M., Greig, A.M., Wark, J.D., Fazzalari, N.L., & Bennell, K.L. (2004). A review of anatomical and mechanical factors affecting vertebral body integrity. *Int. J. Med. Sci*, 1, 170-180.

Brody, D.M. (1987). Running injuries: Prevention and management. *Clin. Symp*, 39, 1-36.

Brown, H. (1992). Javelin throwing British style. *Track Technique*, 3824.

Brown, T. (2006). Getting to the core of the matter. *Strength Cond. J*, 28(2), 50-53.

Burgener, M. (1988). Teaching technique #1: The power clean. *National Strength and Conditioning Journal*, 12(6), 50-52.

Burke, L.M., Cox, G.R., Cummings, N.K., & Desbrow, B. (2001). Guidelines for daily carbohydrate intake. *Sports Med*, 31(4), 267-299.

Burke, L.M. & Read, R.S. (1993). Dietary supplements in sport. *Sports Medicine*, 15, 43-65.

Cairns, M. (1980). Basic points of modern hammer technique. *Track and Field Journal*.

Celejowa, I. & Homa, M. (1970). Food intake, nitrogen and energy balance in Polish weight lifters, during a training camp. *Nutrition and Metabolism*, 12, 259-274.

Chard, M.D. & Lachmann, M.A. (1987). Racquet sports: Patterns of injury presenting to a sports injury clinic. *Br. J. Sports Med*, 21, 150–153.

Chiu, L., Fry, A., Weiss, L., Schilling, B., & Smith, S. (2003). Post-activation potentiation response in athletic and recreationally trained individuals. *The Journal of Strength and Conditioning Research*, Vol. 17, No. 4 (pp. 671–677).

Cholewicki, J., Simons, A., & Radebold, A. (2000). Effects of external trunk loads on lumbar spine stability. *J.Biomech*, 33, 1377-1385.

Chu, D. (1983). Plyometrics: The link between strength and speed. *National Strength and Conditioning Association Journal*, 5(2), 20-21.

Cissik, J.M. (2002). Programming abdominal training, part one. *Strength Cond. J*, 24(1), 9-15.

Clarkson, P.M. (1991). Minerals: Exercise performance and supplementation in athletes. *Journal of Sports Sciences*, 9, 91-116.

Clementz, G., & Dailey, J. (1988). Psychotropic effects of caffeine. *American Family Physician*, 37, 167-172.

Coleman, E. J. (2006). Carbohydrate and exercise. In M. Dunford (Ed.) Sports, cardiovascular and wellness nutritionists dietetic practice group. *Sports Nutrition: A Practice Manual for Professionals* (4th ed.). Chicago, Illinois: American Dietetic Association, 14-32.

Cook, G. (2002). Weak links: Screening an athlete's movement patterns for weak links can boost your rehab and training efforts. *Train Con*, 12(3), 29-37.

Cook, G. & Voight, M. (2001). Essentials in functional exercise: A four-step clinical model for therapeutic exercise prescription. In W.E. Prentice & M.I. Voight (Eds.) *Techniques in Musculoskeletal Rehabilitation* (pp. 87-410). New York, New York: McGraw-Hill, Inc.

Cook, G. (2001). Baseline sports-fitness testing. In B. Foran (Ed.) *High Performance Sports Conditioning* (pp. 19-47). Champaign, Illinois: Human Kinetics.

Cook, G. & Fields, K. (1997). Functional training for the torso. *Strength and Conditioning*, 19(2), 14-19.

Costill, D.L., Dalsky, G.P., & Fink, W.J. (1978). Effects of caffeine ingestion on metabolism and exercise performance. *Medicine and Science of Sports*, 10, 155-158.

Cramer, J., Housh, T., Coburn, J., Beck, T., & Johnson, G. (2006). Acute effects of static stretching on maximal eccentric torque production in women. *Journal of Strength and Conditioning Research*, 20, 354-358.

Csikszentmihalyi, M. (1990). *Flow: The psychology of optimal experience*. New York, New York: Harper and Row.

Dragoo, J.L. (1993). *Handbook of Sports Medicine*. New York, New York: John Wiley and Sons.

Dunn, G. & McGill, K. (1991). *The Throws Manual*. Palo Alto, California: Track and Field News Press.

Dunn, G. (1990). The shot put. In V. Gambetta (Ed.) *The Athletics Congress's Track and Field Coaching Manual* (pp.153-165). Champaign, Illinois: Leisure Press.

Dunford, M. (Ed.). (2006). Sports, cardiovascular, and wellness nutritionists dietetic practice group. *Sports Nutrition: A Practice Manual for Professionals* (4th ed.). Chicago, Illinois: American Dietetic Association, 507.

Economos, C.D., Bortz, S.S., & Nelson, M.E. (1993). Nutritional practices of elite athletes: Practical recommendations. *Sports Medicine*, 16, 381-399.

Espinoza, S. & Stroble, T. (1993). The protein dilemma: real food vs. liquid supplements. *Nephrology News and Issues*, 7, 52-53.

Faigenbaum, A. & Westcott, W. (2000). *Strength and Power for Young Athletes*. Champaign, Illinois: Human Kinetics.

Faries, M.S. & Greenwood, M. (2007). Core training: Stabilizing the confusion. *Journal of Strength and Conditioning Research*, 29(2), 10-25.

Fleck, S.J. & Kraemer, W.J. (1987). *Designing Resistance Training Programs* (1st ed.). Champaign, Illinois: Human Kinetics.

Fleck, S.J. & Kraemer, W.J. (1993). *Strength Training for Young Athletes*. Champaign, Illinois: Human Kinetics.

Foran, B. (Ed). (2001). *High-Performance Sports Conditioning*. Champaign, Illinois: Human Kinetics.

Fredericson, M. & Moore, T. (2005). Core stabilization training for middle-and long-distance runners. *New Stud. Athletics*, 20, 25-37.

Fry, A.C., Kramer, W.J., Stone, M.H., Koziris, L.P. Thrus, J.T., & Fleck, S.J. (2000). Relationships between serum testosterone, cortisol, and weightlifting performance. *Journal of Strength and Conditioning Research*, 14, 338-343.

Fry, R.W., Morton, A.R., & Keast, D. (1992). Periodization of training stress: A review. *Canadian Journal of Sports Science*, 17, 234-240.

Fu, F.H. & Stone, D. A. (1994). *Sports Injuries: Mechanisms, Prevention, Treatment*. Baltimore, Maryland: Williams and Wilkins.

Gambetta, V. & Clark, M. (1999). Hard core training. *Training and Conditioning*, 9, 34-40.

Gambetta, V. (1993). Remedial exercises for the prevention of shoulder injuries in the javelin throw. *New Studies in Athletics*, 3(8), 45-49.

Gambetta, V. & Odgers, S. (1991). *The Complete Guide to Medicine Ball Training*. Sarasota, Florida: Optimum Sports Training.

Gambetta, V. (1996). *Building the Complete Athlete*. Sarasota, Florida: Optimum Sports Training.

Gambetta, V. (1991). *The Gambetta Method: Common Sense Training for Athletic Performance* (2nd ed.). Sarasota, Florida: Optimum Sports Training.

Gambetta, V. (2000). *Pumping Gravity: Functional Strength Training*. Presentation at USATF level III school, Orlando, Florida.

Gibala, M.J. & Howarth, K.R. (2006). Protein and exercise. In Dunford, Marie (ed.) Sports, Cardiovascular, and Wellness Nutritionists Dietetic Practice Group. *Sports Nutrition: A Practice Manual for Professionals* (4th ed.). Chicago, Illinois: American Dietetic Association, 507.

Godina, W. (2006). USATF Level II Curriculum.

Grabiner M.D., Koh, T.J., & Ghazawi A.E. (1992). Decoupling of bilateral paraspinal excitation in subjects with low back pain. *Spine*, 17(10), 1219-1223.

Guyton, A.C. (1994). *The Textbook of Medical Physiology*. Philadephia, Pennsylvania: W.B. Saunders Company.

Haff, G. & Potteiger, J. A. (2001). A brief review: explosive exercises and sports performance. *National Strength and Conditioning Association Journal*, 23(2), 13-20.

Haff, G. (2004). Roundtable discussion: Periodization of training- part 1. *National Strength and Conditioning Association Journal* 26(1), 50-69.

Hagins, M., Adler, K., Cash, M., Daugherty, J., & Mitrani, G. (1999). Effects of practice on the ability to perform lumbar stabilization exercises. *Journal of Orthopaedic & Sports Physical Therapy*, 29, 546-555.

Hanton, S. & Jones, G. (1999). The acquisition and development of cognitive skills and strategies: Making the butterflies fly in formation. *Sport Psychologist*, 13, 1-121.

Haymes, E.M. (1991). Vitamin and mineral supplementation to athletes. *International Journal of Sport Nutrition*, 1, 146-169.

Haywood, K.M. & Getchell, N. (2005). *Lifespan Motor Development* (4th ed.). Champaign, Illinois: Human Kinetics.

Hedrick, A. (1992). Physiological responses to warm-up. *National Strength and Conditioning Journal*, 14, 25-27.

Hedrick, A. (2000). Training the trunk for improved athletic performance. *National Strength and Conditioning Journal*, 22(3), 50-61.

Hesson, J. L. (1991). *Weight Training for Life*. Englewood, Colorado: Morton Publishing.

Hides, J.A., Jull, G.A., & Richardson, C.A. (2001). Long-term effects of specific stabilizing exercises for first-episode low back pain. *Spine*, 26, E243–248.

Hodges, P.W. & Richardson, C.A. (1996). Inefficient muscular stabilization of the lumbar spine associated with low back pain. *Spine*, 21(22), 2640-2650.

Hutchinson, M.R., Laprade, R.F., Burnett, Q.M., Moss, R., & Terpstra, J. (1995). Injury surveillance at the USTA boys' tennis championships: A six-year study. *Med. Sci. Sports Exerc*, 27, 826-830.

Jacobs, K.A. & Sherman, W.M. (1999). The efficacy of carbohydrate supplementation and chronic high carbohydrate diets for improving endurance performance. *Int J Sport Nutr*, 9, 92-115.

Jackson, S.A., & Roberts, G.C. (1992). Positive performance states of athletes: toward a conceptual understanding of the flow experience in elite athletes. *The Sport Psychologist*, 6(2), 156-171.

Johnalagadda, S.S. (2006). Dietary fat and exercise. In Dunford, Marie (Ed.) Sports, Cardiovascular, and Wellness Nutritionists Dietetic Practice Group. *Sports Nutrition: A Practice Manual for Professionals* (4th ed.). Chicago, Illinois: American Dietetic Association; 50-60.

Javorek, I.S. (1998). The benefits of combination lifts. *Strength and Conditioning*, 20(3), 53-57.

Javorek, I.S. (1993). Sport-specific: Specificity in sports conditioning. *National Strength and Conditioning Association Journal*, 15(6), 31-34.

Jensen, J.L., Marstrand, P.C., & Nielsen, J.B. (2005). Motor skill training and strength training are associated with different plastic changes in the central nervous system. *J Appl Physio*, 99, 1558-1568.

Johnson, H. (1999). Stressful motion: Golfers at high risk for low back pain. *Sports Med. Update*, 14, 4-5.

Judge, L.W. (2006). At the core. *Training and Conditioning*, 16(1), 43-48.

Judge, L.W. (Ed). (2006). USATF Level II Throws Curriculum.

Judge, L.W. (2006). Building up your female throwers. *Scholastic Coach*, 75(3).

Judge, L.W. (2004). Big throws. *Training and Conditioning*, 14(2).

Judge, L.W., Burke, J. M, & Moreau, C. (2003). Neural adaptations with sports specific resistance with highly skilled athletes. *Journal of Sport Sciences*, 21, 419-427.

Judge, L.W. & Potteiger, J.A. (2000). A battery of tests to identify overtraining in throwers. *Modern Athlete and Coach*, 38(1).

Judge, L.W. & McAtee, G. (1999). Detecting and correcting technical flaws in the hammer throw. *Modern Athlete and Coach*, 37(2).

Judge, L.W. (1999). Proper technique in the squat. *Coaches Review*, 72(2).

Judge, L.W. (1999). Proper technique in the bench press. *Coaches Review*, 72(1).

Judge, L.W. (1996). Total program for emerging discus thrower from flight to reverse. *Scholastic Coach*, 65(9).

Judge, L.W. & Santino, P. (1995). Detraining and retraining the post-competitive thrower. *American Track and Field*.

Judge, L.W. (1993). Teaching the rotational shot put. *Scholastic Coach*, 62(9).

Judge, L.W., & Potteiger, J.A. (1992). The effect of relative intensity on recovery time following a high intensity workout in males and females. *Track Technique*, 6(3).

Judge, L.W. (1992). Designing a strength and conditioning program for the thrower. *Track and Field Quarterly Review*, 14(3).

Judge, L.W. (1991). Using the dynamic start in the glide. *Track Technique*, 116.

Judge, L.W. (1992). Detecting and correcting technical flaws in young shot putters. *American Athletics*.

Judge, L.W. (1992). Proper execution of the power clean for the track and field athlete. *Track and Field Quarterly Review*, 4(4).

Kerstetter, J.E., Wall, D.E., O'Brien, K.O., Caseria, D.M., & Insogna, K.L. (2006). Meat and soy protein affect calcium homeostasis in healthy women. *J Nut*, 136(7), 1890-1895.

Kleiner, S.M., Bazzarre, T.L., & Litchford, M.D. (1990). Metabolic profiles, diet, and health practices of championship male and female bodybuilders. *Journal of the American Dietetic Association*, 90, 962-967.

Knudson, L.E. (1990). A biomechanical analysis of power vs. speed techniques in shot putting. *Techniques in Athletics*.

Kollody, O. (1975). The training of juniors in the hammer throw. *Track and Field*, 12, 14-15.

Kroll, P.G., Machado, L., Happy, C., Leong, S., & Chen, B. (2000). The relationship between five measures of trunk strength. *J. Back Musculoskeletal Rehabil*, 14, 89-97.

Lamb, D.R. (1984). The nature of exercise physiology. *Physiology of Exercise: Responses and Adaptations* (2nd ed.) (pp. 1-9). New York, New York: Macmillan Publishing Co.

Leetun, D.T., Ireland, M.L., Willson, J.D., Ballantyne, B.T., & Davis, I.M. (2004). Core stability measures as risk factors for lower extremity injury in athletes. *Med. Sci. Sports Exerc*, 36, 926-934.

Lemon, P.W. (1991). Protein and amino acid needs of the strength athlete. *Int J Sport Nutr*, 1(2), 127-145.

Lemon, P.W., Tarnopolsky, M.A., MacDougall, J.D., & Atkinson, S.A. (1992). Protein requirements and muscle mass/strength changes during intensive training in novice bodybuilders. *Journal of Applied Physiology*, 73, 767-775.

Little, T. & Williams, A. (2006). Effects of differential stretching protocols during warm-ups on high-speed motor capacities in professional soccer players. *Journal of Strength and Conditioning Research*, 20, 203-207.

Lombardi, V.J. (1989). *Beginning Weight Training*. Dubuque, Iowa: William C. Brown Publishers.

Luuto, S., Helivaara, M., Hurri, H., & Alaranta, H. (1995). Static back endurance and the risk of low-back pain. *Clin. Biomech*, 10, 323-324.

Mann, D. & Jones, M. (1999). Guidelines to the implementation of a dynamic stretching program. *Strength and Conditioning Journal*, 21, 53-55.

Marieb, E.N. (1992). *The Muscular System. In Human Anatomy and Physiology* (pp. 285-337). Redwood City, California: Benjamin/Cummings Publishing Co.

Matveyev, L. (1981). *Fundamentals of Sports Training*. Moscow: Progress Publishers.

Maughan, R.J., Leiper, J.B., & Shirreffs, S.M. (1997). Factors influencing the restoration of fluid and electrolyte balance after exercise in the heat. *Br Sports Med*, 31(3), 175-182.

McAtee, G. & Judge, L.W. (2006). Implement selection and training design for the hammer throw. *Modern Athlete and Coach*, 44(2).

McCarrol, J.R. & Gioe, T.J. (1982). Professional golfers and the price they pay. *Phys. Sports Med*, 10, 54–70.

McGill, S.M. (2002). *Low Back Disorders: Evidence-Based Prevention and Rehabilitation*. Champaign, Illinois: Human Kinetics.

McGill, S.M. (1998). Low back exercises: Evidence for improving exercise regimens. *Phys. Ther*, 78, 754-765.

McGill, K.A. (1984). Shot put analysis. *Track Technique*, 89.

McMillian, D., Moore, J., Hatler, B., & Taylor, D. (2006). Dynamic vs. static stretching warm up: The effect on power and agility performance. *Journal of Strength and Conditioning Research*, 20, 492-499.

Meichenbaum, D. (1985). *Stress Inoculation Training*. New York, New York: Pergamon.

Miller, E.R., Erlinger, T.P., & Appel, L.J. (2006). The effects of macronutrients on blood pressure and lipids: An overview of the DASH and OmniHeart trials. *Curr Atheroscler Rep*, 8(6), 460-465.

Murphy, A.J., Wilson, G.J., Pryor, J.F., & Newton, R.U. (1995). Isometric assessment of muscular functions: The effect of joint angle. *J. Appl. Biomech*, 11, 205-215.

Murray, B. (2006). Fluid, electrolytes and exercise. In M. Dunford (Ed.) Sports, cardiovascular and wellness nutritionists dietetic practice group. *Sports Nutrition: A Practice Manual for Professionals* (4th ed.). Chicago, Illinois: American Dietetic Association, 94-115.

Nadler, S.F., Wu, K.D., Galski, T., & Feinberg, J.H. (1998). Low back pain in college athletes: A prospective study correlating lower extremity overuse or acquired ligamentous laxity with low back pain. *Spine*, 23, 828-833.

NCAA Injury Surveillance System. (1998-1999). Overland Park, Kansas: National Collegiate Athletic Association.

Nelson, A., Jokkonen, J., & Arnall, D. (2005). Acute muscle stretching inhibits muscle strength endurance performance. *Journal of Strength and Conditioning Research*, 19, 338-343.

Nideffer, R.M. & Sagal, M.S. (2001). Concentration and Attention Control Training. In Williams, J.M. (Ed.) *Applied Sport Psychology: Personal Growth to Peak Performance* (4th ed.). Mountain View, California: Mayfield Publishing Company, 312-313.

Ninos, J. (1995). Guidelines for proper stretching. *Strength and Conditioning*, 17, 44-46.

Norris, C.M. (1999). Functional load abdominal training: part 1. *Journal of Bodywork and Movement Therapies*, 3(3), 150-158.

Noseda, G. (2005). Fats and oils (including omega3, omega6). *Ther Umsch*, 62(9), 625-628.

Nuzzo, J., McCaulley, G., Cormie, P., Cavill, M., & McBride, J. (2008). Trunk muscle activity during stability ball and free weight exercises. *Journal of Strength and Conditioning Research*, 22(1), 95-102.

Oliveta, N. (2004). Establishing volume load parameters: a different look in designing a strength training periodization for throwing events. *Journal of Strength and Conditioning Research*, 26(5). 52–55.

Orlick, T. (1990). *In Pursuit of Excellence: How to Win in Sport and Life Through Mental Training* (2nd ed.). Champaign, Illinois: Leisure Press.

Pagani, T. (1979). The shot put: Mechanic, technique, conditioning, and drills. *Track and Field Quarterly Review*, 79(4).

Pauletto, B. (1987). Understanding the power clean: execution. *Scholastic Coach*, 57(5), 82-85.

Pauletto, B. (1987). Understanding the power clean: guidelines. *Scholastic Coach*, 57(4), 56-57.

Pascoe, D.D., Costill, D.L., Fink, W.J., Robergs, R.A., & Zachwieja, J.J. (1993). Glycogen resynthesis in skeletal muscle following resistive exercise. *Medicine and Science in Sports and Exercise*, 25, 349-354.

Pearson, D.R., Gehlsen, G.M., & Shondell, D.S. (1997). Performance enhancement and training. *Strength and Conditioning*, 19(4), 54-56.

Pedemonte, J. (1986). Foundations of training periodization—part two: The objective of periodization. *NSCA J*, 8(2), 26-28.

Petrov, V. (1980). Hammer throw technique and drills. Translated excerpts from Legkaja Atletika, Moscow: #8.

Pfaff, D. (2005). Alternate methods for developing strength, power and mobility. Clinic handout.

Pfaff, D., (2006). Specific Strength Exercises. Clinic handout.

Phillips, S. (1981). Protein requirements and supplementation in strength. *Nutr*, 20(7-8), 689-695.

Piga, R. (1981). Modern coaching of the shot put. *Tirrenia*, 7-8.

Poliquin, C. (1997). *The Poliquin Principles*. Napa, California: Dayton Writers Group, 5-37.

Poliquin, C. & Patterson, P. (1989). Terminology: classification of strength qualities. *National Strength and Conditioning Association Journal*, 11(6), 48-52.

Potteiger, J.A. & Judge, L.W. (1995). Effects of altering training volume and intensity on body mass, performance, and hormonal concentrations in weight-event athletes. *Track Coach*, 134.

Potteiger, J.A. & Judge, L.W. (1995). Hormonal changes in weight-event athletes. *Journal of Strength and Conditioning Research*, 6(3).

Rankin, J.W., Goldman, L.P., Puglisi, M.J., Nickson-Richardson, S.M., Earthman, C.P., & Gwazdauskas. (2004). Effect of post-exercise supplement consumption on adaptations to resistance training. *J Amer Col Nutr*, 23(4), 322-330.

Reardon, J. & Gordin, R. (1999). Psychological skill development leading to a peak performance "flow state." *Track and Field Coaches Review*, 3(2), 22-25.

Reardon, J. (1995). Relaxation: A necessary skill for competition. *American Athletics*, 3, 50-53.

Reardon, J. (1992). Incorporating mental skills into workouts: learning how to "go with the flow." *American Athletics*, 3, 54-55.

Rennie, M.J. (1996). Influence of exercise on protein and amino acid metabolism. In R. Terjung (Ed.) *Handbook of physiology* (pp. 995-1035). New York, New York: Oxford University Press.

Richardson, C., Jull, G, Toppenburg, R., & Comeford, M. (1992). Techniques for active lumbar stabilization for spinal protection: a pilot study. *Aust. J. Physiother*, 38:105-112.

Riley, D.P. (1997). *Strength Training by the Experts*. Champaign, Ilinois: Leisure Press.

Robinson, R. (1992). The new back school prescription: stabilization training, part I. *Occupt Med*, 7(1), 17-31.

Rockwell, M. (2006). On top of their diets. *Training and Conditioning*, 16(1).

Rockwell, M. (2006). Fluid dynamics. *Training and Conditioning*, 16(4).

Roland, D. (1997). *The Confident Performer*. Sydney, Australia: Currency.

Roy, B.D. & Tarnopolsky, M.A. (1998). Influence of differing macronutrient intakes on muscle glycogen resynthesis after resistance exercise. *J Appl Physiol*, 84, 890-896.

Salmon, P. (1991). Stress inoculation techniques and musical performance anxiety. In G.D. Wilson (Ed.) *Psychology and Performing Arts* (pp. 219-229). Amsterdam: Swets and Zeitlinger.

Santana, J.C. (2000). *Functional Training: Breaking the Bonds of Traditionalism*. Boca Raton, Florida: Optimum Performance Systems.

Saal J. (1990). Dynamic muscular stabilization in the nonoperative treatment of lumbar pain syndromes. *Orthopedic Review*, 19(8).

Santana, C. (2001). Single-leg training for two-legged sports: efficacy of strength development in athletic performance. *National Strength and Conditioning Association Journal*, 23(3), 35-37.

Santino, P. (1989). *Trimming Your Midsection: The Santino System*. Chicago, Illinois: Siara Co.

Sawka, M.N. & Montain, S.J. (2000). Fluid and electrolyte supplementation for exercise heat stress. *Am J Clin Nutr*, 72(2), 564S-572S.

Schmidbleicher, D. (1992). Training for power events. In P. V. Komi (Ed.) *Strength and Power in Sports* (pp. 381-395). London: Blackwell Scientific Publications.

Schmidt, R.A. & Wrisberg, C.A. (2000). *Motor Learning and Performance* (2nd ed.). Champaign, Illinois: Human Kinetics.

Schmidt, R.A. (1975). Schema theory of discrete motor skill learning. *Psychological Review*, 82(4), 225-260.

Schoonen, J.C. & Holbrook, L. (2006). Physiology of anaerobic and aerobic exercise. In M. Dunford (Ed.) Sports, Cardiovascular, and Wellness Nutritionists Dietetic Practice Group. *Sports Nutrition: A Practice Manual for Professionals* (4th ed.). Chicago, Illinois: American Dietetic Association.

Sloan, R. (1992). Glide and rotational shot put. *American Athletics*. Los Altos, California: Pike Creek Press.

Sears, B. (1995). *Mastering the Zone*. New York, New York: Harper Collins.

Selye, H. (1974). *Stress without Distress*. New York, New York: J.B. Lippincott.

Sharp, R.L. (2006). Role of sodium in fluid homeostasis with exercise. *J Am Coll Nutr*, 25(3), 231S-239S.

Siff, M. (2000). Biomechanical foundations of strength and power training. In V. Zatsiorsky (Ed.) *Biomechanics in Sport* (pp. 103-139). London: Blackwell Scientific Ltd.

Sing, R.F. (1984). *The Dynamics of the Javelin Throw*. Overland Park, Kansas: Reynolds Publishing Inc.

Smith Rockwell, M., Nickols-Richardson, S.M., Thye, F.W. (2001). Nutrition knowledge, opinions, and practices of coaches and athletic trainers at a Division I university. *Int J Sport Nutr Exerc Met*, 11:174–185.

Snow-Harter, C.M. (1994). Bone health and prevention of osteoporosis in active and athletic women. *Clin Sports Med*, 13(2), 389-404.

Souza, G.M., Baker, L.L., & Powers, C.M. (2001). Electromyographic activity of selected trunk muscles during dynamic spine stabilization exercises. *Arch. Med. Rehabil*, 82, 1551-1557.

Stanford, M.E. (2002). Effectiveness of specific lumbar stabilization exercises: A single case study. J. Man. Manipulative Ther, 10, 40-46.

Stanton, R., Reaburn, P.R. & Humphries, B. (2004). The effect of short-term Swiss ball training on core stability and running economy. Journal of Strength and Conditioning Research, 18, 522-528.

Stein, K. (2000). High-protein, low-carbohydrate diets: do they work? J Am Dietet Assoc, 100, 760-761.

Steptoe, A., & Fidler, H. (1987). Stage fright in orchestral musicians: A study of cognitive and behavioral strategies in performance anxiety. British Journal of Psychology, 78(2), 241-249.

Stone, M.H. (2004). Explosive Exercise. Presentation at the USATF Level III School, Las Vegas, Nevada.

Stone, M.H., Stone, M.E., Sands, W.A., Pierce, K P., Newton, R.U., Haff, G.G., & Carlock, J. (2006). Maximum strength and strength training: a relationship to endurance? *Strength and Conditioning*, 28(3), 44-53.

Stone, M.R., Stone, M H., Gattone, M., Schilling, B., Pierce, K., & Byrd, R. (2007). Movement pattern specificity/advantages of using pulling movements. *Coaches' Information Service* [online serial]. Available from: http://coachesinfo.com/. Accessed October 1, 2007.

Stone, M.H., Plisk, S., & Collins, D. (2002). Training principle: evaluation of modes and methods of resistance training—a coaching perspective. *Sport. Biomech*, 1, 79-104.

Stone, M.H., O'Bryant, H.S., Schilling, B.K., Johnson, R.L., Pierce, K C., Haff, G.G., Koch, A. J., & Stone, M. (1999). Periodization effects of manipulating volume and intensity: Part 1. *Strength and Conditioning Journal*, 21(2) 56-62.

Stone, M.H., & Fry, A.C. (1997). Increased training volume in strength/power athletes. In R.B. Kreider, A.C. Fry, & M.L. O'Toole (Eds.) *Overtraining in Sport* (pp. 87-106). Champaign, Illinois: Human Kinetics.

Stone, M.H., Moir, G., Glaister, M., & Sanders, R. (2002). How much strength is necessary? *Phys. Ther. Sport*, 3, 88-96.

Stone, M.H. (1990). Muscle conditioning and muscle injuries. *Medicine and Science Exercise*. 22(4), 457-462.

Stone, M.H. & O'Bryant, H. S. (1987). *Weight Training: A Scientific Approach*. Minneapolis, Minnesota: Bellwether Press.

Tarnopolsky, M.A., Atkinson, S A., MacDougall, J.D., Chelsey, A., Phillips, S., & Schwartz, A.P. (1992). Evaluation of protein requirements for trained strength athletes. *J Appl Physiol*, 73, 1986-1995.

Thompson, J. (2003). *The Double Goal Coach: Positive Coaching Tools for Honoring the Game*. New York, New York: HarperCollins Publishers.

Thompson, J.L. Peters. (1991). *Introduction to Coaching Theory*. England: Hazelwood Press Ltd.

Tippett, S.R., & Voight, M.L. (1995). *Functional Progressions for Sport Rehabilitations*. Champaign, Illinois: Human Kinetics.

Tse, M.A., McManus, A.M., & Masters, R.S. (2005). Development and validation of a core endurance intervention program: Implications for performance in college-age rowers. *Journal of Strength and Conditioning Research*, 19, 547–552.

Turk, M. (1997). Building a technical model for the shot put. *Track Coach*, 141.

Unick, J., Kieffer, H., Cheesman, W., & Feeney, A. (2005). The acute effects of static and ballistic stretching on vertical jump performance in trained women. *Journal of Strength and Conditioning Research*, 19, 206-212.

Van Erp-Baart, A.M., Saris, W.H., Binkhorst, R.A., Vos, J.A., & Elvers, J.W. (1989). Nationwide survey on nutritional habits in elite athletes: Part 1: Energy, carbohydrate, protein and fat intake. *Int J Sports Med*, 10(1), 3-10.

Voight, M.L., & Cook, G. (1996). Clinical application of closed kinetic chain exercise. *J. Sport Rehab*, 5, 25-44.

Volpe, S.L. (2006). Vitamins, minerals, and exercise. In M. Dunford (Ed.) Sports, Cardiovascular and Wellness Nutritionists Dietetic Practice Group. *Sports Nutrition: A Practice Manual for Professionals* (4th ed.). Chicago, Illinois: American Dietetic Association.

Wadley, G.H. & Aalbright, J.P. (1993). Women's intercollegiate gymnastics: injury patterns and permanent medical disability. *Am. J. Sports Med*, 21, 314-320.

Walberg, J.L., Leidy, M.K., Sturgill, D.J., Hinkle, D.E., Ritchey, S.J., & Sebolt, D.R. (1988). Macronutrient of a hypoenergy diet affects nitrogen retention and muscle function in weight lifters. *Int J Sports Med*, 9(4), 261-266.

Wardlaw, G.M. (1999). *Perspectives in Nutrition* (4th ed.). Boston, Massachusetts: WCB McGraw-Hill.

Wardle, A. (1975). Behavior modification by reciprocal inhibition of instrumental music performance anxiety. In C.K. Madsen, R D. Greer, & C.H. Madsen (Eds.) *Research in Music Behavior: Modifying Basic Behavior in the Classroom* (pp. 191-205). New York Teachers College.

Watson, M.D. & DiMartino, P.P. (1987). Incidence of injuries in high school track and field athletes and its relation to performance ability. *Am J Sports Med*. 15:251–254.

Whitaker, J. (2004). Abdominal ultrasound imaging of pelvic floor muscle function in individuals with low back pain. *J. Man. Manipulative Ther*, 12, 44-49.

Williams, M.H. (1994). The use of nutritional ergogenic aids in sports: is it an ethical issue? *International Journal of Sport Nutrition*, 4, 120-131.

Wilson, J.D., Dougherty, C.P., Ireland, M.L., & Davis, I.M. (2005). Core stability and its relationship to lower extremity function and injury. *J. Am. Acad. Orthop. Surg*, 13, 316-325.

Winchester, J.B., Erickson, T.M., Black, J.B., & McBride, J.M. (2005). Changes in bar-path kinematics and kinetics after power-clean training. *Journal of Strength and Conditioning Research*, 19, 177-182.

Wrisberg, C. (2007). *Sport Skill Instruction for Coaches*. Champaign, Illinois: Human Kinetics.

Yamaguchi, T. & Ishii, K. (2005). Effects of static stretching for 30 seconds and dynamic stretching on leg extension power. *Journal of Strength and Conditioning Research*, 19, 677-683.

Young, M. (2004). *Critical Factors in Shot Putting*. Presentation at the USATF Elite Shot Put Summit, Columbus, Ohio.

Young, W.B. (2006). Transfer of strength and power training to sports performance. *Int. J. Sports Physiol. Performance*, 1(2), 74.

Zawadzki, K.M., Yaspelkis, B.B., & Ivy, J.L. (1992). Carbohydrate-protein complex increases the rate of muscle glycogen storage after exercise. *Journal of Applied Physiology*, 72, 1854-1859.

Zetnz, C., Fees, M., Medhi, O., & Decker, A. (1998). Incorporating resistance training into the precompetition warm-up. *Strength and Conditioning*, 20, 51-55.

Larry Judge, Ph.D., CSCS, is an assistant professor and the coordinator of the graduate coaching program at Ball State University in Muncie, Indiana. He is the USA Track and Field national chairman for coaches education in the throws, and he lectures throughout the United States at various camps and clinics, including USA Track and Field Level II and Level III coaching education schools. He also lectures in the IAAF coaches' education program. Judge is a USATF Master Coach.

Judge competed as a shot-putter for Indiana State University, was an NCAA championship finalist, and has a personal best of 19.00m (62'3"). He still holds the school record in the shot put at Indiana State University.

Judge earned his Master of Science degree in exercise science and sports management at Indiana State University in Terre Haute, Indiana, before going on to complete his Ph.D. in education administration.

Widely recognized as the premiere throws coach in the United States, Larry Judge has tutored over 100 NCAA Division I All-Americans, 11 NCAA national champions, 16 USATF champions, eight Olympians, two American record-holders, three collegiate record-holders, three American collegiate record-holders, and two world records .

Judge just completed his 18th year of collegiate coaching with the University of Florida in 2005. Under Judge's direction, the Florida throws group has reached the pinnacle of the sport, amassing unparalleled honors. In just five years at UF, Judge has tutored nine All-Americans, five Southeastern Conference champions, two NCAA champions, and three Olympians, adding to an already impressive resume. Gator throwers have collected an astounding 34 All-American honors, 16 individual SEC titles, and six individual NCAA titles since Judge's arrival in Gainesville prior to the 2000-01 season.

Besides his teaching, service, and research responsibilities at Ball State University, Coach Judge continues to train a group of elite throwers, including Laquanda Cotten, Erin Gilreath, Rachel Longfors, Candice Scott, and Liz Wanless. He has established a throwing club, Club Chuck It, which athletes of all ages can join. Coach Judge has produced a series of DVDs and videos on training for the throwing events and strength and conditioning for the throws athlete.

About the Author

Athletes Coached

- Christy Barrett (USA): 1993 world championships, shot put
- Brad Synder (Canada): 1996 Olympian, 1997 world championships, shot put
- Lisa Misipeka (American Samoa): 1995 world championships, 1996 Olympic Games, shot put
- Dawn Ellerbe (USA): World record 20-lb weight, American record-holder, hammer and 20-lb weight, 1999 world championships, 2000 Olympic Games (7th)
- Jesseca Cross (USA): 2000 Olympic Games, shot put and hammer
- Jason Gervais (Canada): 1999 world championships, 2000 Olympic Games, discus
- Candice Scott (Trinidad and Tobago): 2003 (9th) and 2005 (8th) world championships, 2004 Olympic Games (9th), hammer
- Kim Barrett (Jamaica): 2004 Olympic Games, shot put
- Erin Gilreath (USA): World record 20-lb, American record-holder hammer and 20-lb weight, 2006 (6th) World Cup, 2005 (10th) world championships, 2004 Olympic Games
- Liz Wanless (USA): 2005 world championships, shot put

Coaching Awards

- USTCA National Assistant Coach of the Year, throws (2004)
- USATF Coaches Education National Coach/Educator of the Year (2005)

Certifications

- 2004, USATF, master coach
- 2003, USATF, level III coach, throws
- United States Weight Lifting Federation, regional Olympic lifting coach
- 1991, American College of Sports Medicine, health fitness instructor
- 1991, American Council on Exercise, certified personal trainer
- 1991, USATF, level I and level II coaches' education, lead instructor
- 1990, USATF, level II coaching certification, throws
- 1990, USATF, level I coaching certification
- 1989, National Strength and Conditioning Association, CSCS
- 1988, USATF, certified track and field official, national level

To find out more about Coach Judge or to contact him, you can log onto his website: www.coachlarryjudge.com.

Coach Judge with his post-collegiate training group (from left to right): Erin Gilreath, Candice Scott, Laquanda Cotten, and Liz Wanless

Coach Judge and Erin Gilreath at the 2006 World Athletics final